# Adobe® Premiere® Elements 2.0

## Illustrated

MT Cozzola

THOMSON
COURSE TECHNOLOGY™

Australia • Canada • Mexico • Singapore • Spain • United Kingdom • United States

THOMSON
COURSE TECHNOLOGY

**Adobe® Premiere® Elements 2.0 – Illustrated**
MT Cozzola


**Executive Editor:**
Rachel Goldberg

**Senior Acquisitions Editor:**
Marjorie Hunt

**Product Manager:**
Jane Hosie-Bounar

**Developmental Editor:**
Barbara M. Waxer

**In-House Product Manager:**
Christina Kling Garrett

**Production Editor:**
Philippa Lehar

**Associate Product Manager:**
Shana Rosenthal

**Editorial Assistant:**
Janine Tangney

**QA Reviewers:**
Jeff Schwartz
Ashlee Welz

**Text Designer:**
Joseph Lee, Black Fish Design

**Compositor:**
GEX Publishing Services

**Copy Editor:**
Mary Kemper

**Proofreader:**
Chris Clark

**Indexer:**
Rich Carlson





Printed in the United States of America

1 2 3 4 5 6 7 8 9 BM 10 09 08 07 06

For more information, contact Thomson Course Technology, 25 Thomson Place, Boston, Massachusetts, 02210.

Or you can visit us on the World Wide Web at www.course.com





Some video footage courtesy of Fig Media, Inc.
Some video footage courtesy of Flying Leap Radio Theater
Some video footage courtesy of Dave Belden
A Grey Day in Seaham.mp3, Fantastic Plastic.wav, Singer Strange Theme.mp3, and Twelve Empty Cups.mp3 written and performed by Derek R. Audette
Theme song.mp3 written and performed by Mark Kmit (used with permission)
The Pharaos Theme.wav written and performed by the Pharaos
Lord McDonald Medley.wav traditional folk music performed by Michael Coleman and Ed Geoghegan
RunninWild.mp3 written and performed by James Cole's Washboard Four





ISBN-13: 978-1-4188-6017-2
ISBN-10: 1-4188-6017-4

# The Illustrated Series Vision

Teaching and writing about computer applications can be extremely rewarding and challenging. How do we engage students and keep their interest? How do we teach them skills that they can easily apply on the job? As we set out to write this book, our goals were to develop a textbook that:

- works for a beginning student
- provides varied, flexible and meaningful exercises and projects to reinforce the skills
- serves as a reference tool
- makes your job as an educator easier, by providing resources above and beyond the textbook to help you teach your course

Our popular, streamlined format is based on advice from instructional designers and customers. This flexible design presents each lesson on a two-page spread, with step-by-step instructions on the left and screen illustrations on the right. This signature style, coupled with high-caliber content, provides a comprehensive yet manageable introduction to Adobe® Premiere® Elements 2.0—it is a teaching package for the instructor and a learning experience for the student.


## ACKNOWLEDGMENTS

Thanks to everyone at Thomson Course Technology who made this book a reality. Through the vision and support of Marjorie Hunt, Christina Kling Garrett, and Janine Tangney, writing this book was rewarding and hassle-free from start to finish. The Quality Assurance team of Jeff Schwartz and Ashlee Welz weeded out technical errors, while production editor Philippa Lehar and copyeditor Mary Kemper brought consistency and clarity to the pages. I'm also grateful to academic reviewers Johnny Sue Bauer and Donna Teel for their valuable input.

Special thanks to project manager Jane Hosie-Bounar for guiding this process with sound advice and good humor. And gratitude isn't enough for my developmental editor, Barbara Waxer. She is the best problem-solver, sounding board, traffic manager, and creative consultant a writer could have, and I am forever in her debt.

I am deeply indebted to my friends in the theatre and filmmaking communities for lending resources for various projects in this book, especially: James Gustin and Fig Media Inc. (yes, Fig really is a hip production company, and you can visit them at www.figmediainc.com); performers Dan Griffiths and Stephen Chipps, composer Mark Kmit, and Kapoot Clown Theatre; Adam, Emily, Jay, Tamara, and everyone at Flying Leap Radio Theatre; and last but not least, filmmaker Dave Belden. Dave shot most of the footage used in the Genoa Stock video, as well as some of the films in the Film Fest project. Thanks also to everyone at the Adobe Premiere Elements User Forum (www.adobe.com/support/forums)—especially James J. Johnson, for his advice regarding images, title clips, and project portability. A final thanks goes to Shannon Wolfe for graciously sharing her farm, flocks, and infectious intensity. Like Dave, Linda, Tom, Lana, Mary Joan, Rich and Pat, I too am a student of Shannon's, and can testify that everything she says about dogs and training is true.

—MT Cozzola

# Preface

Welcome to *Adobe Premiere Elements 2.0—Illustrated.* This highly visual book offers users a hands-on introduction to Adobe Premiere 2.0 and also serves as an excellent reference for future use.

## Organization and Coverage

This text is organized into seven units. In these units students learn how to use automatic features, edit a movie, add transitions and effects, work with sound, add titles and credits, and output a movie.

## About This Approach

What makes the Illustrated approach so effective at teaching software skills? It's quite simple. Each skill is presented on two facing pages, with the step-by-step instructions on the left page and large screen illustrations on the right. Students can focus on a single skill without having to turn the page. This unique design makes information extremely accessible and easy to absorb and provides a great reference after the course is over. This hands-on approach also makes it ideal for both self-paced and instructor-led classes.

## Additional Features

The two-page lesson format featured in this book provides the new user with a powerful learning experience. Additionally, this book contains the following features:

### Real-World Case

The case study used throughout the book, a fictitious video production company called Ty Media, is designed to be "real-world" in nature, and introduces the kinds of activities that students will encounter when working with Premiere Elements. With a real-world case, the process of solving problems is more meaningful to students.

Each two-page spread focuses on a single skill or skill set.

Concise text that introduces the basic principles in the lesson and integrates the brief case study (indicated by the paint palette icon).

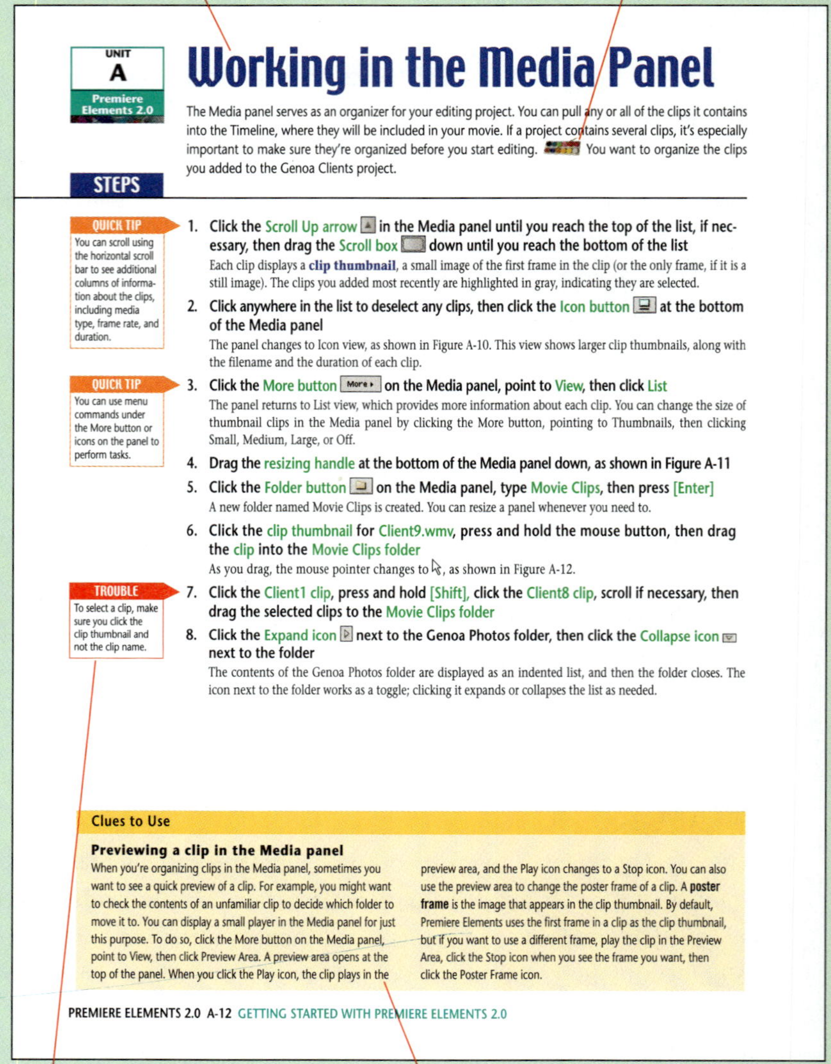

UNIT A Premiere Elements 2.0

STEPS

## Working in the Media Panel

The Media panel serves as an organizer for your editing project. You can pull any or all of the clips it contains into the Timeline, where they will be included in your movie. If a project contains several clips, it's especially important to make sure they're organized before you start editing. You want to organize the clips you added to the Genoa Clients project.

QUICK TIP: You can scroll using the horizontal scroll bar to see additional columns of information about the clips, including media type, frame rate, and duration.

QUICK TIP: You can use menu commands under the More button or icons on the panel to perform tasks.

TROUBLE: To select a clip, make sure you click the clip thumbnail and not the clip name.

1. **Click the Scroll Up arrow in the Media panel until you reach the top of the list, if necessary, then drag the Scroll box down until you reach the bottom of the list**
   Each clip displays a **clip thumbnail**, a small image of the first frame in the clip (or the only frame, if it is a still image). The clips you added most recently are highlighted in gray, indicating they are selected.
2. **Click anywhere in the list to deselect any clips, then click the Icon button at the bottom of the Media panel**
   The panel changes to Icon view, as shown in Figure A-10. This view shows larger clip thumbnails, along with the filename and the duration of each clip.
3. **Click the More button on the Media panel, point to View, then click List**
   The panel returns to List view, which provides more information about each clip. You can change the size of thumbnail clips in the Media panel by clicking the More button, pointing to Thumbnails, then clicking Small, Medium, Large, or Off.
4. **Drag the resizing handle at the bottom of the Media panel down, as shown in Figure A-11**
5. **Click the Folder button on the Media panel, type Movie Clips, then press [Enter]**
   A new folder named Movie Clips is created. You can resize a panel whenever you need to.
6. **Click the clip thumbnail for Client9.wmv, press and hold the mouse button, then drag the clip into the Movie Clips folder**
   As you drag, the mouse pointer changes to , as shown in Figure A-12.
7. **Click the Client1 clip, press and hold [Shift], click the Client8 clip, scroll if necessary, then drag the selected clips to the Movie Clips folder**
8. **Click the Expand icon next to the Genoa Photos folder, then click the Collapse icon next to the folder**
   The contents of the Genoa Photos folder are displayed as an indented list, and then the folder closes. The icon next to the folder works as a toggle; clicking it expands or collapses the list as needed.

**Clues to Use**

**Previewing a clip in the Media panel**

When you're organizing clips in the Media panel, sometimes you want to see a quick preview of a clip. For example, you might want to check the contents of an unfamiliar clip to decide which folder to move it to. You can display a small player in the Media panel for just this purpose. To do so, click the More button on the Media panel, point to View, then click Preview Area. A preview area opens at the top of the panel. When you click the Play icon, the clip plays in the preview area, and the Play icon changes to a Stop icon. You can also use the preview area to change the poster frame of a clip. A **poster frame** is the image that appears in the clip thumbnail. By default, Premiere Elements uses the first frame in a clip as the clip thumbnail, but if you want to use a different frame, play the clip in the Preview Area, click the Stop icon when you see the frame you want, then click the Poster Frame icon.

PREMIERE ELEMENTS 2.0 A-12 GETTING STARTED WITH PREMIERE ELEMENTS 2.0

Hints as well as troubleshooting advice, right where you need it–next to the step itself.

Clues to Use and Production Matters boxes provide concise information that either expands on the major lesson skill or describes an independent task or production consideration that in some way relates to the major lesson skill.

Every lesson features large, full-color representations of what the screen should look like as students complete the numbered steps.

FIGURE A-6: Capture workspace

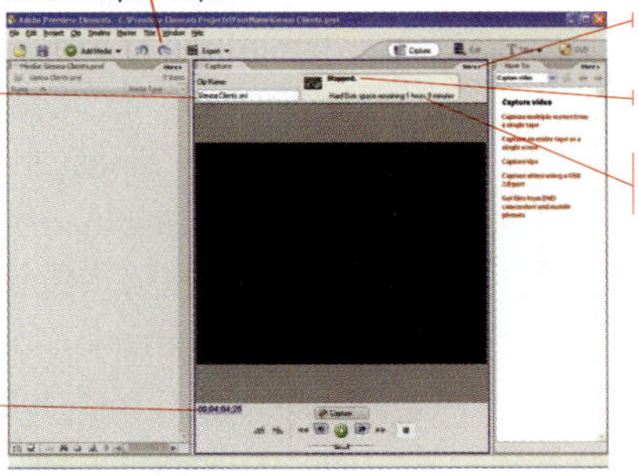


FIGURE A-7: Capturing video

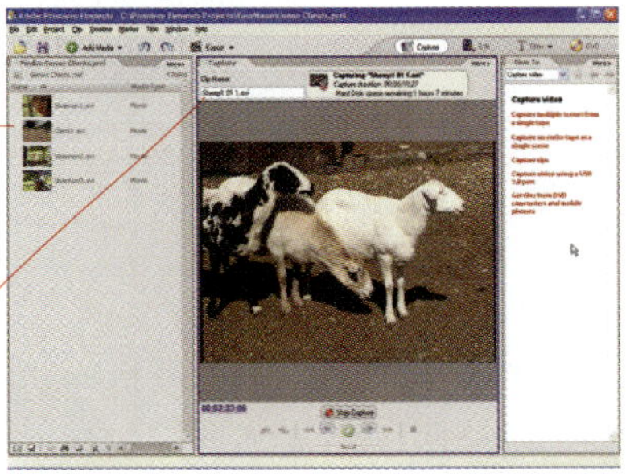


TABLE A-2: Capture panel device controls

| control | name | used to |
|---|---|---|
| Capture | Capture | Begin transferring video |
| | Previous Scene | Jump to the beginning of the previous detected scene on tape |
| | Next Scene | Jump to the beginning of the next detected scene on tape |
| | Rewind | Reverse through the tape |
| | Step Back | Move back one frame at a time in the tape |
| | Play | Begin playing the tape in video preview area |
| | Step Forward | Move ahead one frame at a time in the tape |
| | Fast Forward | Move quickly ahead through the tape |
| | Stop | Stop playing or capturing tape |
| | Shuttle | Drag left or right to move tape forward or back |

Premiere Elements 2.0

GETTING STARTED WITH PREMIERE ELEMENTS 2.0 PREMIERE ELEMENTS 2.0 A-9

Quickly accessible summaries of key terms, toolbar buttons, or keyboard alternatives connected with the lesson material. Students can refer easily to this information when working on their own projects at a later time.

The pages are numbered according to unit. A indicates the unit, 9 indicates the page.

## End-of-Unit Material

Each unit concludes with a Concepts Review that tests students' understanding of what they learned in the unit. The Concepts Review is followed by a Skills Review, which provides students with additional hands-on practice of the skills.

The Skills Review is followed by Independent Challenges, which pose case problems for students to solve using creativity and critical thinking. Independent Challenges 1 through 3 increase in difficulty, with the first being the easiest (most step-by-step with detailed instructions). Independent Challenges 2 and 3 become increasingly open-ended, requiring more independent thinking and problem solving. Independent Challenge 4, the E-Quest, asks students to use the World Wide Web to find media or research a topic to complete a project. All Independent Challenges build from unit to unit, with students editing different types of videos as they learn skills throughout the book.

The Visual Workshop follows the Independent Challenges and helps students further develop critical thinking skills. Students are shown a screen or a project in the Premiere Elements workspace and are asked to recreate it.

## Data and Source Files

To complete the exercises in this book, students need Data and Source Files. These files are provided to the instructor as part of the Instructor Resources. These files are also available on a Review Pack CD, which can be bundled with the book. To order the Review Pack, speak to your sales representative. Due to the large size of the Data and Source files, they are not available for download on the www.course.com Web site.

# Instructor Resources

The Instructor Resources CD is Course Technology's way of putting the resources and information needed to teach and learn effectively into your hands. With an integrated array of teaching and learning tools that offers you and your students a broad range of technology-based instructional options, we believe this CD represents the highest quality and most cutting edge resources available to instructors today. Many of these resources are available at www.course.com. The resources available with this book are:

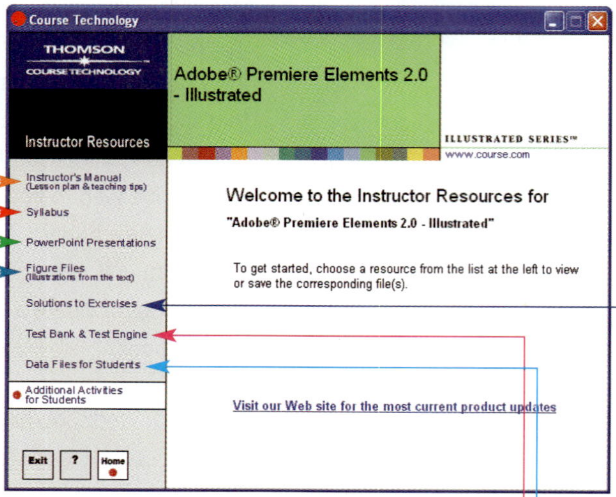


- **Solutions to Exercises**—These contain every file students are asked to created or modify in the lessons and End-of-Unit material. A Help file on the Instructor Resources CD includes information for using the Solution Files. There is also a document outlining the solutions for the End-of-Unit Concepts Review, Skills Review, and Independent Challenges.

- **PowerPoint Presentations**—Each unit has a corresponding PowerPoint presentation that you can use in lecture, distribute to your students, or customize to suit your course.

- **Instructor's Manual**—Available as an electronic file, the Instructor's Manual includes unit overviews and detailed lecture topics with teaching tips for each unit.

- **Sample Syllabus**—Prepare and customize your course easily using this sample course outline.

- **Figure Files**—The figures in the text are provided on the Instructor Resources CD to help you illustrate key topics or concepts. You can create traditional overhead transparencies by printing the figure files. Or, you can create electronic slide shows by using the figures in a presentation program such as Microsoft Office PowerPoint.

- **ExamView**—ExamView is a powerful testing software package that allows you to create and administer printed, LAN-based, and Internet-based exams. ExamView includes hundreds of questions that correspond to the topics covered in this text, enabling students to generate detailed study guides that include page references for further review. The computer-based and Internet testing components allow students to take exams at their computers, and also save you time by grading each exam automatically.

- **Data Files and Source Clips for Students**—To complete most of the units in this book, your students will need **Data Files** and **Source Clips** (containing movie clips). Put them on a file server for students to copy. The Data Files and Source Clips are available on the Instructor's Resources CD and the Review Pack which can be bundled with the book for student purchase. To bundle the Review Pack with the book, speak to your sales representative.

Instruct students to use the **Data Files List** located at the back of this book and on the Instructor Resources CD. This list gives instructions on copying and organizing files.

# Brief Contents

# Contents

# Read This Before You Begin

## Working with Premiere Elements

Minimum System Requirements:

- Intel® Pentium® 4, M, D, Extreme Edition or AMD or AMD Athlon XP, XP-M, Opteron, Athlon 64
- Microsoft® Windows® XP (Home, Pro, Media Center) running Service Pack 2
- 256 MB of RAM
- 2 GB of available hard disk space for installation
- DVD-ROM drive (compatible DVD writer required to burn DVDs)
- 1024x768, 16-bit (XGA) display
- Microsoft DirectX 9 compatible sound and display drivers
- For video capture and transfer:
    - DV/i.LINK/FireWire/IEEE 1394 interface to connect a Digital8 or DV camcorder
    - USB2 interface with a compatible DV via USB DV camcorder
    - Other video devices (supported via Media Downloader)

When estimating your hard disk space needs, note that one minute of digital video requires approximately 250 MB of space; it's also recommended that at least 20% of your hard disk space be free, to ensure smooth data transfer. Most newer computers meet the minimum hard disk speed of 7200 necessary to transfer digital video.

Each workspace in the Premiere Elements program window is comprised of several panels, such as the Monitor panel and the Timeline panel. Depending on your monitor size and resolution, the panels on your screen may be larger or smaller than those shown in the figures in this book.

## Working with Data Files

Data Files have been supplied for completing the exercises in this book. Premiere Elements files work with source clips. Source files are video files, audio clips, and still image clips that can be used in a project file as part of a movie. A project file in Premiere Elements uses links to these source files so that you can work in the program, then uses the actual source files to create the finished movie. When you open a Data File or other project file, Premiere Elements needs to load all the source clips used in the file.

Every source clip used in a Data File provided is located in a single folder—named Source Clips—on the CD that comes with this book. (There are two subfolders within the Source Clips folder that contain source clips as well.) To locate all of the clips used in a Data File, navigate to the Source Clips folder and select the first item being asked for. Premiere Elements will then find all of the additional source clips in the same location, if necessary.

Editing is a progressive process, and this is reflected in the exercises in this book. Projects build from unit to unit, in the lesson assignments as well as the end-of-unit projects. Therefore, the Data File that a student opens in one unit may be similar to the solution they created in the previous unit. However, the Data File is not the same as the Solution File from the preceding unit; additional edits are made to further refine the project, so it cannot be used as the solution to a previous exercise.

In Independent Challenges 2 and 4, students are expected to provide their own source files. Therefore, they are expected to open their own solution file from the previous unit in these exercises.

If students do not have access to camera equipment for Independent Challenge 2, or access to the Internet for public domain media in Independent Challenge 4, the instructor can provide the source files from the appropriate solutions folder for these projects. Keep in mind that even with the same source files, the student's results will vary quite a bit from the solutions provided.

Source files for the solutions to Independent Challenge 2 and 4 are provided only once, to minimize disk space. The source files for Independent Challenge 2 are located in the Unit B solutions folder, and the source files for Independent Challenge 4 are located in the Unit C solutions folder. Instructors will need to navigate to those folders when prompted, to open those solutions in later units.

In Unit F, students insert an image in a title clip. When checking solutions, instructors may see a generic logo placeholder instead of the inserted image if they open the project from a location other than where the student saved it. The logo appears because the link to the image is not maintained, and the program cannot locate the file. To see the image, open the file from the student's saved location.

## Working with Rendered Projects

When you render a project, Premiere Elements processes the edits you've made, compresses the information, and displays a preview of the movie. During the rendering process, the program generates preview files for the rendered movie and and stores them in an Adobe Elements Preview Files folder. Due to file size considerations and folder location differences from computer to computer, the Data Files and Solution Files provided with this book do not contain preview files or any of the supplemental folders and files that are generated with a project. When you open or render a provided file, Premiere Elements generates all necessary folders and files on your computer.

If you open a project that was rendered on a computer other than the one you're using, Premiere Elements prompts you to locate the render files so it can generate a rendered preview. If this happens, click Skip Previews so that Premiere Elements does not attempt to display the rendered previews. In all cases where students are instructed to render a project, the accompanying solution is rendered, to mimic the intended output from the student. Therefore, each time you open a provided solution file, you'll need to click Skip Previews.

If you want to be able to access your students' rendered files when opening their solutions, you can do one of the following:

- Have students save projects to a location that you have access to.
- Have students archive their solution files, using the Project Archiver command on the Project menu. However, note that this option requires a lot of disk space, because each archived file includes a copy of each source files used in each project (i.e., if 30 students archive a project that includes source files equaling 20 MB, the projects take up 600 MB plus the size of the project files; if they simply save the files, the projects take up only 20 MB plus the size of the project files).

UNIT A
Premiere Elements 2.0

# Getting Started with Premiere Elements 2.0

## OBJECTIVES

- Understand video editing software
- Start Premiere Elements and create a new project
- Adjust project settings
- Capture video
- Add media files
- Work in the Media panel
- Get Help
- Close a project and exit Premiere Elements

Adobe Premiere Elements is a video editing program that gives you the power to create great-looking videos, complete with transitions, special effects, and credits, and to distribute the videos on DVD, over the Web, or on tape. In this unit, you learn about video editing, start working in Premiere Elements, and create a new project. You have just been hired as an assistant editor at Ty Media, a company that produces digital videos for commercial, corporate, and individual clients. Luis Rojas, a producer at Ty Media, meets with you to tell you about a new client, Genoa Stock & Training. Genoa Stock trains herding dogs for stock and competition, and they want a promotional video to post on their Web site and distribute on DVD in their press kits. You'll be editing this movie, so Luis suggests you prepare by familiarizing yourself with Premiere Elements.

UNIT
A
Premiere Elements 2.0

# Understanding Video Editing Software

**Video editing** software includes tools for putting together footage recorded with a DV (digital video) camcorder, along with existing video, audio, and image files, to create a finished video and distribute it on DVD, videotape, or over the Internet. As a consumer-level video editing program, Premiere Elements does not contain all the advanced features of professional-level programs, such as high-definition TV and multicamera support. But for many filmmakers, the combination of ease-of-use, sophisticated features and effects, and affordability make Premiere Elements the perfect editing solution. You meet with your production team for the Genoa Stock & Training video and learn that video editing is only part of the overall video creation process. The group, which includes a producer, a director, and a videographer, among others, explains how your role as editor fits into the big picture.

DETAILS

### The video editing process consists of the following elements:

- **Preproduction**

  **Preproduction** involves all the work you do before you start shooting a movie. This can include the producer creating a budget, the director and screenwriter developing a story or concept, the screenwriter writing the script, the director casting and rehearsing the actors, the location scout finding suitable locations, the production designer overseeing set and costume design, and the director of photography planning the camera angles and sequences. Figure A-1 shows a typical screenplay used for a narrative film. Depending on the budget, the preproduction crew can be as large as hundreds of people or as few as one.

  Even for projects with little or no budget, preproduction is crucial. If you take on a simple documentary project like creating a video of your friend's wedding, you likely won't need to write a script or build a set, but you should visit the locations ahead of time, develop a concept (such as a fast-paced music video or a slow, stately progression of scenes), and test your camera angles and sound equipment. Spending sufficient time and effort on preproduction usually makes the difference between an amateurish video and a well-crafted work of art.

**QUICK TIP**
You can use screenwriting programs such as Final Draft and Cinovation Scriptware to create and edit scripts in standard film and video formats.

- **Production**

  The production stage involves the **shooting** itself—essentially, using a DV camcorder to record the action. The **production crew** might consist of just one **camera operator** holding one camera, or the crew might have multiple operators running multiple cameras, a **gaffer** heading up a team of lighting and electrical professionals, **set dressers** to decorate the set, sound recordists, production assistants, and more.

**QUICK TIP**
You can also edit footage recorded with a digital still camera, camera cell phone, or MPEG-4 video recorder in Premiere Elements. To edit footage recorded with an analog video camera, you need to first convert the footage into digital format.

- **Postproduction**

  Postproduction involves several steps, and Premiere Elements includes tools to help you complete each one, right from your computer. First, you use it to transfer the **source footage** (that is, the recorded videotape) into the computer and to organize it and any additional **source material**, such as video files, audio files, and image files. Next, you use tools in Premiere Elements to **edit** the footage, assembling the moments you want to keep in the order you want, adding any special transitions and effects (such as dissolves or slow motion) where you want them, and adding a music soundtrack or making other audio enhancements. Then it's time to add **titles**, such as the name of your movie and the list of cast and crew. Finally, Premiere Elements guides you through the process of outputting your movie to DVD, videotape, or file for transfer over the Internet. See Table A-1 for a description of the workspaces available to you in Premiere Elements. Although the term "movie" is traditionally used to designate a work shot on film from one shot on videotape, Premiere Elements refers to the finished videos you make as **movies**, as do many filmmakers. Another common term for a video is a **digital film**.

FIGURE A-1: Sample screenplay created with screenwriting software

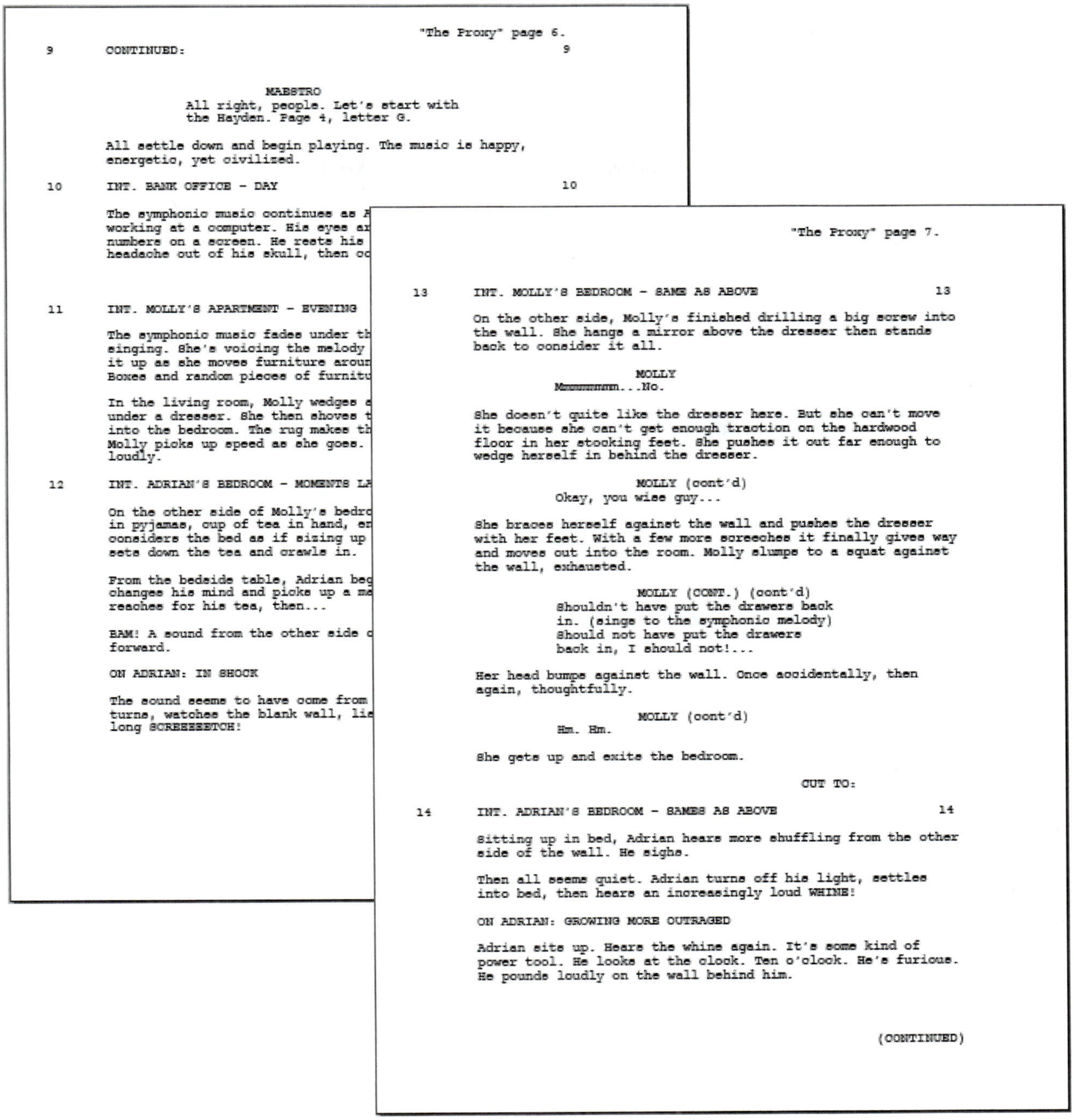

"The Proxy" page 6.

9 CONTINUED: 9

MAESTRO
All right, people. Let's start with the Hayden. Page 4, letter G.

All settle down and begin playing. The music is happy, energetic, yet civilized.

10 INT. BANK OFFICE - DAY 10

The symphonic music continues as A working at a computer. His eyes ar numbers on a screen. He rests his headache out of his skull, then oc

11 INT. MOLLY'S APARTMENT - EVENING

The symphonic music fades under th singing. She's voicing the melody it up as she moves furniture aroun Boxes and random pieces of furnitu

In the living room, Molly wedges a under a dresser. She then shoves t into the bedroom. The rug makes th Molly picks up speed as she goes. loudly.

12 INT. ADRIAN'S BEDROOM - MOMENTS LA

On the other side of Molly's bedro in pyjamas, cup of tea in hand, en considers the bed as if sizing up sets down the tea and crawls in.

From the bedside table, Adrian beg changes his mind and picks up a ma reaches for his tea, then...

BAM! A sound from the other side o forward.

ON ADRIAN: IN SHOCK

The sound seems to have come from turns, watches the blank wall, lis long SCREEEEETCH!

"The Proxy" page 7.

13 INT. MOLLY'S BEDROOM - SAME AS ABOVE 13

On the other side, Molly's finished drilling a big screw into the wall. She hangs a mirror above the dresser then stands back to consider it all.

MOLLY
Mmmmmmmm...No.

She doesn't quite like the dresser here. But she can't move it because she can't get enough traction on the hardwood floor in her stocking feet. She pushes it out far enough to wedge herself in behind the dresser.

MOLLY (cont'd)
Okay, you wise guy...

She braces herself against the wall and pushes the dresser with her feet. With a few more screeches it finally gives way and moves out into the room. Molly slumps to a squat against the wall, exhausted.

MOLLY (CONT.) (cont'd)
Shouldn't have put the drawers back in. (sings to the symphonic melody) Should not have put the drawers back in, I should not!...

Her head bumps against the wall. Once accidentally, then again, thoughtfully.

MOLLY (cont'd)
Hm. Hm.

She gets up and exits the bedroom.

CUT TO:

14 INT. ADRIAN'S BEDROOM - SAMES AS ABOVE 14

Sitting up in bed, Adrian hears more shuffling from the other side of the wall. He sighs.

Then all seems quiet. Adrian turns off his light, settles into bed, then hears an increasingly loud WHINE!

ON ADRIAN: GROWING MORE OUTRAGED

Adrian sits up. Hears the whine again. It's some kind of power tool. He looks at the clock. Ten o'clock. He's furious. He pounds loudly on the wall behind him.

(CONTINUED)

TABLE A-1: Workspaces in Premiere Elements

| workspace | used to | default panels |
|---|---|---|
| Capture | Convert video footage from a DV camera into editable clips | Media, Capture, How To |
| Edit | Assemble, cut, and enhance video and audio clips | Media, Monitor, Effects and Transitions, How To, Properties, Timeline |
| Titles | Add titles and credits | Media, Monitor, Titler, How To, Titler Styles, Timeline |
| DVD | Create DVD menus and burn DVDs | Media, Monitor, DVD Layout, How To, Properties, Timeline |

UNIT
A
Premiere Elements 2.0

# Starting Premiere Elements and Creating a Project

To start working in Premiere Elements, you need to start the program and then open or create a file for your video. In Premiere Elements, this file is called a **project**. Your first project for Genoa Stock focuses on satisfied clients and their dogs. You start Premiere Elements and create a project for this video.

## STEPS

**QUICK TIP**
In this book, we use the default video preset, for North America NTSC Standard 48Hz.

1. **Click the Start button on the Windows taskbar, point to All Programs, then click Adobe Premiere Elements 2.0**

   The Premiere Elements Welcome Screen opens, as shown in Figure A-2. The three large icons let you choose whether to start a new project, work on an existing one, or capture video. Links to recently opened projects appear in the Recent Projects list. (If you have not yet created any projects in Adobe Premiere Elements, this list is blank.) The Tutorials icon opens a project included with the Premiere Elements Help system, and the Setup icon opens a dialog box for changing between the presets NTSC and PAL, the two main standards for broadcast video formats.

2. **Click the New Project icon**

   The New Project dialog box opens. The default project name "Untitled" appears in the Name text box, and a default folder is specified as the location for saving the project.

3. **Click the Name text box, select the text Untitled, if necessary, then type Genoa Clients**

   This project will store all the content and editing information for the video you create about Genoa Stock & Training.

**QUICK TIP**
The file format for a Premiere Elements project is **.prel** (Adobe Premiere Elements Project); other video editing programs have their own proprietary project file format, such as .ppj (Adobe Premiere Project) in Adobe Premiere Pro, and .wswmm (Windows Movie Maker Project) in Windows Movie Maker.

4. **Click Browse, navigate to the location in which you are saving files for this book, click Make New Folder, type YourName (your first and last name, without spaces), press [Enter], click OK, then click OK in the New Project dialog box**

   The project is saved to the location you specified and opens in the Edit workspace, as shown in Figure A-3. The project filename appears last in the **title bar** at the top of the screen. Below it is the **menu bar**, where Premiere Elements commands are organized into menus. The **toolbar** contains buttons for commonly used commands. The **task bar** contains buttons to switch among the four workspaces in Premiere Elements, one for each major stage in the editing process. A **workspace** is an arrangement of **panels**, smaller windows containing commands or tools for completing tasks or obtaining information. The Edit workspace contains six panels: the **Media panel**, for organizing the source clips you want to include in a movie; the **Timeline panel**, for assembling clips and enhancing them; the **Effects and Transitions panel**, for choosing special effects and other modifications; the **Monitor panel**, for viewing footage; the **How To panel**, for help on the current task; and the **Properties panel**, for viewing and changing attributes of the currently selected item on the Timeline (because the Timeline is blank, this panel is blank). The status bar at the bottom of the screen displays instructions on the current task when available.

**TROUBLE**
Video is measured in frames per second—the number of frames that pass over the play head in one second.

5. **Click the Capture button on the task bar**

   The Capture workspace opens, containing an arrangement of panels to help you transfer video footage from your camcorder to your computer's hard drive.

6. **Click the Edit button on the task bar**

7. **Point to the resizing handle at the bottom of the How To panel; when the pointer changes to ↕, drag a few inches down the screen, then release the mouse button**

   The How To panel increases in size. Panels in Premiere Elements are adjustable and configurable. You can resize, move, or hide them to make more room on the screen, and you can display additional panels even if they are not part of the current workspace.

8. **Click Window on the menu bar, point to Restore Workspace, then click Edit**

   The default panel settings for the workspace are restored.

FIGURE A-2: Premiere Elements Welcome Screen

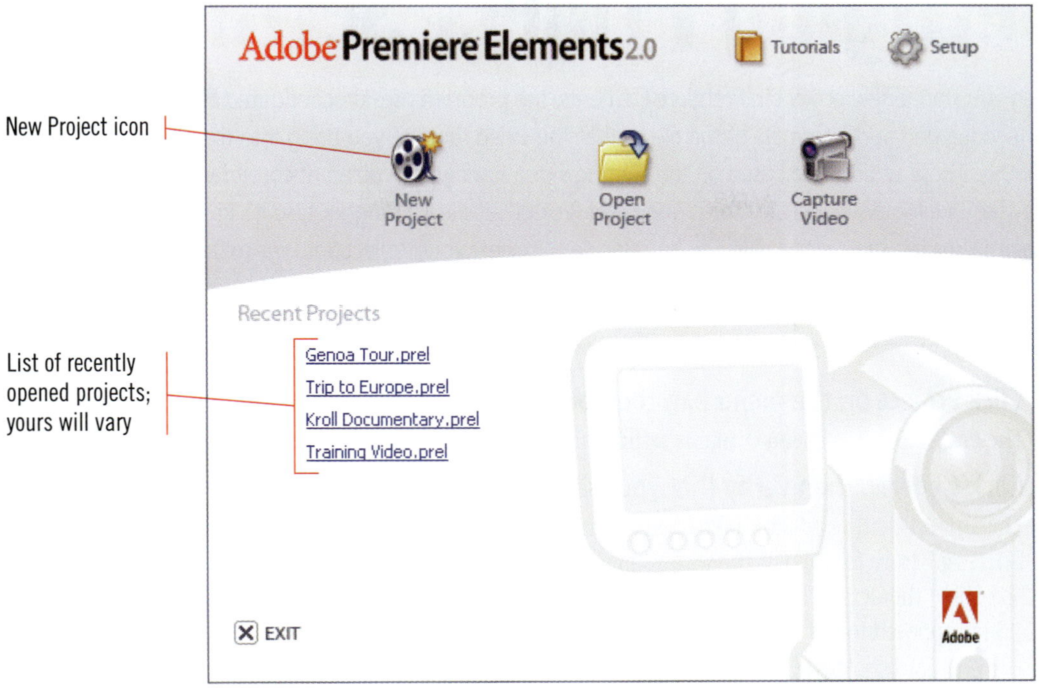


FIGURE A-3: Edit workspace

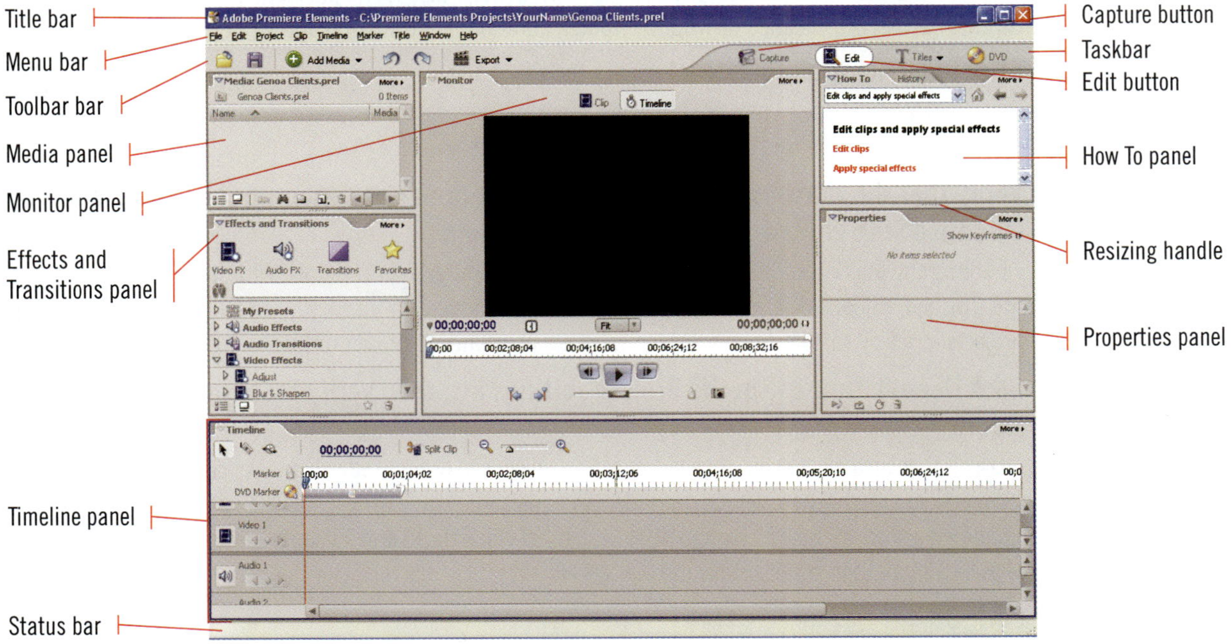


Premiere Elements 2.0

UNIT
**A**
Premiere Elements 2.0

# Verifying Project Settings

When you start a new project in Premiere Elements, the program uses preconfigured **Project Settings** to specify the video and audio formats of the file so that the video footage you bring into the file looks right and plays smoothly. These settings are based on the existing video standards in different countries and on the requirements of your source footage. This book uses one set of Project Settings throughout, so it's important to make sure your program uses the same ones. You decide to review your Project Settings to familiarize yourself with the editing modes available in Premiere Elements.

## STEPS

1. **Click Project on the menu bar, then point to Project Settings**
   The Project Settings menu contains settings for four categories.
2. **Click General, then verify that your settings match those shown in Figure A-4**
   The Project Settings dialog box opens with the General category displayed. Premiere Elements offers an **Editing Mode** for each of the world's major broadcast standards, NTSC and PAL. The settings in this dialog box show the default settings for video processing and playback under the NTSC standard, with a standard 4:3 (as opposed to the wide-screen 16:9) ratio. That's the format we use throughout this book.
3. **Click Playback Settings**
   The Playback Settings dialog box opens, where you can select options for how you want to preview your work as you edit it.
4. **Verify that both the Desktop Video check box and the Disable video output when Premiere Elements is in the background check box contain checkmarks, then click OK**
5. **Click Capture in the Project Settings list, then verify that the Capture Format is DV Capture**
   The lone setting for Capture is displayed. This setting affects how Premiere Elements transfers video from your DV camcorder to the computer. By default, DV Capture is the only option available, but if additional capture devices are installed on your computer, additional options will appear here.
6. **Click Video Rendering in the Project Settings list**
   **Rendering** is a process Premiere Elements goes through to apply the edits you make to each frame of video, compress the information, and display the results in the Monitor panel.
7. **Verify that the Maximum Bit Depth check box does not contain a checkmark and that the Optimize Stills check box does include a checkmark**
   Disabling the Maximum Bit Depth speeds up your computer's performance without sacrificing the quality of the finished video. The Optimize Stills option tells Premiere to insert still images, such as photographs, in projects in a way that conserves disk space while maintaining proper timing alongside moving images.
8. **Click Default Timeline in the Project Settings list, then verify that your screen matches Figure A-5**
   A **track** is an area where you place video and audio clips in order to edit them. Depending on the complexity of a project, you might use as few as one video and one audio track, or several dozen of each. You can click the up and down arrows in the list boxes to display up to 99 video tracks and 99 audio tracks on the Timeline, but three of each is more than sufficient for most projects.
9. **Click OK**
   The Project Settings dialog box closes and you return to the Project window.

**TROUBLE**

If you need to adjust the Editing Mode, click Cancel, click File on the menu bar, click Close, click the Setup button in the Welcome Screen, then click standard 48kHz in the Available Presets list. For additional assistance, consult your instructor.

**QUICK TIP**

You can change the display style of any track to show more or less information; to change the style of a video track, click the Set Video Track Display Style button on the Timeline, then switch among displaying the thumbnail image at the beginning of a clip, at the beginning and end of a clip, along the entire clip, or not at all.

FIGURE A-4: General Project Settings dialog box

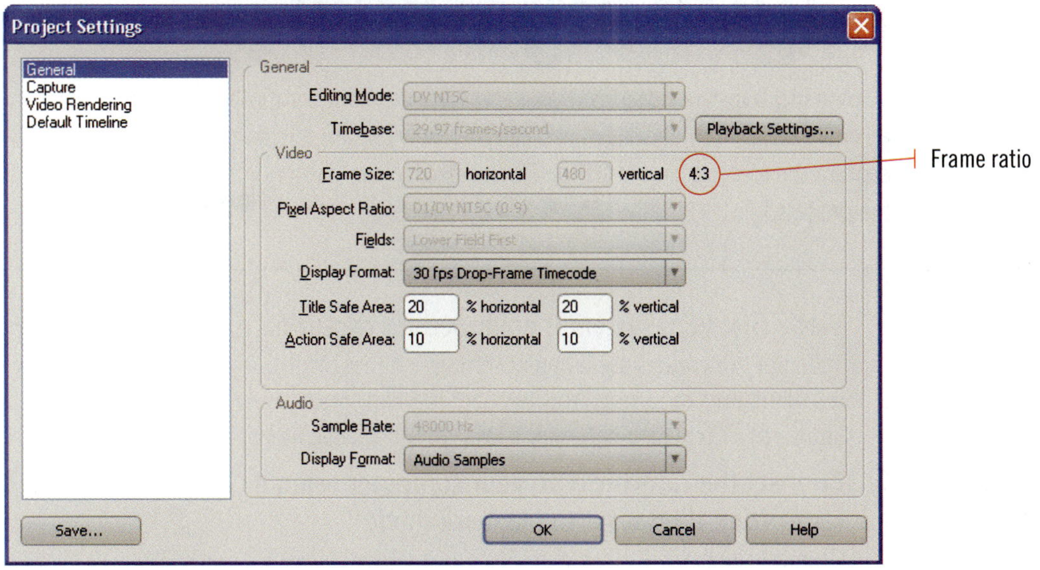


FIGURE A-5: Default Timeline Project Settings

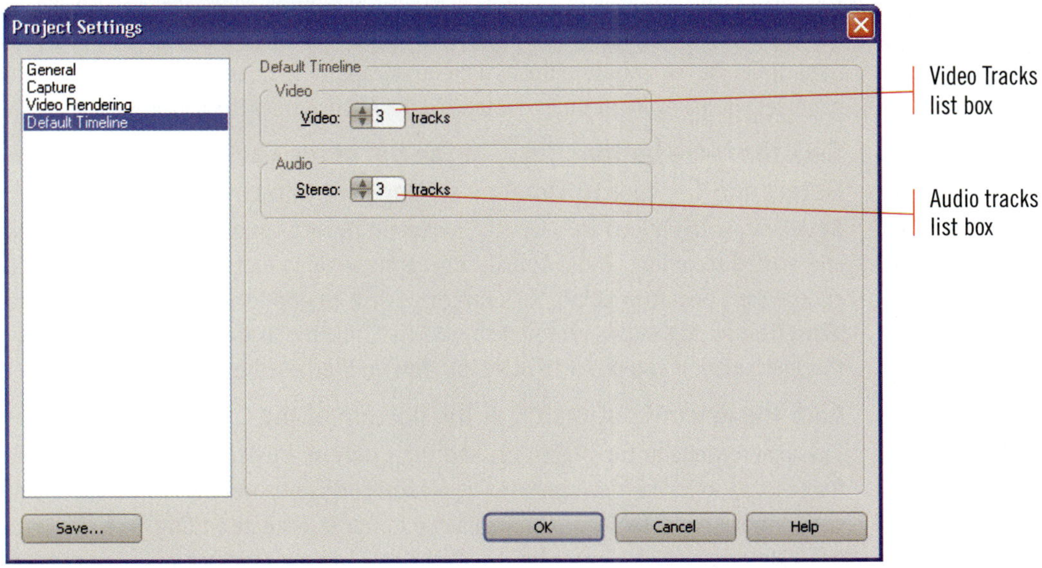


## Production Matters

### Understanding NTSC and PAL

Since the emergence of television and video technology, two different broadcast standards have emerged throughout the world. **NTSC**, which stands for **National Television Standards Committee**, is the broadcast standard in the Americas, Japan, the Caribbean, and Taiwan, while **PAL**, which stands for **Phase Alternating Line**, is used in most of the rest of the world. These standards specify the pixel aspect ratio, frame rate, and other elements that control how an image is composed and displayed on your screen. For example, the **pixel aspect ratio** measures the ratio between the width and height of a **pixel**, which is simply a picture element—one of the tiny dots that make up a video image. The NTSC standard uses an almost square pixel, while in PAL the pixel is slightly more rectangular. These differences can cause all sorts of distortion problems if you try to record using one standard and play using another, or if you try playing a PAL-based video in an NTSC-based VCR. Within these two standards, there are two **frame aspect ratios** defined in each broadcast standard; the 4:3 aspect ratio produces the traditional television-style video frame that is only slightly wider than it is tall, while the 16:9 aspect ratio results in a more cinematic "wide-screen effect." Premiere Elements supports both frame aspect ratios in both standards, but you must select a setting before you create a project; you cannot change mid-project. To change to a different standard, click the Setup icon in the Welcome Screen.

UNIT
**A**
**Premiere Elements 2.0**

# Capturing Video

**Capturing** transfers video from your camcorder to your computer's hard drive. You can capture the contents of an entire tape automatically, or you can manually choose the parts you want to transfer. You prepare to capture the footage for the Genoa Stock video. (*Note*: Capturing requires actual videotape; this lesson describes the process.)

## STEPS

**QUICK TIP**

If you are capturing video you did not record, confirm that the footage was shot using the same broadcast standard and frame aspect ratio as the Editing Mode selected in your Project Settings.

**QUICK TIP**

The NTSC standard is actually 29.97 frames per second, not 30, but Premiere Elements adjusts for this slight discrepancy to keep the timecode numbering system simple.

**QUICK TIP**

When capturing automatically, Premiere Elements stops the capture process when it reaches the end of the recorded tape.

1. **Verify that your system is equipped for capturing digital video footage**
   Different camcorders use different settings when recording, so it's a good idea to use the same camcorder for recording and capturing. You connect the camcorder using either an IEEE 1394 cable (more commonly known as a **FireWire cable**) or a USB 2.0 cable, depending on the port.
2. **Connect the camcorder to your computer using an IEEE 1394 or USB 2 cable, turn on the camcorder, then set it to playback mode**
   On most camcorders, the playback mode is labeled either VTR or VCR.
3. **In Premiere Elements, click the Capture button [Capture] on the task bar**
   The Capture workspace opens, as shown in Figure A-6. The status area at the top of the Capture panel shows the default Clip Name, which will be used for the captured video file; a status line that indicates the state of the camcorder (such as Stopped or Playing); and the estimated amount of video that fits on your computer's hard drive. The More button opens a menu of capture settings. Device controls at the bottom of the Capture panel let you navigate through the tape. Table A-2 describes the controls.
4. **Click the More button [More ▸] at the top of the Capture panel, then verify that the Scene Detect and Capture to Timeline settings contain checkmarks**
   By default, both options are selected. The **Scene Detect** option detects each point where the camera stopped and started recording, and automatically captures video footage in separate clips. If you want to manually choose start and stop points for capturing, click the option to remove the checkmark. The **Capture to Timeline** setting moves captured clips to the Timeline in the order in which they were recorded. Remove this checkmark if you prefer to place the clips on the Timeline yourself.
5. **Click the Rewind button [◂◂] at the bottom of the Capture panel, if necessary**
   The tape rewinds to the beginning, and the **Current Position Timecode display** indicates the current frame location in the video preview area. **Timecode** measures the location of each frame of video, allowing you to move frame by frame through a clip for more accurate editing. In NTSC format, one second of video has 30 frames, so a display reading of 00;28;05;27 indicates the frame is 28 minutes, 5 seconds, and 27 frames into the recorded tape. Timecode is added to videotape only when the camera records.
6. **Click the Capture button [Capture] at the bottom of the Capture panel**
   Premiere Elements begins capturing the videotape and creating clips, and displays the capture in the video preview area. See Figure A-7. The Clip Name text box displays a default name, based on the project name, for the clip that is being captured. To give the clip a more meaningful name, click the text box and type a new name before clicking the Capture button.
7. **Use the device control buttons to pause or move to specific scenes, then click the Stop button [■] when finished**
   The video clips appear in the Media panel.

FIGURE A-6: Capture workspace

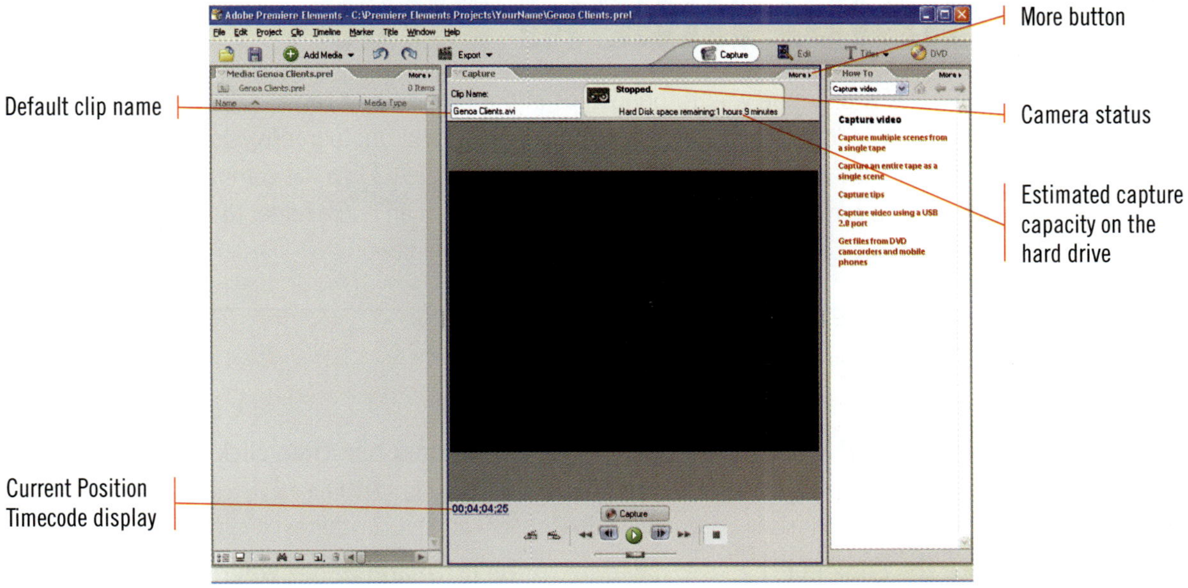


FIGURE A-7: Capturing video

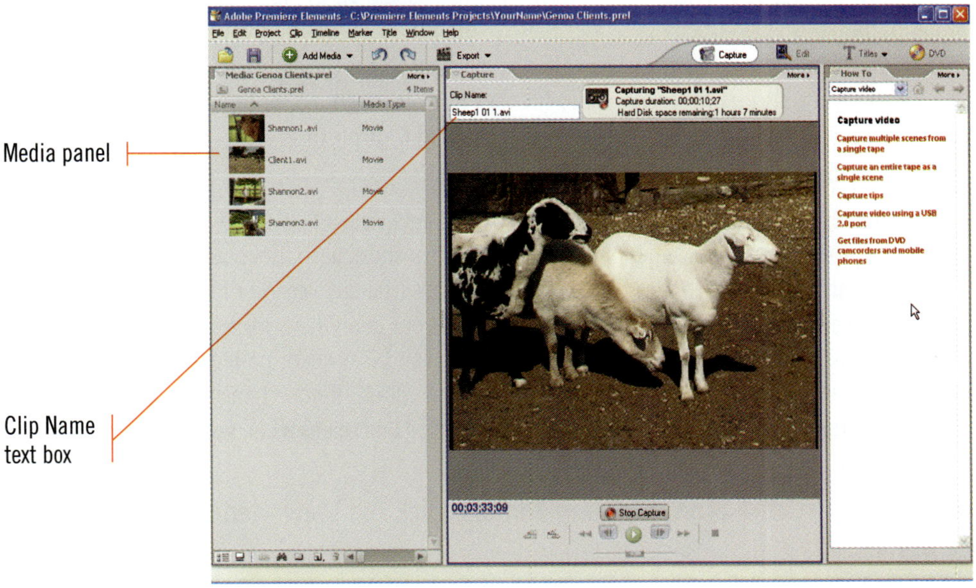


TABLE A-2: Capture panel device controls

| control | name | used to |
| --- | --- | --- |
| Capture | Capture | Begin transferring video |
| | Previous Scene | Jump to the beginning of the previous detected scene on tape |
| | Next Scene | Jump to the beginning of the next detected scene on tape |
| | Rewind | Reverse through the tape |
| | Step Back | Move back one frame at a time in the tape |
| | Play | Begin playing the tape in video preview area |
| | Step Forward | Move ahead one frame at a time in the tape |
| | Fast Forward | Move quickly ahead through the tape |
| | Stop | Stop playing or capturing tape |
| | Shuttle | Drag left or right to move tape forward or back |

# Adding Media Files

Capturing files is only one way to bring clips into a project. You can also bring in existing files such as QuickTime or Windows Movie Maker movies, graphics, and photographs, along with audio files such as songs, music, voice-over narration, and sound effects. Table A-3 lists the compatible file types you can add to a project. You can add an individual file, multiple files, or an entire folder to a project. You need to add clips to the Genoa Stock project before you begin editing.

## STEPS

1. **Click the Edit button on the task bar**

   The Edit workspace opens.

2. **Click the Add Media button on the task bar, then click From Files and Folders**

   The Add Media dialog box opens. You can also add media from a DV Camera or removable hard drive. **Media** is a catchall term encompassing video, audio, and images—in short, anything you might want to include in a video.

3. **Click the Look in list arrow, navigate to the drive and folder where your Data Files are located, then double-click the Source Files folder**

   The files in the Source Files folder appear in the file list, as shown in Figure A-8. This folder contains image (.bmp and .jpg) and video (.wmv and .avi) files. While Audio Video Interleave (.avi) is the native video file format of Premiere Elements and many other video editing programs, in this book we use the Windows Media Video (.wmv) format for many video files because although it supports less color and image detail, it allows us to keep file sizes small for quicker uploading and transporting.

4. **Click Client1.wmv, then click Open**

   The Add Media dialog box closes, and a reference to the Client1.wmv file is added in the Media panel. When you add a file to a project, Premiere Elements adds a **reference** or shortcut to the source file, rather than copying the actual file to your project. Video files are typically very large (the .avi version of the Client1 clip is 60.9MB), so importing source files into a project would likely overtax your computer's memory and could even cause your computer to crash. Using reference files addresses resource and disk space problems, but does require that you know the location of the source files for any project you work on. If you change the location or filename of a source file, and then open a project that uses that file, a dialog box opens when you open the project, asking you to locate it.

5. **Click Add Media, click From Files and Folders, click the View Menu button, then click Details**

   The Add Media dialog box displays the contents of the last folder you worked with, in Details view and in alphabetical order. Detailed information about the files appears, including file size, type, and date modified.

6. **Click Client2, press and hold [Shift], click Client10, then click Open**

   All the selected clips are added to the Media panel. Pressing and holding [Shift] selects all the adjacent files between the first and last file you click; pressing and hold [Ctrl] selects files individually, whether they are next to each other or not. Notice that an asterisk appears next to the filename in the title bar. This indicates that the project has changed since it was last saved.

7. **Click Add Media, click From Files and Folders, click the Genoa Photos folder, then click Add Folder**

   The entire folder is added to the Media panel, as shown in Figure A-9. Depending on your monitor size and resolution, your screen might display more or fewer items in the Media panel.

8. **Click the Save button on the toolbar**

   Your changes are saved to disk.

**QUICK TIP**

You can also add files by dragging them from another program window on your computer to the Media panel in Premiere Elements.

**QUICK TIP**

In this book, all source files are contained in the Source Files folder.

**TROUBLE**

If your files are not listed in alphabetical order, click the Name column header to alphabetize them; if you click the column header when the files are in alphabetical order, you will sort them in reverse alphabetical order.

**FIGURE A-8: Add Media dialog box**

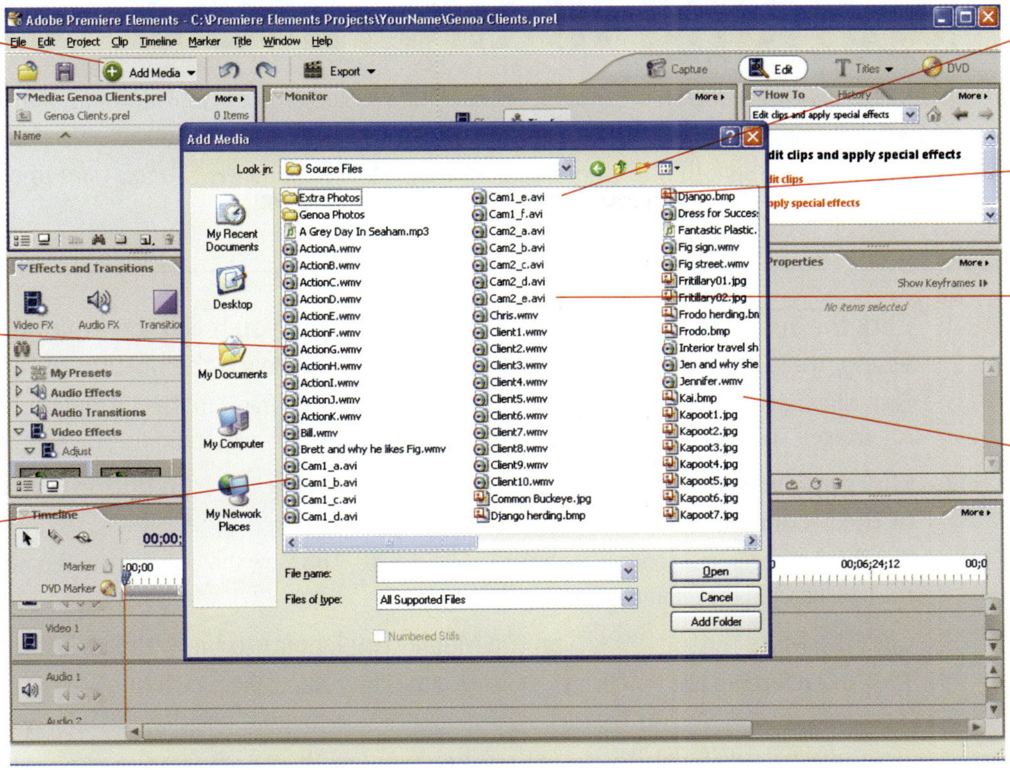


**FIGURE A-9: Clips added to Media panel**

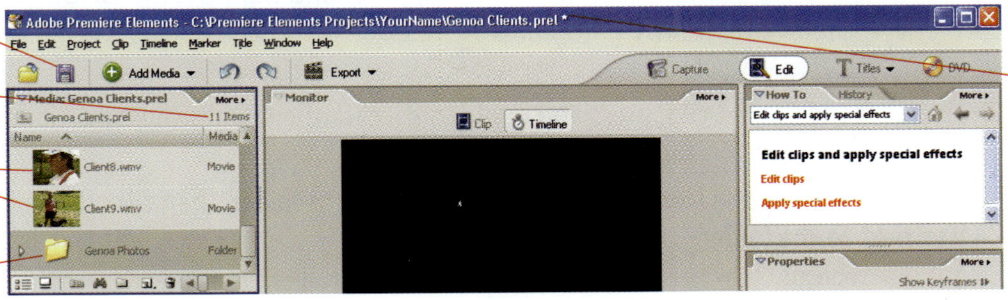


**TABLE A-3: Compatible media file types**

| media type | file types | file extensions |
|---|---|---|
| **Video** | AVI, Filmstrip, MPEG, QuickTime, Windows Media | .avi, .flm, .mpeg/vob/mod/mpe/mpg/m2v/mp2/ mpv/m2p/m2t, .mov/3gp/3g2/mp4/m4v, .wmv/asf |
| **Image** | Adobe Illustrator, Adobe Title Designer, Bitmap, GIF, Encapsulated Postscript, Icon, JPEG, Macintosh PICT, PCX, Photoshop/Photoshop Elements, Portable Network Graphic, TIFF, Truevision Targa | .ai, .prtl, .bmp/dib/rle, .gif, .eps, .ico, .jpg/jpeg/jpe/jfif, .pct/pic/pict, .pcx, .psd, .png, .tif/tiff, .tga/icb/vst/vda |
| **Audio files** | Dolby AC-3, Macintosh Audio AIFF, mp3 Audio, MPEG Audio, QuickTime, Windows Media, Windows WAVE | .ac3, .aif/aiff, .mp3, .mpeg/mpg/mpa/mp3/m2a, .mov/m4a, .wma, .wav |

UNIT
A
Premiere Elements 2.0

# Working in the Media Panel

The Media panel serves as an organizer for your editing project. You can pull any or all of the clips it contains into the Timeline, where they will be included in your movie. If a project contains several clips, it's especially important to make sure they're organized before you start editing. You want to organize the clips you added to the Genoa Clients project.

## STEPS

1. **Click the Scroll Up arrow in the Media panel until you reach the top of the list, if necessary, then drag the Scroll box down until you reach the bottom of the list**
   Each clip displays a **clip thumbnail**, a small image of the first frame in the clip (or the only frame, if it is a still image). The clips you added most recently are highlighted in gray, indicating they are selected.
2. **Click anywhere in the list to deselect any clips, then click the Icon button at the bottom of the Media panel**
   The panel changes to Icon view, as shown in Figure A-10. This view shows larger clip thumbnails, along with the filename and the duration of each clip.
3. **Click the More button More ▸ on the Media panel, point to View, then click List**
   The panel returns to List view, which provides more information about each clip. You can change the size of thumbnail clips in the Media panel by clicking the More button, pointing to Thumbnails, then clicking Small, Medium, Large, or Off.
4. **Drag the resizing handle at the bottom of the Media panel down, as shown in Figure A-11**
5. **Click the Folder button on the Media panel, type Movie Clips, then press [Enter]**
   A new folder named Movie Clips is created. You can resize a panel whenever you need to.
6. **Click the clip thumbnail for Client9.wmv, press and hold the mouse button, then drag the clip into the Movie Clips folder**
   As you drag, the mouse pointer changes to , as shown in Figure A-12.
7. **Click the Client1 clip, press and hold [Shift], click the Client8 clip, scroll if necessary, then drag the selected clips to the Movie Clips folder**
8. **Click the Expand icon next to the Genoa Photos folder, then click the Collapse icon next to the folder**
   The contents of the Genoa Photos folder are displayed as an indented list, and then the folder closes. The icon next to the folder works as a toggle; clicking it expands or collapses the list as needed.

**QUICK TIP**
You can scroll using the horizontal scroll bar to see additional columns of information about the clips, including media type, frame rate, and duration.

**QUICK TIP**
You can use menu commands under the More button or icons on the panel to perform tasks.

**TROUBLE**
To select a clip, make sure you click the clip thumbnail and not the clip name.

### Clues to Use

#### Previewing a clip in the Media panel

When you're organizing clips in the Media panel, sometimes you want to see a quick preview of a clip. For example, you might want to check the contents of an unfamiliar clip to decide which folder to move it to. You can display a small player in the Media panel for just this purpose. To do so, click the More button on the Media panel, point to View, then click Preview Area. A preview area opens at the top of the panel. When you click the Play icon, the clip plays in the preview area, and the Play icon changes to a Stop icon. You can also use the preview area to change the poster frame of a clip. A **poster frame** is the image that appears in the clip thumbnail. By default, Premiere Elements uses the first frame in a clip as the clip thumbnail, but if you want to use a different frame, play the clip in the Preview Area, click the Stop icon when you see the frame you want, then click the Poster Frame icon.

FIGURE A-10: Media panel in Icon view

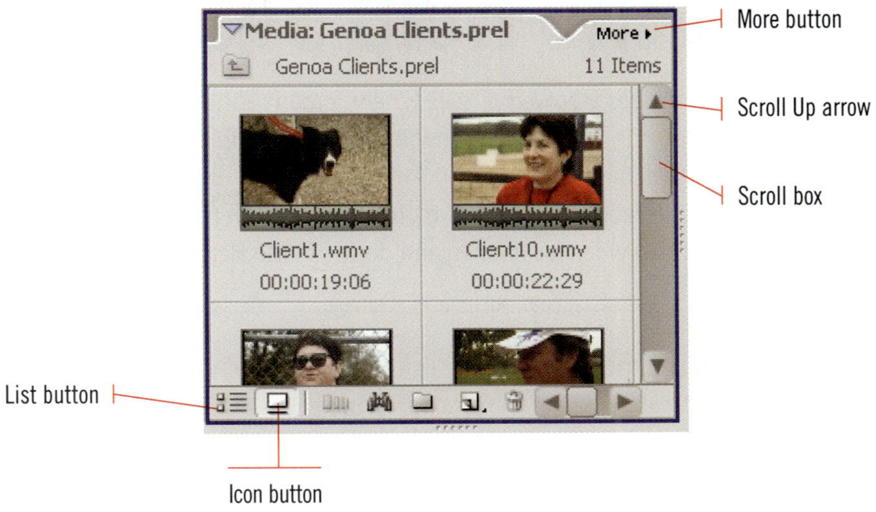


FIGURE A-11: Resizing the Media panel

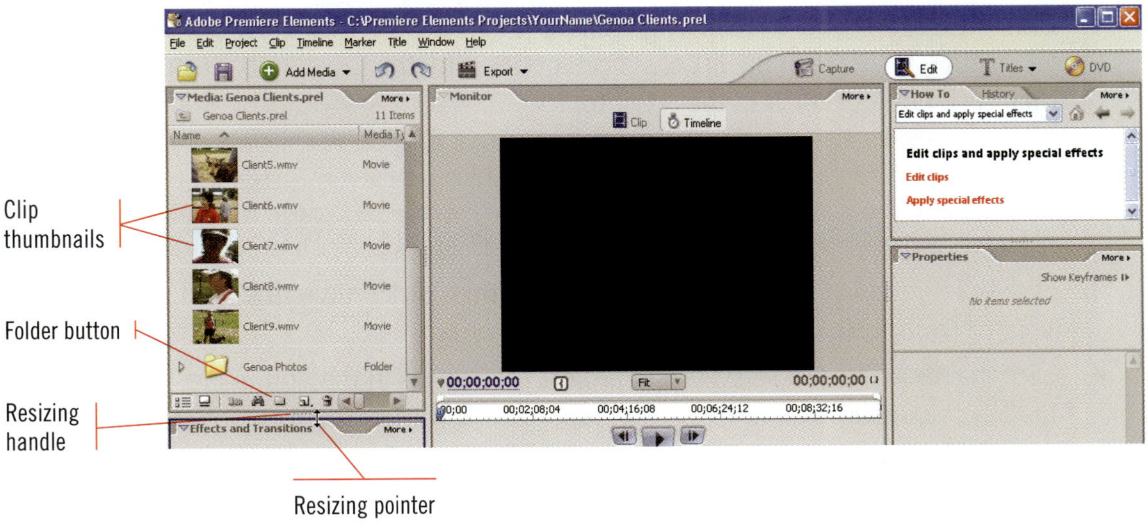


FIGURE A-12: Moving a clip to a folder

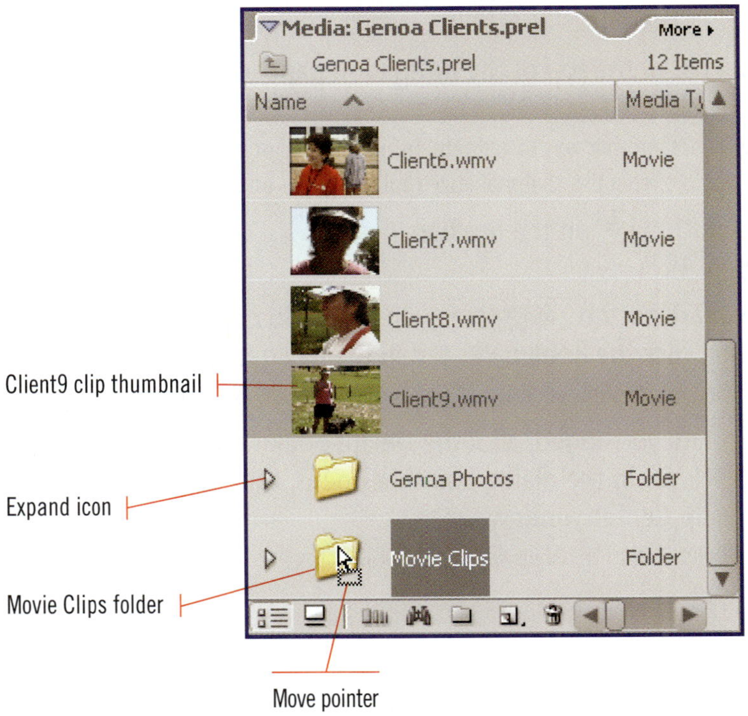

UNIT
A
Premiere Elements 2.0

# Using the Help System

Premiere Elements includes a powerful Help system, organized so that you can get the answers you need quickly and easily. You can get help by browsing through a table of contents, looking through an index, searching for a key term, or referring to a bookmarked topic you saved previously. You can also access additional types of help; see Table A-4 for more information. You've been thinking about how to output your Genoa Clients video when it's finished and decide to use Help to understand how to create a DVD.

## STEPS

1. **Click Help on the menu bar, then click Premiere Elements Help**
   The Adobe Help Center window opens, as shown in Figure A-13. You can resize the Help window by dragging any edge or corner. Adobe Help Center functions like a Web page, with hyperlinks to other pages and a toolbar for navigating the interface and printing. Below the toolbar are two panes. The **navigation pane** on the left provides links to help contents, displayed in the right pane. At the top of the navigation pane are four tabs, each of which lets you access help in a different way.

**QUICK TIP**
You can expand and collapse any category or subcategory by clicking the Expand or Collapse icon or the topic name.

2. **Click the Contents tab in the navigation pane if necessary, click the Expand icon next to Creating DVDs, read the list of subcategories, click the Creating DVDs subcategory, then click Types of DVDs in the list of topics**
   Information on this topic appears in the right pane, as shown in Figure A-14. In the navigation pane, a list of topics appears in the list, indented beneath the Creating DVDs subcategory. The Contents tab functions in a hierarchical fashion, similar to a table of contents. Instead of chapters, content is organized into categories and subcategories, and then broken into topics. Underlined text indicates a hyperlink to another page.
3. **Click the Print button Print on the toolbar, then click Print in the Print dialog box**
   A copy of the topic is printed based on your printer's default settings.

**QUICK TIP**
You can also get help right in the Premiere Elements workspace, by using the How to panel. Links in this panel display instructions for typical tasks in the current workspace.

4. **Click the About project settings and project presets link in the right pane**
   The linked page opens in the right pane and the new topic is highlighted in the navigation pane.
5. **Click in the Search For text box on the toolbar, type auto-play DVDs, then press [Enter]**
   The Search tab opens in the navigation pane, and lists the search results for "auto-play DVDs." The first topic in the results list appears in the right pane. When you know just what information you're looking for, you might prefer to use the Search tab in Help; when you want to browse through several topics to find what you want, the Contents tab might serve you better.

**QUICK TIP**
The Bookmarks tab functions like a Favorites list in a Web browser; you can access favorite topics in the Bookmarks tab and manage your bookmarks using the buttons at the bottom of the navigation pane.

6. **Click the Index tab at the top of the navigation pane, click the letter D, then click the DVD file type topic**
   The Index tab provides another way to get help. Information is organized by letter, like a book index, and you can click any letter to open a list of alphabetized subcategories and topics.
7. **Click the Back button on the toolbar**
   You return to the previous page.
8. **Click the Bookmark button Bookmark on the toolbar, click OK in the New Bookmark dialog box, then click the Bookmarks tab in the navigation pane**
   A bookmark for the current topic is added to the Bookmarks tab, as shown in Figure A-15.

**QUICK TIP**
If you are sharing a computer with other users, you should delete bookmarks and other program customization as a courtesy to others.

9. **Click the bookmark you added, click the Delete Bookmark icon at the bottom of the navigation pane, click Yes in the dialog box that opens, then click the Close button at the top of the Adobe Help Center window**
   The bookmark is deleted, and the Help window closes.

**FIGURE A-13: Adobe Help Center**

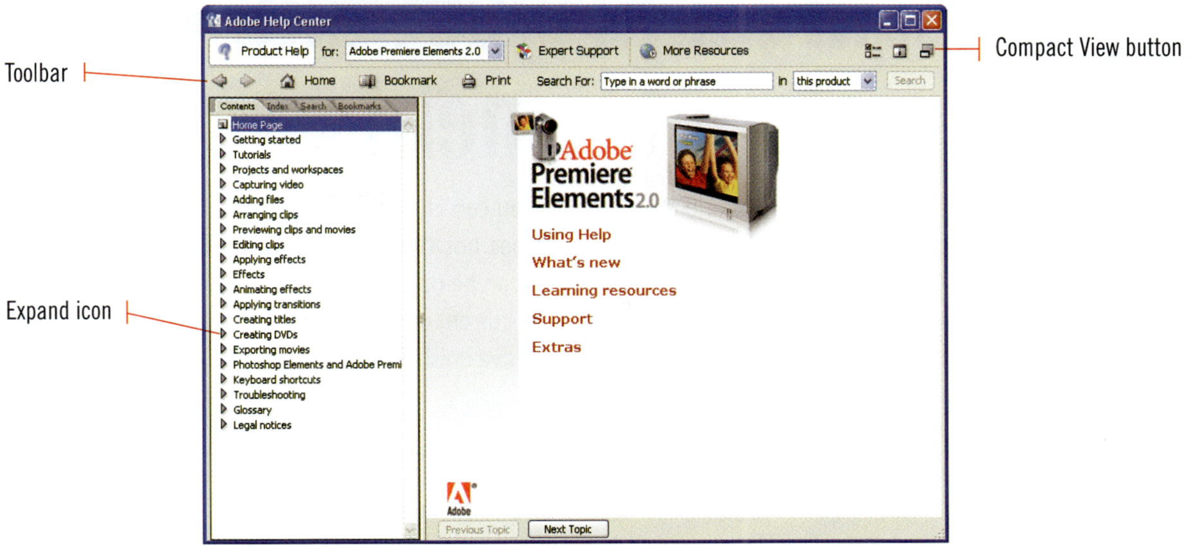


**FIGURE A-14: Contents tab**

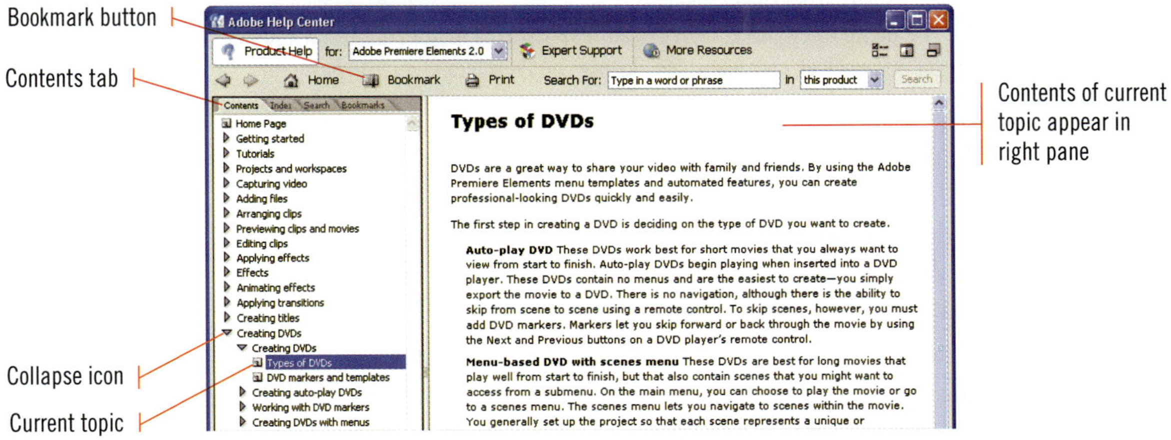


**FIGURE A-15: Bookmarks tab**

**TABLE A-4: Additional Help options**

| option | provides |
|---|---|
| Product Help | Help on the current Adobe product |
| Product Help | Technical support from Adobe, available over the Internet or by phone<br>Click Expert Support button in Adobe Help Center (contract required) |
| More Resources | Online resources to training, user forums, and other sites accessible through the Adobe Web site<br>Click More Resources button |
| | Shrinks Adobe Help Center to Compact view; Help stays open while your work is resized; the Help Center is out of the way and displays only the current topic with fewer navigation buttons |

UNIT A
Premiere Elements 2.0

# Closing a Project and Exiting Premiere Elements

When you have finished working on a project, you can close it and open another project, or you can close Premiere Elements entirely. Closing a project does not close the Premiere Elements program window; it closes only the current project. Only one project can be open in Premiere Elements at a time, so if you want to work on a different project, you must close the current one. It's good practice to save and close your project before exiting Premiere Elements. You've finished working on the Genoa Clients project and are ready to quit editing for the day.

## STEPS

1. **Click the Save Project button on the toolbar**
   Get in the habit of saving your work frequently. Premiere Elements prompts you to save a project before closing, if necessary.
2. **Click File on the menu bar**
   The File menu opens, as shown in Figure A-16. This menu contains a Close command for closing the current project and an Exit command for closing the Premiere Elements program.
3. **Click Close**
   The project closes, but the Premiere Elements Welcome Screen remains open. You can create or open another project or close the program.
4. **Click File on the menu bar**
   The menu does not open. Menu commands are not available unless a project is open, so you only use the File menu to close the program when a project is open.
5. **Click the Exit button EXIT on the Welcome Screen**
   Premiere Elements closes. If you exit Premiere Elements when a project is open, Premiere Elements prompts you to save changes to the project.

**QUICK TIP**

You must use the Exit button on the Welcome Screen to exit when no project is open; the Exit command on the File menu is accessible only when a project is open.

FIGURE A-16: File menu

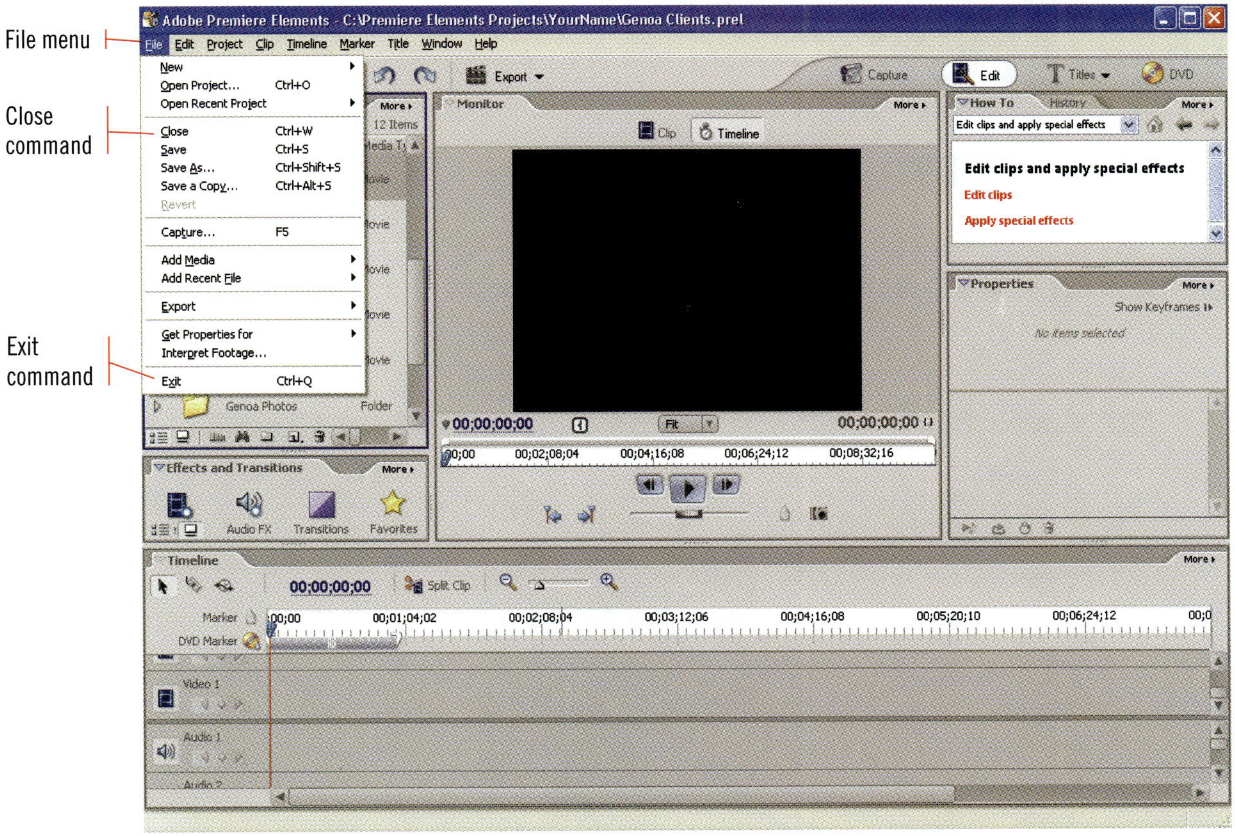


## Clues to Use

### Auto saving a project

To protect your work in case of a power outage, system crash, or other mishap, you can use the Auto Save option. Auto Save automatically saves a version of your project at a specified time interval, and can save multiple versions of the file, so that you have several versions available if you need them. To make sure Auto Save is turned on, click Edit on the menu bar, point to Preferences, then click Auto Save. The Preferences dialog box opens with the Auto Save category in front, as shown in Figure A-17. Click to add a checkmark to the Automatically Save Projects check box if necessary; removing this checkmark turns the Auto Save feature off. Enter a time interval (in minutes) such as 10 or 20 in the Automatically Save Every text box, enter a maximum number of versions such as 5 or 10 that you want Premiere Elements to save in the Maximum Project Versions text box, then click OK. Saving multiple versions of a project does not cost much in disk space, because you are not saving additional versions of your source files; and having multiple versions available means you can step back to a much earlier point in your edit, even one from a few days or weeks back. After you have manually saved a project once, Auto Save begins saving at the assigned interval, and saves up to the maximum number of versions, discarding the oldest one first.

FIGURE A-17: Setting Auto Save preferences

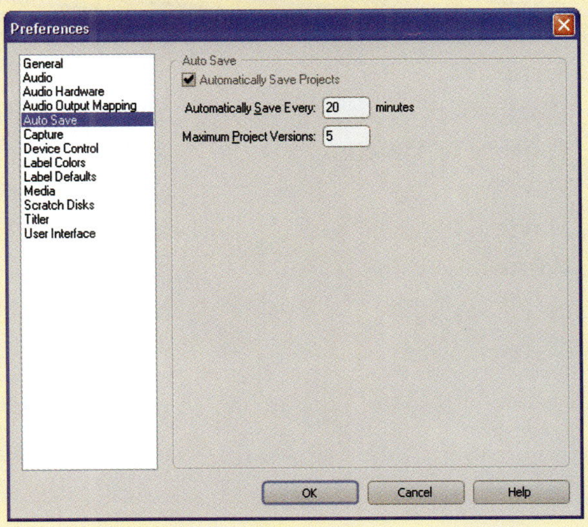

# Practice

## ▼ CONCEPTS REVIEW

**Label the elements of the Premiere Elements program window shown in Figure A-18.**

FIGURE A-18

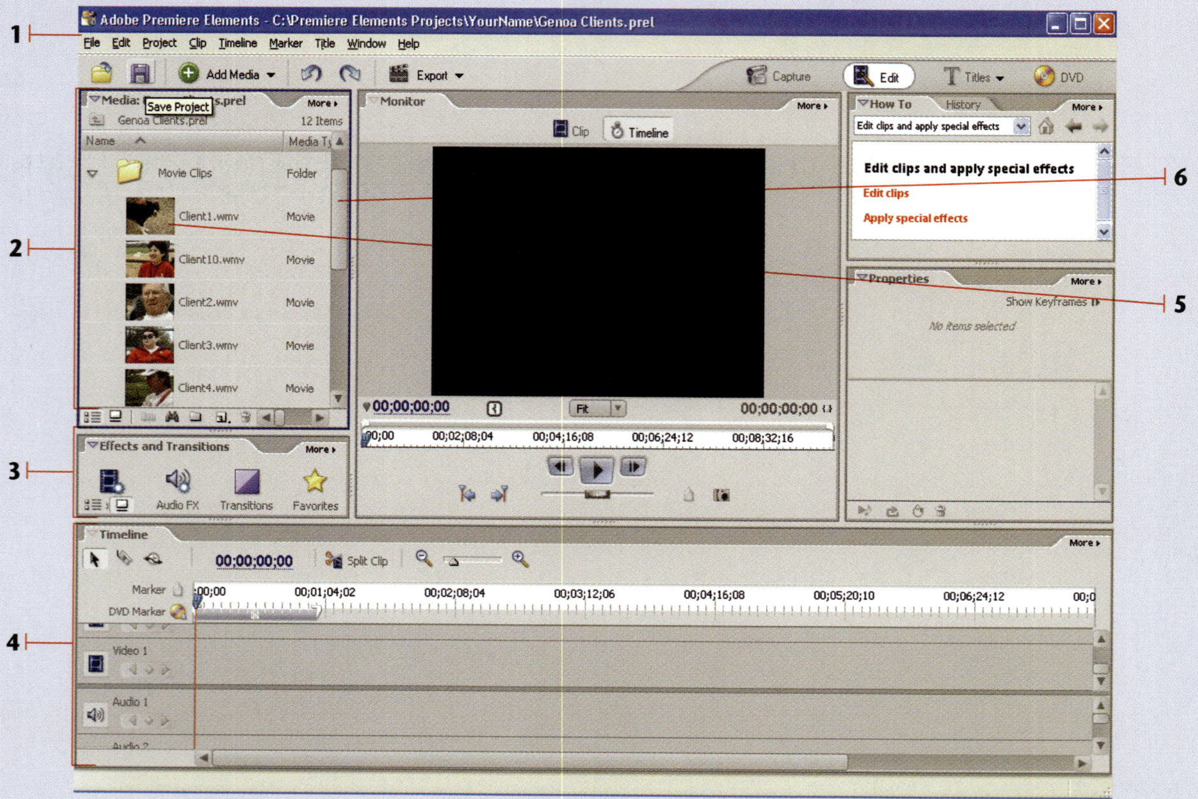


**Match each term with the statement that best describes it.**

**7. Media**
**8. Preproduction**
**9. Scene**
**10. Workspace**
**11. Capture to Timeline**
**12. Shooting**
**13. Movie**
**14. Postproduction**

**a.** Setting that automatically moves clips into the Timeline once they are captured
**b.** Any sources, including video, audio, and/or images, that you might want to include in a video
**c.** The stage of video production when you plan the project
**d.** An arrangement of panels for completing tasks in Premiere Elements
**e.** Filmmaking term that means using the camera to record action
**f.** The name Premiere Elements gives to digital films
**g.** The stage of video production when you edit the final piece
**h.** In filmmaking, a sequence of one or more smaller units of action

**Select the best answer from the list of choices.**

**15. What is NTSC?**

- **a.** A broadcast standard
- **b.** A file format
- **c.** A workspace in Premiere Elements
- **d.** A frame aspect ratio

**16. What is rendering?**

- **a.** The process of converting recorded footage to an .avi file
- **b.** The process a video editing program goes through to capture video
- **c.** The process an editor goes through to choose which shots to include in a video
- **d.** The process a video editing program goes through to apply edits, compress information, and display results

**17. In which panel do you organize your source clips?**

- **a.** Transitions panel
- **b.** Media panel
- **c.** Monitor panel
- **d.** Timeline panel

**18. What specification is always included in a broadcast standard?**

- **a.** Frame rate
- **b.** Maximum file size
- **c.** Minimum clip volume
- **d.** Clip length

**19. Which person in a production crew is in charge of the lighting and electrical staff?**

- **a.** Gaffer
- **b.** Screenwriter
- **c.** Set dresser
- **d.** Camera operator

**20. How many project files can be open at once in Premiere Elements?**

- **a.** Five
- **b.** Ten
- **c.** One
- **d.** Varies, depending on your system settings

## ▼ SKILLS REVIEW

**1. Understand video editing software.**

- **a.** Define video editing software.
- **b.** Identify the three stages of video production.
- **c.** Editing footage is one postproduction task that Premiere Elements helps you perform. Name two other postproduction tasks you can complete using this program.

# ▼ SKILLS REVIEW (CONTINUED)

2. **Start Premiere Elements and create a new project.**
   a. Start Premiere Elements.
   b. Start a new project.
   c. Name the new project **Clown PR**, save it in the *YourName* folder where you are saving files for this book, then click OK.
   d. In the Premiere Elements program window, identify each panel in the Edit workspace.
   e. Switch to the DVD workspace, then click Cancel in the DVD Templates dialog box.
   f. In the DVD workspace, drag the lower-right corner of the DVD Layout panel approximately two inches down and to the right.
   g. Restore the default layout of the DVD workspace.
   h. Switch to the Capture workspace.

3. **Adjust project settings.**
   a. Open the General category of the Project Settings dialog box, then review the information.
   b. Switch to the Capture category, then review the information.
   c. Switch to the Video Rendering category, then review the information.
   d. Switch to the Default Timeline category, change the number of Video tracks to 2, then change the number of Audio tracks to 1.
   e. Click OK in the Project Settings dialog box.

4. **Capture video.**
   a. If possible, connect a video camera to your computer.
   b. Turn on the camera, then set it to playback mode.
   c. Insert a DV tape containing test footage into the camera.
   d. In the Capture workspace, click the Play button in the Capture panel, then review some footage.
   e. After reviewing some footage, click the Stop button without capturing footage.

5. **Add media files.**
   a. Click the Add Media button on the taskbar, then click From Files and Folders.
   b. Navigate to the drive and folder where your Data Files are located, then add the following eight JPEG image files to the project: Kapoot1.jpg, Kapoot2.jpg, Kapoot3.jpg, Kapoot4.jpg, Kapoot5.jpg, Kapoot6.jpg, Kapoot7.jpg, and Kapoot8.jpg.
   c. Add the Extra Photos folder to the project.
   d. Save your changes to the project.

6. **Work in the Media window.**
   a. Scroll through the Media panel and view the clip thumbnail for each image you added.
   b. Switch to Icon view.
   c. Switch to List view.
   d. Resize the Media panel so it is as large as possible.
   e. Create a new folder in the Media panel called **Audience Photos**.
   f. Move the following images into the Audience folder: Kapoot6.jpg, Kapoot7.jpg, and Kapoot8.jpg.
   g. Expand the Audience folder and verify that it contains three images. Compare your screen to Figure A-19.
   h. Collapse the Audience folder.
   i. Expand the Extra Photos folder, verify that it contains two images, then collapse the folder.

FIGURE A-19

## SKILLS REVIEW (CONTINUED)

**7. Get Help.**

- **a.** Open the Adobe Help Center window.
- **b.** Open the Contents pane, if necessary.
- **c.** Scroll to and expand the Projects and workspaces category.
- **d.** Expand the Projects and project settings category.
- **e.** Click the About projects topic.
- **f.** Click the About workspaces and panels link, then read the topic.
- **g.** In the About workspaces and panels topic, click the Inserting clips link.
- **h.** Bookmark the Inserting clips topic.
- **i.** Go back to the previous page.
- **j.** Delete the bookmark you added, then close the Help window.

**8. Close a project and exit Premiere Elements.**

- **a.** Save your changes to the Clown PR project.
- **b.** Close the Clown PR project.
- **c.** Exit Premiere Elements.

## INDEPENDENT CHALLENGE 1

The city's Department of Cultural Affairs has hired you to help promote the annual film festival. You've been asked to create a movie trailer, featuring clips from several films premiering at the fest. The trailer will be posted on the city's Web site. The city has provided you with clips of several films from the festival. You need to create a project and add the clips so that you can create this video.

- **a.** Start Premiere Elements.
- **b.** Create a new project called **Film Fest** in the *YourName* folder where you are saving files for this book.
- **c.** Import the following files, located in the Source Files folder: Tax Help.wmv, Muffin Control.wmv, Silent Breakfast.wmv, Dress for Success.wmv, Sad Song.wmv, Still from Dress for Success.bmp, and Still from the Mountaineer.bmp.
- **d.** In the Media panel, create a Stills folder and a Movies folder.
- **e.** Move the .mwv clips into the Movies folder and the .bmp clips into the Stills folder.
- **f.** Expand the Movies folder.

**Advanced Challenge Exercise**

- Open the preview area.
- View the Tax Help.wmv clip in the preview area, as shown in Figure A-20.
- Close the preview area.

- **g.** Save and close the project, then exit Premiere Elements.

FIGURE A-20

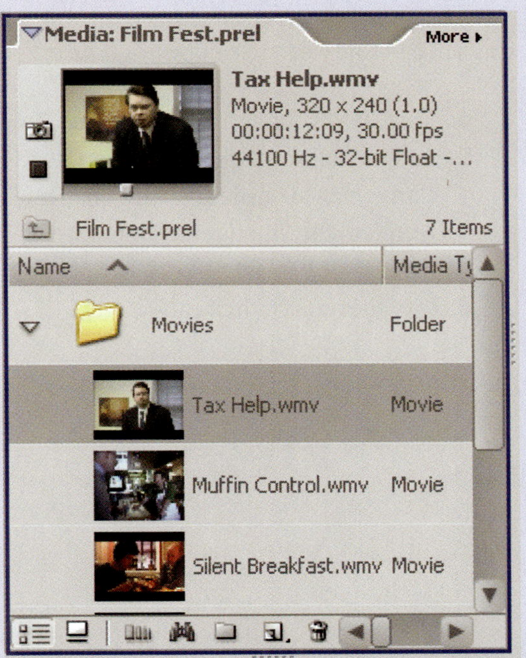

## ▼ INDEPENDENT CHALLENGE 2

As an ambitious video artist, you are working on a new documentary that you plan to direct, shoot, and then edit in Adobe Premiere Elements. You begin shooting the piece next week. You want it to include a variety of interesting visual effects, but your budget is limited. You decide to learn more about the effects available in Premiere Elements so you can take full advantage of them once you begin editing.

**a.** Start Premiere Elements.
**b.** Create a new project called **My First Movie** in the *YourName* folder where you are saving files for this book.
**c.** Open the Adobe Help Center window.
**d.** Use the Contents pane or the Index pane to find information on the topic **applying effects**.
**e.** Follow the link to the topic **Gallery of video effects**.
**f.** Read and print the information, then circle three effects you find interesting.

**Advanced Challenge Exercise**

- Use the Search tab to search for information on each of the three effects you circled.
- Print the topic for each of the three effects.

**g.** Write your name at the top of each printout, close the project without saving changes, then exit Premiere Elements.

## ▼ INDEPENDENT CHALLENGE 3

After a lot of effort, you've landed a dream internship at a hip video production company located in the heart of the city. The company is so impressed with your work that they've decided to expand their internship program. Jim, president of the company, has asked you to create a video that introduces new interns to the staff and the office. In the following units of the book, you will edit this video to complete a finished piece.

**a.** Create a new project named **Dream Job** in the *YourName* folder where you are saving files for this book.
**b.** Add the following clips from the Source Clips folder to your project: Why Megan likes Fig.wmv, Megan.wmv, Chris.wmv, Michelle and why she likes Fig.wmv, Brett and why he likes Fig.wmv, Jen and why she likes Fig.wmv, Jennifer.wmv, Interior travel shot.wmv, Fig sign.wmv, Fig street.wmv, Staff pan.wmv, and Bill.wmv.
**c.** Create a new folder called **Staff**, then move all the clips into the folder.
**d.** Save the project, then close it.

## ▼ INDEPENDENT CHALLENGE 4

To grow as an editor, you should understand the complex jobs that must be completed in the making of a film or video. From producing to art direction, from sound to lighting design, a large production can require hundreds of professionals; in smaller productions, all those roles might be filled by just one or two people. The media barrages us with stories about famous actors, directors, and even producers and screenwriters, but many equally important jobs go unheralded. Expand your knowledge of the complex process of film and video production by learning more about what goes into some of the less publicized roles of video and film production.

**a.** Choose one of the following production roles to research:
- Line producer
- Casting director
- Art director
- Cinematographer

**b.** Use your favorite search engine to search the Web for information on the role you've chosen. Look for descriptions of the term, interviews with professionals in the field, and links to Web sites of your chosen role. See Figure A-21 for an example.

**c.** Print relevant Web pages and add your name to the top of each printout.

FIGURE A-21

## ▼ VISUAL WORKSHOP

Create a new project called **Butterfly Lecture** in the *YourName* folder in which you are saving files for this book. Add the files shown and arrange the workspace so your screen matches Figure A-22. When you are finished, save your changes to the project, press [PrtScr], paste the image into a word processing program, print a copy, then exit the word processor and Premiere Elements.

**FIGURE A-22**

# Using Auto Features

## OBJECTIVES

- Open and save an existing project
- Create a slideshow for a rough cut
- Preview a movie
- Render a movie
- Adjust clips for a rough cut
- Create a slideshow for still images
- Change the default transition
- Add a soundtrack to a slideshow

Premiere Elements includes auto features that allow you to create movies with a minimum of steps, even if you're new to the program. You can use the Create Slideshow command to automatically create a video with movie clips or still images. You can customize these automatic movies with clip choices, transitions, and even a music track. Using auto features provides a friendly introduction to the whole editing process, so you're familiar with workspaces and editing tasks when it comes time to use manual controls. Shannon Wolfe, president of Genoa Stock, is speaking at a training seminar next week. She needs a video featuring Genoa Stock clients that she can play at the seminar before her presentation. She also wants to post, on a kiosk in the hotel conference room, pictures of students herding dogs. You decide to create a rough cut of some video footage Shannon can use at the seminar and a slideshow for the kiosk.

UNIT
**B**
**Premiere Elements 2.0**

# Opening and Saving an Existing Project

When you want to work with an existing project, you need to **open** it to load its references, edits, and scratch files. A **scratch file** is a file Premiere Elements generates automatically to improve performance while you edit. Only one project can be open at a time, so if you try to open a project while another is open, Premiere closes the current project. The file format for a Premiere Elements project is **.prel** (Adobe Premiere Elements Project). Like Premiere Elements, most video editing programs have their own proprietary project file format; in Adobe Premiere Pro, for example, the format is .ppj (Adobe Premiere Project), and in Windows Movie Maker it's .wswmm (Windows Movie Maker Project). When you open a project, you can save a copy of it with a new name to leave the original unchanged. You open the Genoa Stock Clients project and continue working on it.

## STEPS

**QUICK TIP**
You can also open a project by clicking File on the menu bar and then clicking Open, or by pressing [Ctrl][O].

1. **Start Premiere Elements, then in the Welcome Screen click the Open Project icon**
   The Open Project dialog box opens.
2. **Click the Look In list arrow, then navigate to the drive and folder where your Data Files are located**
   The list of available files appears in the file list, as shown in Figure B-1.
3. **Click the Files of type list arrow, view the list, then click the arrow again to close the list**
   Only one file type, Adobe Premiere Elements project, is listed. You can add many types of media files to a Premiere Elements project, but you can open only Premiere Elements project files in this program.

**TROUBLE**
If prompted to locate a file, navigate to the Source Files folder in the drive and folder where your Data Files are located, click the filename, then click Select.

4. **Click the file PE B-1.prel, then click Open**
   The project opens in the Edit workspace. You can also open a project by double-clicking its name in the list.
5. **Click File on the menu bar, then click Save As**
   The Save Project dialog box opens.
6. **If necessary, navigate to the drive and folder in which you are saving files for this book, then double-click the *YourName* folder**
   The Save Project dialog box opens and the projects you have created so far appear in the file list box, as shown in Figure B-2. In addition, a minimum of three folders appear: Adobe Premiere Elements Preview Files, Encoded Files, and Media Cache Files. If the Auto Save feature is turned on and a file has been saved once, an Adobe Premiere Elements Auto Save folder appears as well. Premiere Elements automatically generates these folders when you first open or create a project if they do not already exist in the current folder, and it generates similar folders as needed to organize the scratch files for a project. You rarely need to work directly with these folders, but they make your video editing life much easier. For example, the Adobe Premiere Elements Preview Files folder stores video preview files, so that you can quickly view the results of your edits instead of re-rendering the work area each time you make a change. You can save project files to any drive and folder you want; if you save a project in a folder that does not contain existing scratch folders, Premiere Elements creates the folders as needed.

**QUICK TIP**
To open a project you used recently, click File on the menu bar, click Open Recent Project, then click the name of the project in the list.

7. **Select the text PE B-1.prel in the File name text box, type Genoa Clients Rough Cut 1, then press [Enter]**
   Premiere Elements saves a copy of the project under the new name Genoa Clients Rough Cut 1. This project contains a Movie clips folder and a Still images folder, visible in the Media panel.

FIGURE B-1: Open Project dialog box

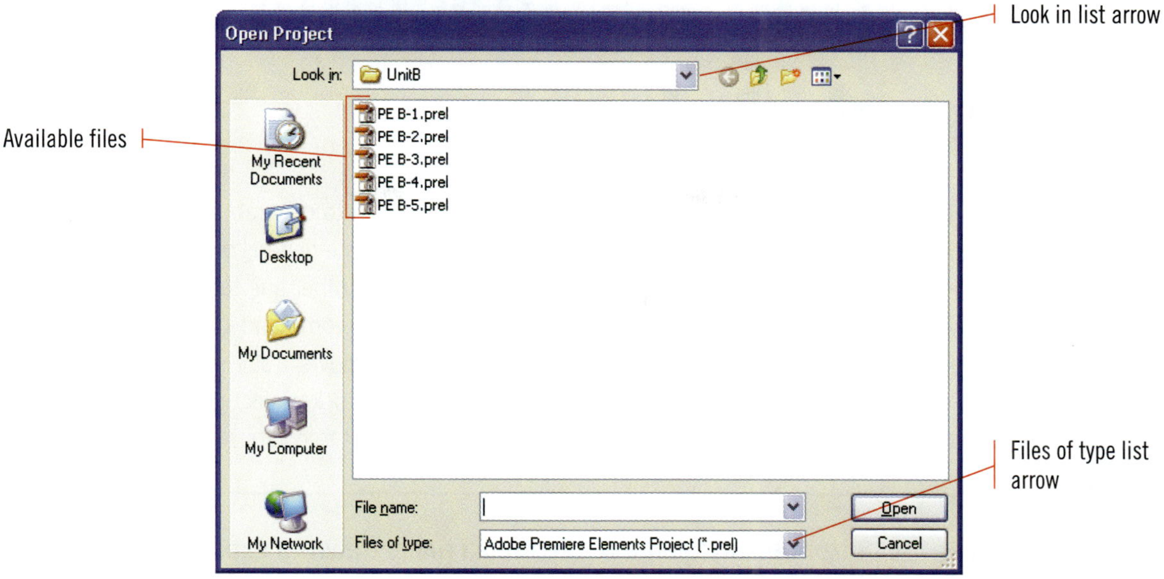


FIGURE B-2: Save Project dialog box

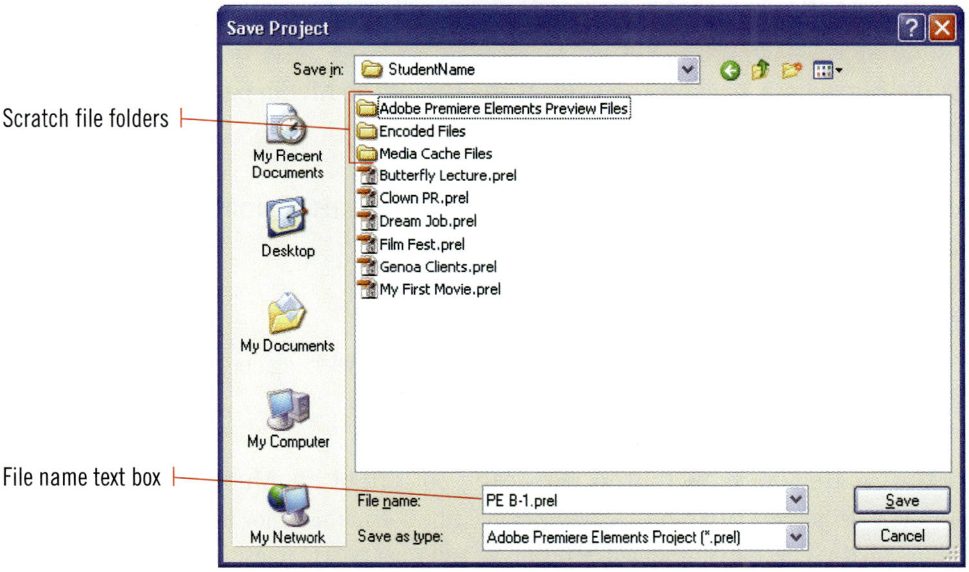


## Clues to Use

### Improving performance with scratch disks

By default, scratch files such as video preview files and Auto Save files are saved in the same location as your project file. The more video projects you work on, the more footage you capture, the more space your system will require for storing source files and the scratch files. If you have more than one hard disk available, you can save disk space on your primary hard drive by selecting different save locations for scratch files in the Preferences dialog box. To do so, click Edit on the menu bar, point to Preferences, then click Scratch Disks. This dialog box lets you change the location to which you save captured video, captured audio, video previews, audio previews, media cache files (generated during editing to improve performance), and DVD encoding files (used for creating a DVD). To change the scratch disk location, click the Browse button for any Scratch disk, navigate to a new location, then click OK. You should use your fastest hard drive for the Captured Video, Captured Audio, and Media Cache folders. It is not recommended that you use network drives, because the data transfer rate is generally not fast enough; nor should you use removable drives, because the Premiere Elements program must have constant access to these folder locations.

UNIT
**B**
Premiere Elements 2.0

# Creating a Slideshow for a Rough Cut

In Premiere Elements, you can use the Create Slideshow command to generate a rough cut. A **rough cut** is an assembly of all the clips you plan to use in a movie arranged in the general order you plan to use them, in the state before you've edited the clips and applied transitions and other fine-tuning. You can use the Create Slideshow command with movie clips, stills, and audio clips. This command takes the clips you select and assembles them on the Timeline automatically, creating an instant movie, a still image presentation, or a combination of the two. The camera operator for the Genoa Stock project provided you with some clips of Genoa Stock clients talking about the training program. You want to create a rough cut using these clips.

## STEPS

1. **Drag the bottom sizing handle of the Media panel down to expand the panel, then double-click the Movie Clips folder**
   The Movie Clips folder opens displaying seven clips, sorted by filename, starting with Client1 and ending with Client7, as shown in Figure B-3. Expanding a folder by clicking the Expand icon displays the folder's contents along with the other files and folders in a project, whereas opening a folder displays the contents *and* activates the folder; any new media you add is automatically added to the folder.

> **TROUBLE**
> If the clips are not sorted starting with Client1, click the Sort icon at the top of the list.

2. **Click the Move up a level button at the top of the Media panel**
   The folder closes.

3. **Double-click the Still Images folder, verify that it contains 10 images, then click**
   You want to include only the movie clips in the rough cut.

> **TROUBLE**
> To select a folder, make sure you click the folder icon itself and not the Expand icon next to it. If you accidentally expand the folder, click the Collapse icon and then try again.

4. **Click the Movie Clips folder to select it**
   You can create a slideshow using all the clips in the Media panel selecting one or more clips, or selecting one or more folders.

> **QUICK TIP**
> Information at the bottom of the dialog box provides tips and advice on the current task.

5. **Click the Create Slideshow button at the bottom of the Media panel**
   The Create Slideshow dialog box opens, as shown in Figure B-4. In this dialog box, you specify settings for the slideshow, such as how the clips should be organized and what type of transition to place between each clip.

6. **Click the Ordering list arrow, then click Sort Order, if necessary**
   This setting arranges clips based on their order in the Media panel list.

7. **Click the Media list arrow, then click Take Video and Audio, if necessary**
   With this setting, Premiere Elements includes both the video and audio in the movie clips, rather than just including one or the other. If you planned to create a music video, for instance, you might want to just take the video from several movie clips and add separate audio later.

8. **Click OK**
   All the video and audio clips in the Movie Clips folder are added to the Timeline, as shown in Figure B-5. The Timeline shows a thumbnail of each clip, or as much of it that will fit in the current zoom range and monitor size. The first frame of the first clip in the Timeline is displayed in the Monitor panel.

9. **Click the Save Project button on the toolbar**

**FIGURE B-3: Movie Clips folder open in Media panel**

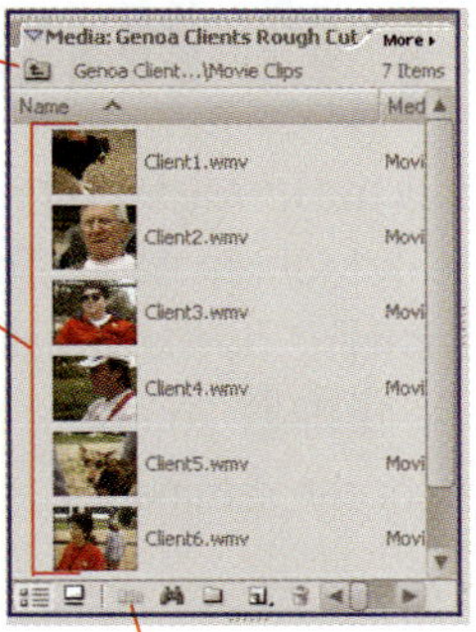


**FIGURE B-4: Create Slideshow dialog box**

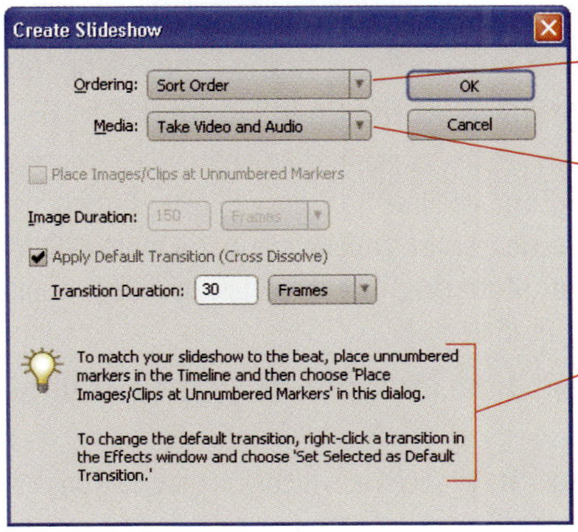


**FIGURE B-5: Completed rough cut**

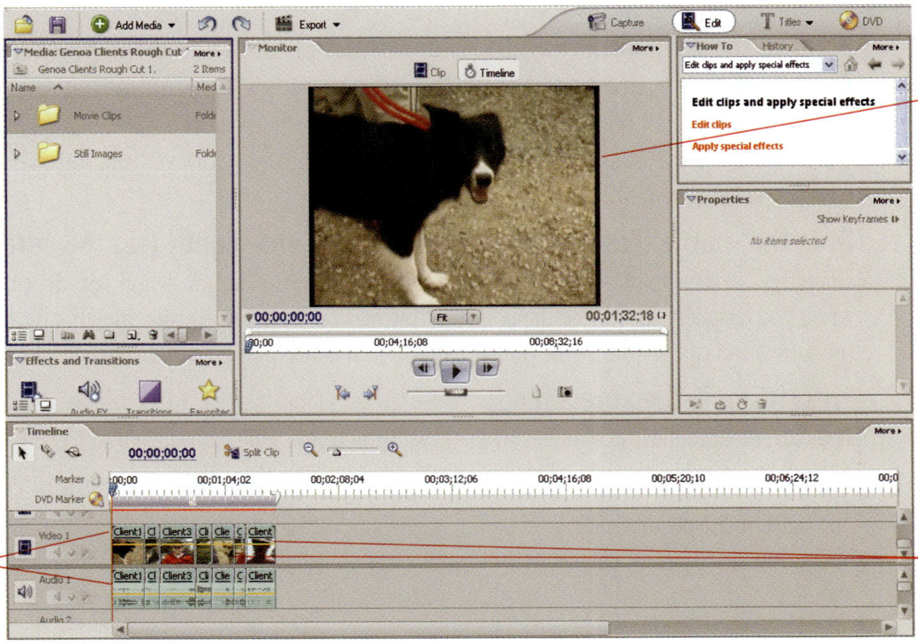

UNIT B
Premiere Elements 2.0

# Previewing a Movie

You can use the Monitor panel to preview the movie you are editing at any time. To start and stop the movie you can use the controls in the Timeline or Monitor panel. To move to a specific point in the movie, you can use the current-time indicator in the Timeline or the Timeline view of the Monitor panel, or you can use additional controls in the Monitor panel. You want to preview the Genoa Clients Rough Cut to see whether it will suit Shannon's purposes for the seminar.

## STEPS

1. **Click the Play button on the Monitor panel**

   The movie plays in the Monitor panel, and the changes to a Pause button, as shown in Figure B-6. The Slideshow command inserts a transition between each clip, so each clip blends into the next. Depending on your computer, the movie may not play smoothly; that's all right for now. When the movie finishes, it stops on the last frame of the last clip. The **time ruler** on both the Timeline and the Monitor panel measures the movie length. It displays a **current-time indicator**, which shows the exact frame in the Timeline and which you can use to navigate to any frame. The **time display** above the time ruler shows the exact frame location of the, which is 00:01;32;15, or 1 minute, 32 seconds, and 15 frames; your frame location will differ.

2. **Click the Zoom In button as many times as necessary until the clips on the Timeline fill the available space, as shown in Figure B-7**

   Unlike in a word-processing or graphic design program, the zoom level in Premiere Elements does not show you more or less of the document or image; instead, it changes your view of the Timeline. **Zooming in** shows a smaller portion of the Timeline, but at a more detailed level so that you can navigate more easily from frame to frame. **Zooming out** shows less detail but displays more of the Timeline so that you can easily jump minutes ahead or back.

3. **Drag the current-time indicator to the left until the time display is approximately 00;00;30;03**

   The movie progresses at the speed at which you drag, so you can hear some sound and see the frames moving in the Monitor. Depending on your monitor's display and zoom setting, the time ruler displays different time marker milestones. As long as you set the indicator to a frame near 30 seconds into the movie, don't worry about reaching this precise frame.

4. **Press [Spacebar], view the movie for a few seconds, then press [Spacebar] again**

   The movie plays from the current point forward until you press [Spacebar]; you can use [Spacebar] instead of the controls on the Monitor panel to start and stop playing.

5. **Point to the time display on the Monitor panel, then when the pointer changes to the scrub pointer, drag right until the time display is approximately 00;00;50;00**

   As you drag, is not visible. You can move back and forth in the Timeline by dragging the time display with. You can see the frames progressing in the Monitor panel; however, the sound does not play when you navigate using this method.

6. **Drag the shuttle slider on the Monitor panel slightly left, then drag it slightly right**

   Dragging the shuttle plays the movie with audio in forward motion when you drag right, or reverse motion when you drag left. The speed depends on how far you drag the shuttle; dragging far to the right or left plays the movie in fast motion, while dragging a slight distance plays it more slowly.

7. **Press [Home], then press [End]**

   The current-time indicator moves to the beginning of the movie, and then to the end.

8. **Click the Go to Previous Edit Point button on the Monitor panel**

   The current-time indicator moves to the beginning of the current clip, Client7, as shown in Figure B-8. The beginning of the new clip is superimposed over the last frame of the previous clip because the Create Slideshow command applied a transition to this frame.

**QUICK TIP**

Depending on your monitor size, your zoom percentage will vary from the figures shown in this book; adjust your zoom level as necessary as you work.

**QUICK TIP**

To move to a specific frame, you can click the time display in the Timeline or Monitor panel, type the desired frame number, then press [Enter].

**QUICK TIP**

You can also view a movie in reverse by dragging the left in either time ruler.

**FIGURE B-6: Previewing a movie**

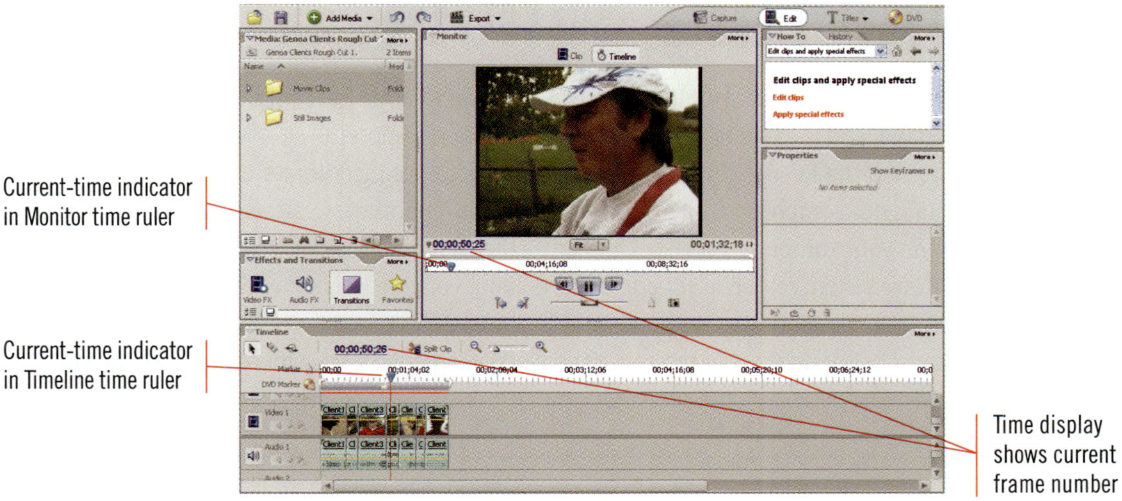


**FIGURE B-7: Zooming in on the Timeline**

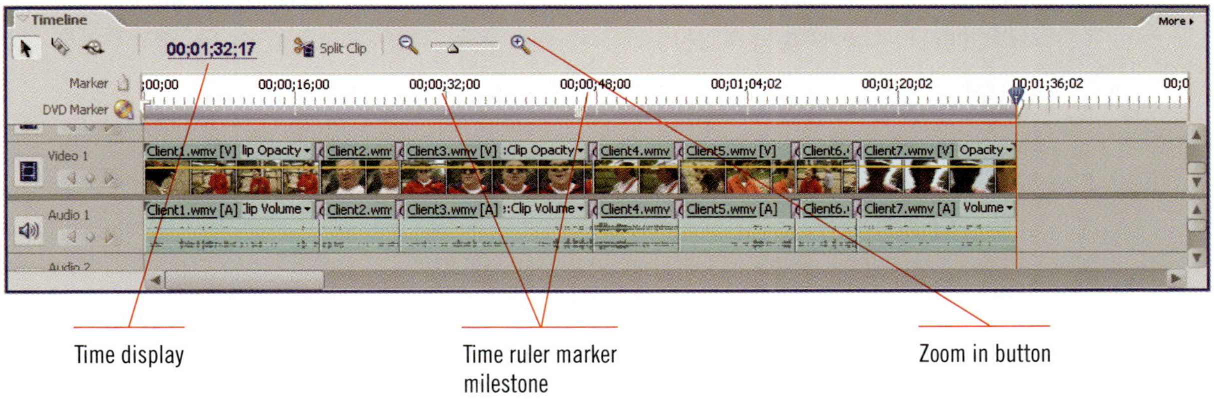


**FIGURE B-8: Moving to a previous edit point**

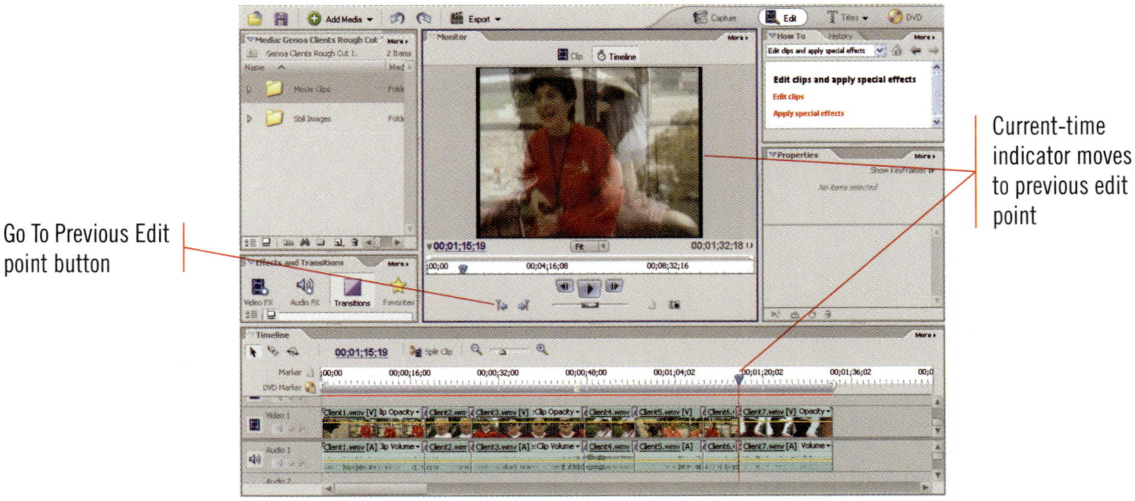

UNIT B

Premiere Elements 2.0

# Rendering a movie

The **Render** command processes the edits you've made to a movie, compresses the information, recalculates each frame, and displays the results in final form when you preview it. When you preview a movie without first applying the Render command, the preview does not incorporate the edits applied to each frame and the data is not compressed. Therefore, the degree of smoothness you see in the Monitor window varies depending on your computer's speed, RAM, and other system resources. To obtain the smoothest playback and to conserve system resources for additional editing, you need to render the contents of the Timeline (or any portion of it that you want to preview in final form). The **work area bar** indicates the portion of a movie that will be rendered. You can resize the work area bar to render more or less of the contents on the Timeline. You want the Genoa Stock movie to play as smoothly as possible, so you render it.

## STEPS

1. **Verify that the work area bar extends from the beginning to the end of the footage on the Timeline; if it does not, drag the start-of-movie marker to the first frame of the movie, then drag the end-of-movie marker to the last frame of the movie**

   The work area bar is the gray band directly beneath the time ruler on the Timeline panel. By default, this bar adjusts to extend over any new footage added to the Timeline, as shown in Figure B-9. Sometimes you need to adjust it to accommodate added clips or to render only part of a movie, such as when you are working on a long movie and don't need to see a rendered preview of the whole thing. The red line below the work area bar indicates unrendered footage.

2. **Click Timeline on the menu bar, then click Render Work Area**

   Depending on the speed of your computer, rendering may take a few seconds or a few minutes. When the edits (in this case, the transitions generated with the Create Slideshow command) are applied and the data compressed, the red line changes to green, indicating that the footage has been rendered, as shown in Figure B-10. After rendering, the current-time indicator moves to the beginning of the rendered footage, the line returns to green, and the rendered footage plays in the Monitor panel.

3. **View the rendered movie for a few seconds, then press [Spacebar] to pause it**

   The movie plays more smoothly than it did before it was rendered. In general, you don't need to render every time you add clips or make an edit, but if you want the movie to play as smoothly as possible, especially when working with larger files, you may find it useful to render the footage whenever you make a change that creates unrendered footage, which is indicated by the red line.

4. **Press [Page Down] to go to the next edit point, press [Spacebar] to play the movie, then after you watch the transition, press [Spacebar] to pause the movie**

   The transition from clip to clip plays more smoothly.

5. **Press [End]**

   The current-time indicator moves to the end of the movie.

6. **Click the Save Project button on the toolbar**

   The edits to the movie are saved.

**QUICK TIP**

You can monitor the rendering process by watching the red line turn to green on the Timeline.

**QUICK TIP**

You can press [Page Up] to move to the previous edit point.

FIGURE B-9: Unrendered work area

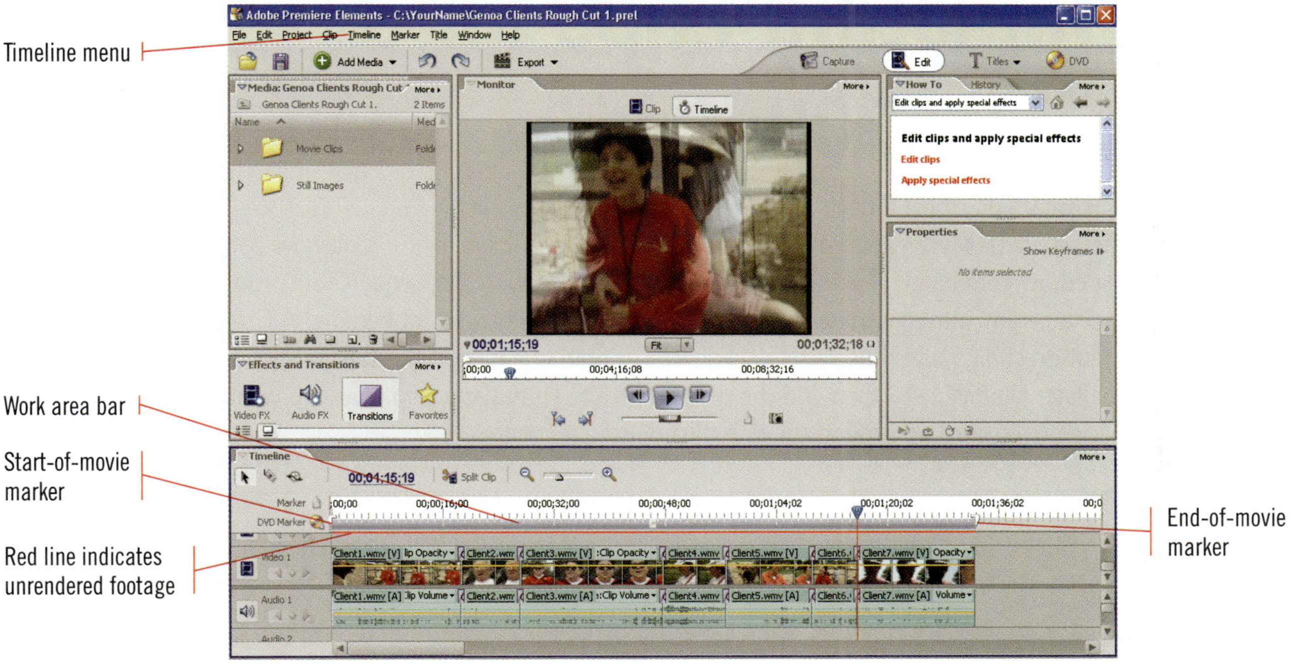


FIGURE B-10: Rendered work area

UNIT B
Premiere Elements 2.0

# Adjusting Clips for a Slideshow

You can modify some aspects of a slideshow before you use auto features. This allows you more control over the results. For example, you can change the order of clips in the slideshow before using the Create Slideshow command. You aren't quite satisfied with the Genoa Clients rough cut. Currently, the movie begins with a client enthusiastically discussing the benefits of herding. A later clip shows the same client describing an unsuccessful experience. To grab the attention of the audience, you want to position the later clip first, and then end the movie with the enthusiastic clip. You also want to delete a clip. You decide to create a new rough cut with this adjusted sequence.

## STEPS

1. **Click File on the menu bar, point to Open Recent Project, then click PE B-1.prel**
   The Genoa Clients Rough Cut project closes and the PE B-1 project opens.
2. **Click File, click Save As, then save the project as Genoa Clients Rough Cut 2**
3. **Double-click the Movie Clips folder, click the Icon View button at the bottom of the Media panel, then drag the resizing handles on the bottom and right edge of the panel until all the clips are visible**
   In Icon view, you can rearrange or delete clips as desired. This view provides a **storyboard** format, a set of pictures that shows the visual progression of the movie. You can use the pictures to help you plan the movie before creating it on the Timeline. Enlarging the panel gives you more room to work.
4. **Click the Client1 clip thumbnail, press and hold the mouse button, then drag the thumbnail to the right of the Client7 clip, as shown in Figure B-11**
   As you drag, the pointer changes to and a black border appears to the right of the Client7 clip, indicating where the dragged object will be placed; the border appears on the left if the dragged clip will be inserted to the clip's left.
5. **Click the Client6 clip thumbnail, press and hold the mouse button, then drag the thumbnail to the right of the Client2 clip**
   When you release the mouse button, the clip is inserted between the Client2 clip and the Client3 clip.
6. **Drag the Client6 clip thumbnail to the empty placeholder to the left of the Client2 clip**
   When you can drag a clip to an empty placeholder instead of between two clip thumbnails, the placeholder is highlighted in black to indicate where the dragged object will be placed. Compare your screen to Figure B-12.
7. **Click the Client2 clip thumbnail, then press [Delete]**
   The Client2 clip is deleted from the Media panel and the project. The source file remains on your computer, so you can add it to or reuse it in this project or in a new one.
8. **Click the Client6 clip thumbnail in the folder, press and hold [Shift], click the Client1 clip thumbnail, click the Create Slideshow button , verify that the Ordering list reads Sort Order, then click OK**
   The clips are arranged in the Timeline in the order in which they appear in the Media panel. Compare your screen to Figure B-13.
9. **Save your changes, drag the resizing handle on the Monitor panel to enlarge it, then play the new movie**

**QUICK TIP**

You don't have to drag the resizing handle to resize a panel; you can also drag anywhere on the edge of a panel that contains a resizing handle, or drag a corner formed by two edges that contain resizing handles.

**FIGURE B-11: Moving a clip in the Media panel**

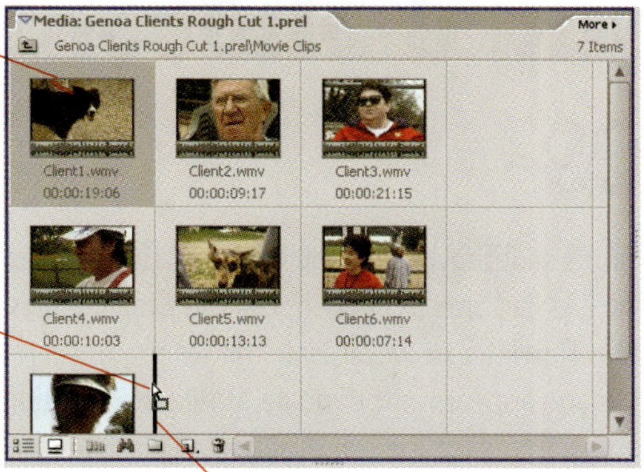


**FIGURE B-12: New clip order in Media panel**

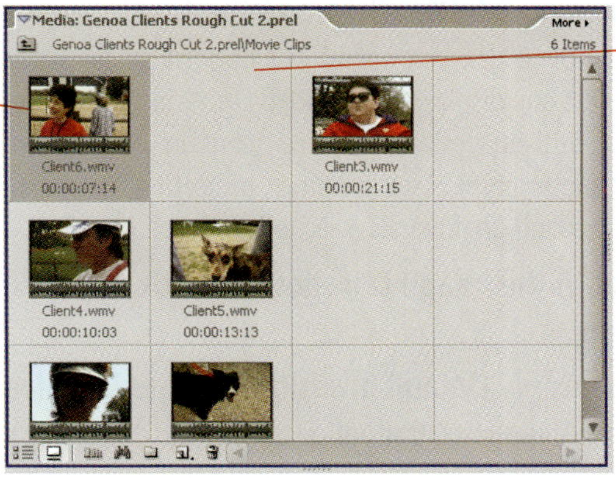


**FIGURE B-13: New rough cut**

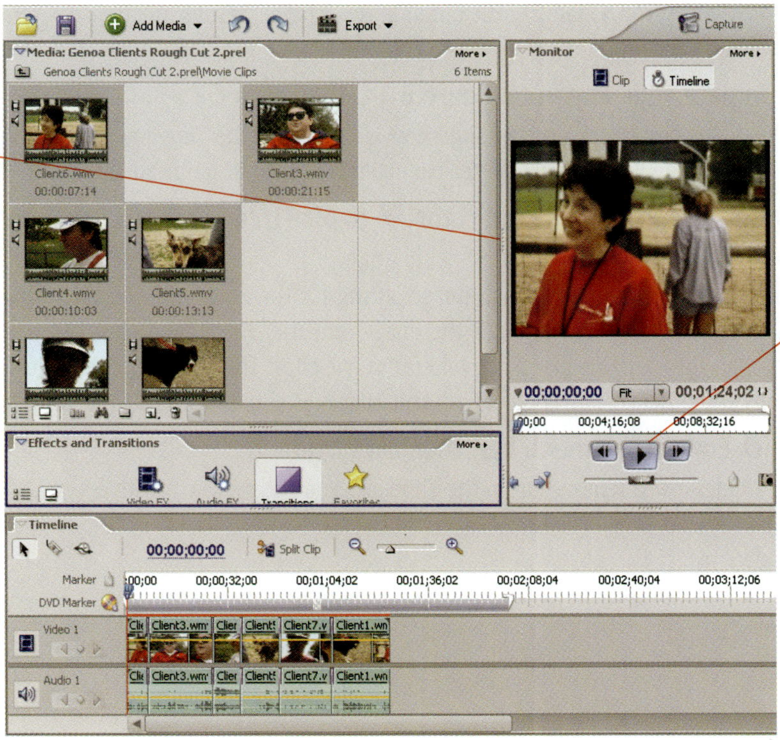

UNIT B
Premiere Elements 2.0

# Creating a Slideshow for Still Images

The process of creating a slideshow using still images is the same as creating one using movie clips. You can rearrange them in the Media panel as needed, use the Create Slideshow command to create the movie, and then preview it on the Timeline. However, still images present a few additional considerations, such as the length of time each image appears in the movie. While the duration of a movie clip is self-explanatory—it is the length of the clip—you determine the duration still images are displayed. You might want images in a slideshow to stay on screen for just a fraction of a second or for several seconds. You are ready to create the still image slideshow that Shannon requested for her seminar.

## STEPS

1. **Close the Movie Clips folder**
2. **Select the Still Images folder, then click the Create Slideshow button on the Media panel**
   The Create Slideshow dialog box opens. The options in the dialog box pertain to still clips instead of movie clips. The Media list box displays "Take Video Only" instead of "Take Video and Audio" because you selected a folder containing still images which do not contain an audio track. The Image Duration text box displays "150," and the Duration type is set to Frames, indicating that each image will remain on screen for 150 frames. At 30 frames per second, that equals 5 seconds for each image.
3. **Select the text in the Image Duration text box, type 90, then verify that the Duration type is set to Frames**
4. **Verify that the Apply Default Transition (Cross Dissolve) check box contains a check mark**
   As with movie clip slideshows, this option applies the default transition to the beginning of each clip following the first one. The name of the default transition appears in parentheses. If you want to change this transition type, you must first change the default transition, which you will learn in the next lesson.
5. **Select the text in the Transition Duration text box, then type 15**
   Because you shortened the duration of each clip, you want the dissolve transition between each clip to occur more quickly, too. Changing the duration to 15 frames results in a transition that takes half a second instead of a whole second.
6. **Compare your screen to Figure B-14, then click OK**
   The dialog box closes, and the slideshow is created on the Timeline just after the rough cut you created earlier. See Figure B-15. The work area bar extends to the last frame added.
7. **Drag the current-time indicator to 00;01;24;02, then click the Play button on the Monitor panel**
   The slideshow plays, with each image lasting for three seconds and each dissolve transition between clips lasting half a second. Although the images are still, the time display and current-time indicator progress through the Timeline just as they do for movie clips. This means you have just as much control over transitions and other editing choices with still images as you do with moving video.
8. **Click Edit on the menu bar, then click Undo**
   The slideshow is removed from the Timeline. You will replace it with a new slideshow in the next lesson.

**QUICK TIP**

You can also create slideshows that contain both movie clips and still images; after selecting the clips you want to include, adjust the options in the Create Slideshow dialog box, making sure that the Take Audio and Video option is selected in the Media list.

**FIGURE B-14: Create Slideshow dialog box**

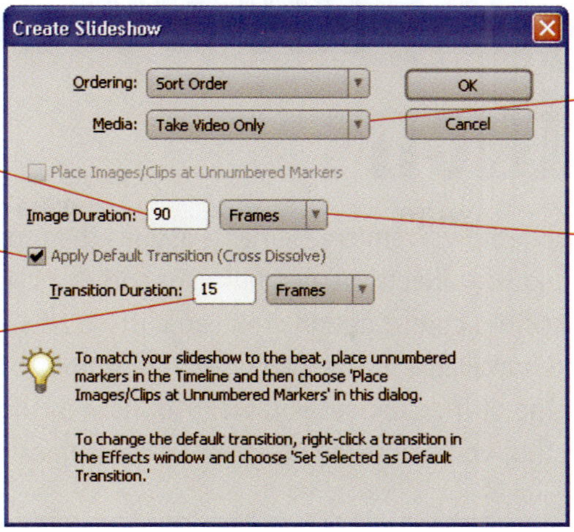


**FIGURE B-15: Still image slideshow added to Timeline**

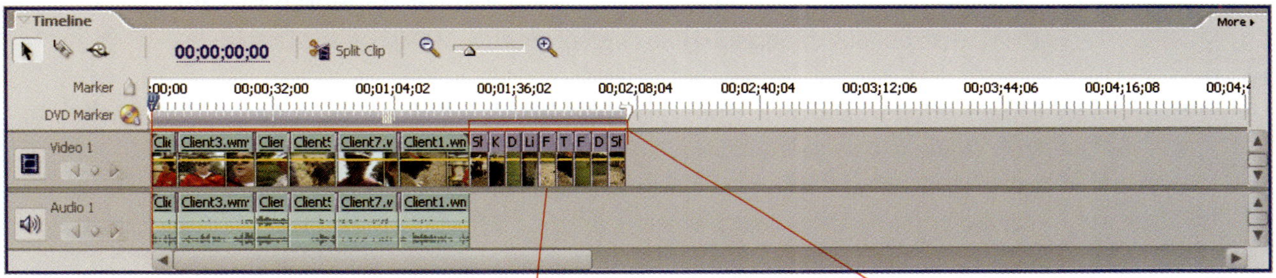


## Clues to Use

### Arranging clip order using the mouse

If you want to change the order in which clips appear in a slideshow, but don't want to rearrange clips on the Media panel, you can press [Ctrl] while clicking clips to set the order of the clips instead. Pressing and holding [Ctrl] allows you to select multiple **nonadjacent** clips—clips that are not next to each other. This method does not allow you to see the order in which clips will appear in a movie, but it's a faster method and allows you to maintain the current order of clips in the Media panel. For instance, you may be working with a project that contains dozens of clips. You want to include only six of them in a rough cut, and you know the order in which you want the clips to appear. Instead of creating a folder, moving those six clips into it, changing to Icon view, and then dragging to arrange the clips in the proper order, you can use the mouse and [Ctrl] instead. In the Media panel, click the first clip you want in the slideshow, press and hold [Ctrl], then click each additional clip in the order that you want them to appear. It's important that you click in the order you want, because Premiere Elements "remembers" the order in which you clicked. When you've selected all your clips, open the Create Slideshow dialog box. Click the Ordering list arrow, then click Selection Order. Make any additional changes in the Create Slideshow dialog box, then click OK. The slideshow is created with the clips appearing in the order in which you clicked them.

# Changing the Default Transition

When you create a slideshow, Premiere Elements assigns the program's default transition to the clips. A **transition** is a setting that affects the beginning or end of a clip; it can be as simple as a fade to black or as complex as a custom cutout design. You can customize a slideshow by choosing a different transition from the dozens available in the Effects and Transitions panel, and then setting it as the default transition. One of the changes you want to make in the Genoa clients slideshow is the transition. To accomplish this, you adjust the program's default transition.

## STEPS

1. **Drag the resizing handles on the Effects and Transitions panel to enlarge it**
   This panel contains categories for both video and audio effects and transitions. The program's default audio transition is Constant Power, which creates a smooth effect where the volume in the previous clip fades down gradually as the volume in the new clip fades up. You do not change the default audio transition at this time.

2. **Click the Transitions button, then click the Video Transitions Expand icon ▶**
   The video transitions are organized into categories, such as 3D Motion and Dissolve.

3. **Click ▶ next to Dissolve, then click the Icon View button if necessary to switch to Icon view**
   The available Dissolve transitions are listed, and the current default video transition, Cross Dissolve, is surrounded by the dark blue border, as shown in Figure B-16. A **cross dissolve** transition creates the effect of the previous image fading away while another appears on top of it and gradually replaces it.

4. **Click Cross Dissolve in the Dissolve list**
   You can preview a transition by clicking its icon. The letters A and B represent the two clips that will interact. The transition is surrounded by a light blue border and a dark blue border, shown in Figure B-16. The light blue border indicates the transition is selected and the dark blue border indicates it is the default transition

5. **Click the Collapse icon ▼ next to Dissolve, then click ▶ next to Page Peel**
   The transitions in this category create effects similar to a page turning in a book.

6. **Click each transition in this category to preview the effect**
   As you click each transition, the light blue selection border surrounds it. The dark blue border is not visible because Cross Dissolve in the Dissolve category is still the default transition.

7. **Click the Page Turn transition, click the More button More ▸ on the Effects and Transitions panel, then click Set Selected as Default Transition, as shown in Figure B-17**
   The Page Turn transition is surrounded by both dark and light blue borders.

8. **Resize the Media panel if necessary, click the Still Images folder on the Media panel, click the Create Slideshow button, then change the values in the Create Slideshow dialog box so they match Figure B-18**

9. **Click OK, then save your changes to the project**
   The new slideshow is added to the Timeline, and your changes are saved to disk.

**QUICK TIP**
If a different transition is selected as the default transition on your computer, you will not see this selection border.

**QUICK TIP**
You can click the List view button on the Effects and Transition panel to display the items in List format.

**QUICK TIP**
You can also set the default transition by right-clicking a transition, then clicking Set Selected as Default Transition in the shortcut menu.

FIGURE B-16: Viewing the default transition

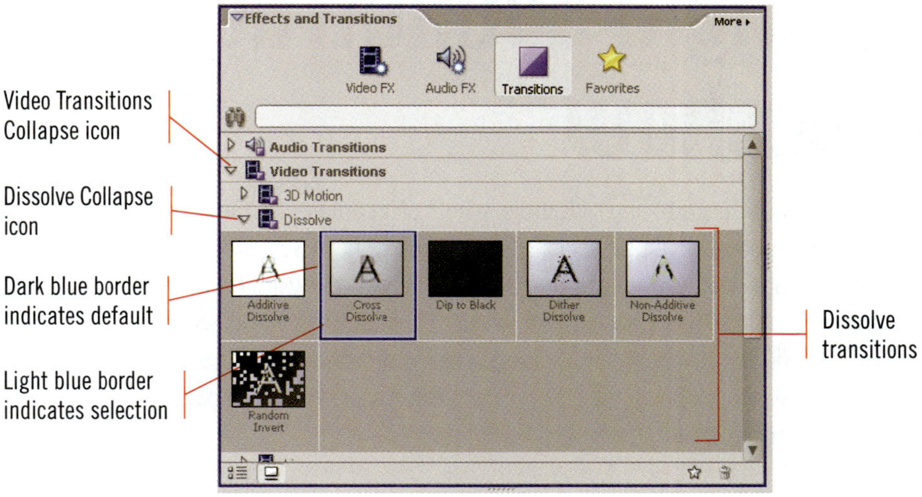


FIGURE B-17: Changing the default transition

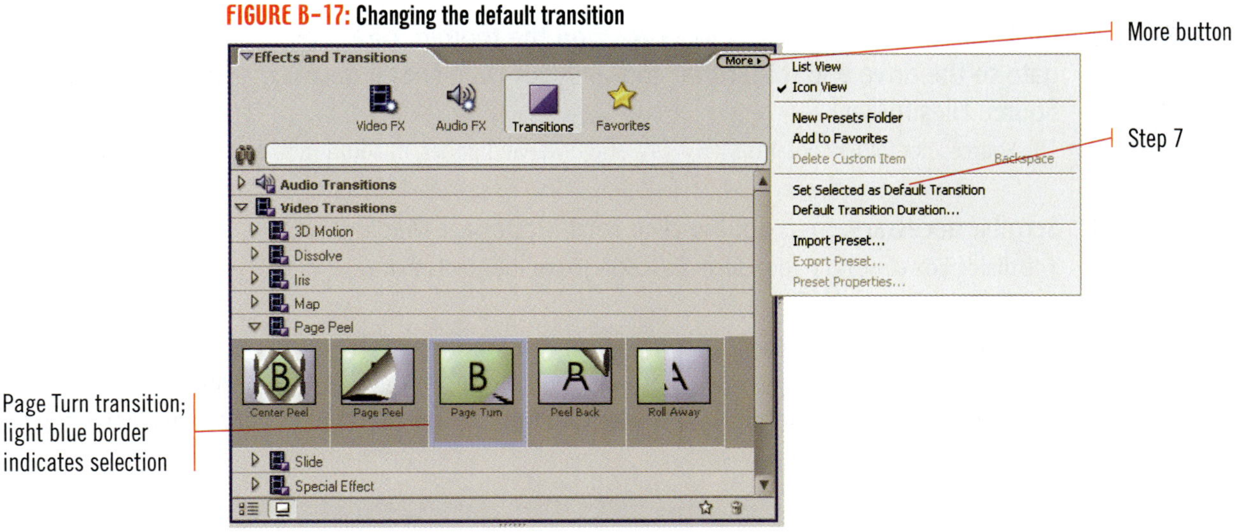


FIGURE B-18: Completed Create Slideshow dialog box

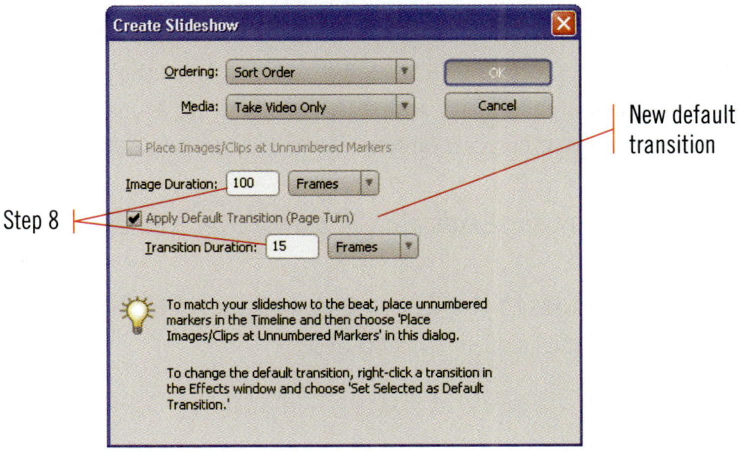

UNIT
**B**
Premiere Elements 2.0

# Adding a Soundtrack to a Slideshow

You can add a soundtrack to any slideshow, whether it contains movie clips, still images, or a mix of both. A rough cut may not need music, because you already have sound from the movie clips, but still image slideshows can be greatly enhanced by adding narration or music. To add a soundtrack to a slideshow, you select the audio file along with any movie or still image clips you want to include before creating the slideshow. You want the new Genoa Clients slideshow to contain a soundtrack, and have located a song you think will work perfectly. First you want to restore the workspace so you can see the Timeline and Monitor panels more easily.

## STEPS

**QUICK TIP**
You can also restore the Edit workspace by pressing [Shift][F8].

1. **Click Window on the menu bar, point to Restore Workspace, click Edit, then drag the Zoom slider on the Timeline to the left, as shown in Figure B-19,so you can see the new slideshow you added**

**QUICK TIP**
You can also open the Add Media dialog box by pressing [Ctrl][I].

2. **Click the Add Media button Add Media on the toolbar, click From Files or Folders, navigate to the drive and folder that contain your Data Files if necessary, then open the Source Files folder**
   The Source Files folder contains MP3, WAV, and other audio files, in addition to movie and still image clips.

3. **Scroll if necessary, then double-click Lord McDonald Medley.wav**
   The dialog box closes and the added file is selected in the Media panel.

4. **Click the Create Slideshow button on the Media panel**
   The Create Slideshow dialog box opens, as shown in Figure B-20. The options in the dialog box allow you to Take Audio Only, because an audio file is selected. The Image Duration and Transition Duration options are not available for audio files.

5. **Click OK**
   The audio clip is added to the first blank area of the Timeline on the Audio 1 track.

6. **Drag the end-of-movie marker on the work area bar until it extends to the end the of the new audio clip, as shown in Figure B-21, click Timeline on the menu bar, then click Render Work Area**

**TROUBLE**
The smoothness at which a rendered movie plays depends upon your system resources. Even if your computer meets the application's system requirements, it may not be fast enough to preview footage smoothly; however, this should not affect the final movie when you export it.

7. **Pause the movie, move to frame 00;02;24;02, then play the slideshow with the soundtrack**
   The rendered slideshow plays with the accompanying soundtrack. The music ends abruptly, but the slideshow serves your purposes for now. You will learn how to fade audio in a future unit.

8. **Drag the current-time indicator slowly over frames 00;01;26;00 through 00;01;28;00**

9. **Save your changes to the Genoa Clients Rough Cut 2 project, then press [Ctrl][Q]**
   Both the project and Premiere Elements close.

FIGURE B-19: Dragging the Zoom slider

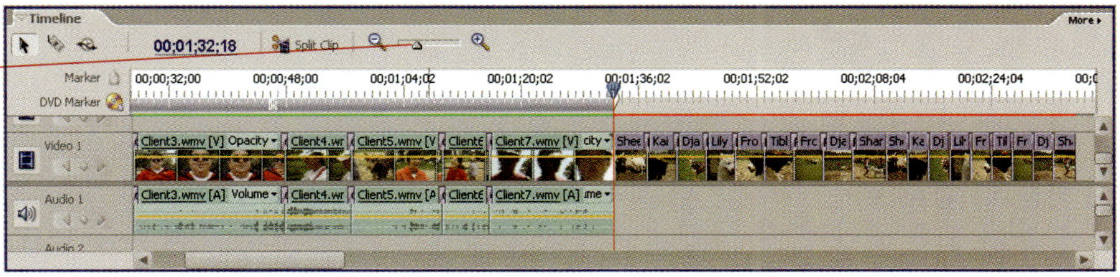


FIGURE B-20: Adding a soundtrack to a slideshow

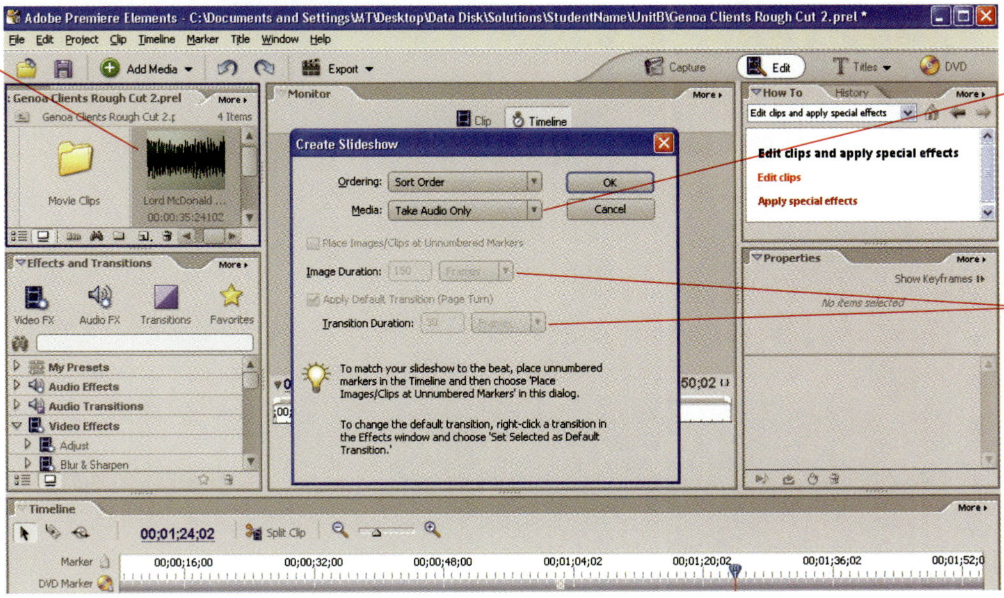


FIGURE B-21: Soundtrack added to slideshow

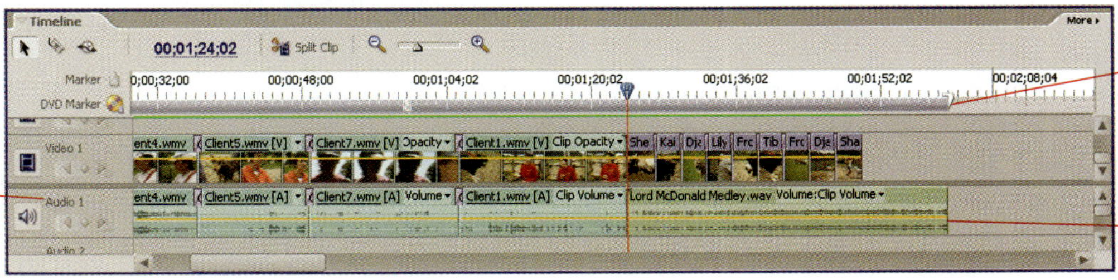

# Practice

## ▼ CONCEPTS REVIEW

**Label the elements of the Premiere Elements program window shown in Figure B-22.**

FIGURE B-22

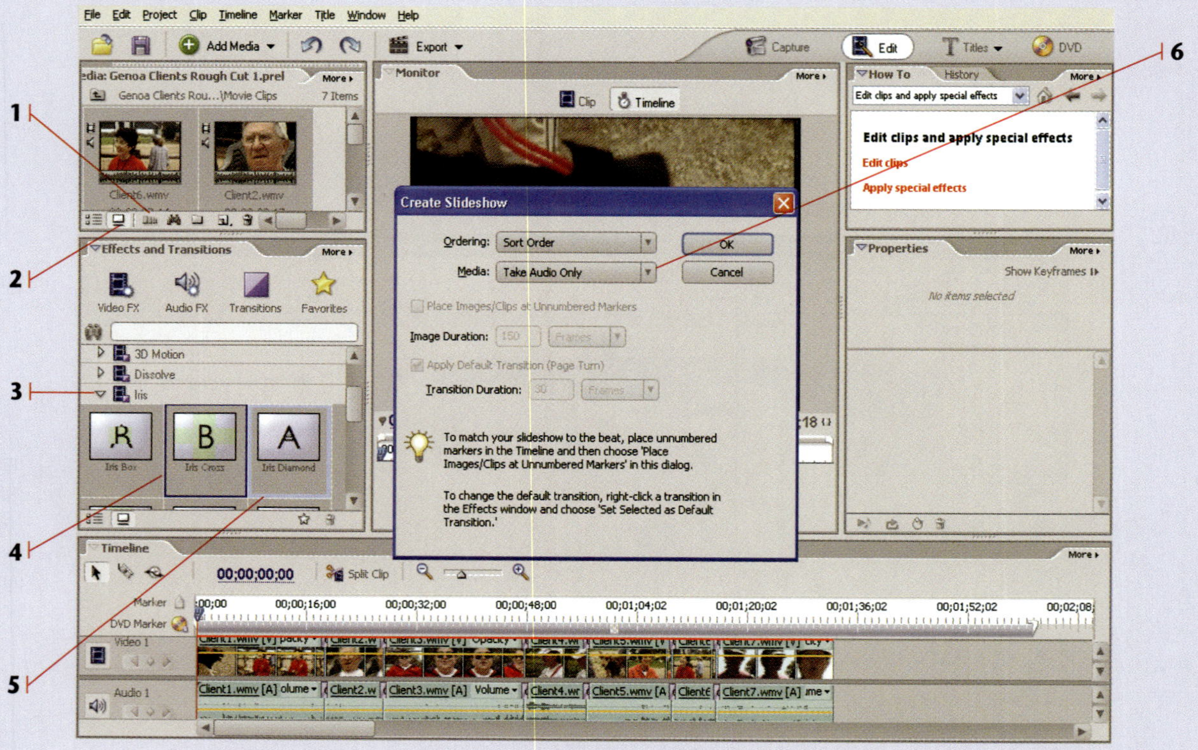


**Match each term with the statement that best describes it.**

7. **Slideshow**
8. **Rough cut**
9. **Time ruler**
10. **Time display**
11. **Current-time indicator**
12. **Red line at bottom of time ruler**
13. **Green line at bottom of time ruler**
14. **Monitor panel**

**a.** Measures movie length in time increments
**b.** Displays a preview of the contents of the Timeline
**c.** Assembled movie of all clips in a folder or project
**d.** Displays the current frame location of a movie on the time ruler
**e.** Displays the current frame location of a movie in numeric format
**f.** Indicates footage is rendered
**g.** Presentation of still images
**h.** Indicates footage is unrendered

**Select the best answer from the list of choices.**

**15. If you want to see a smaller portion of the Timeline at a more detailed level you should:**
- **a.** Zoom out.
- **b.** Zoom up.
- **c.** Zoom in.
- **d.** Close the Timeline panel.

**16. Which key do you press to move to the beginning of a movie on the Timeline?**
- **a.** [Home]
- **b.** [End]
- **c.** [Spacebar]
- **d.** [Tab]

**17. If you want footage on the Timeline to play as smoothly as possible, what should you do?**
- **a.** Close the Monitor panel.
- **b.** Choose a different default transition.
- **c.** Render the footage.
- **d.** Close the project.

**18. What happens when you delete a clip on the Media panel?**
- **a.** The clip and source file are deleted from the current project only.
- **b.** The clip is deleted from the current project, but the source file remains intact.
- **c.** The clip and source file are deleted from all projects.
- **d.** The source file is deleted, but the clip remains in the current project.

**19. To rearrange clips in the Media panel:**
- **a.** Switch to List view.
- **b.** Display the Preview Area.
- **c.** Close all open folders.
- **d.** Switch to Icon view.

**20. To change the transition used in a slideshow:**
- **a.** Delete the current transition in the Timeline panel.
- **b.** Change the default transition in the Effects and Transitions panel.
- **c.** Add a new transition in the Media panel.
- **d.** Delete the current transition in the Monitor panel.

## ▼ SKILLS REVIEW

**1. Open and save an existing project.**
- **a.** Start Premiere Elements.
- **b.** Click the Open Project icon in the Welcome screen.
- **c.** Navigate to the drive and folder where your Data Files are located, then open the file **PE B-2.prel**.
- **d.** Save the file as **Clown Rough Cut 1** in the *YourName* folder where you are saving files for this book.

**2. Create a slideshow for a rough cut.**
- **a.** Open the Movie Clips folder, verify that it contains eight .avi movie clips, then close it.
- **b.** Double-click the Photos folder and verify that it contains eight photos, then close it.
- **c.** Select the Movie Clips folder.
- **d.** Click the Create Slideshow button on the Media panel.

## ▼ SKILLS REVIEW (CONTINUED)

e. In the Create Slideshow dialog box, verify that the Ordering list box reads Sort Order, that the Media list box reads Take Video and Audio, and that the Apply Default Transition (Page Turn) check box contains a check mark.
f. Create the slideshow.
g. Save your changes to the project.

**3. Preview a movie.**

a. Play the movie.
b. When the movie ends, zoom in on the Timeline until the clips fill the available space.
c. Drag the current-time indicator to move to approximately frame **00;00;28:00**.
d. Press [Spacebar], view the movie for a few seconds, then press [Spacebar].
e. Drag the scrub pointer on the Timeline time display to the right to move to frame **00;00;58;15**.
f. Drag the shuttle slider on the Monitor panel to play the movie slowly in reverse motion.
g. Move to the beginning of the movie, then to the end of the movie.
h. Move to the previous edit point on the Timeline.

**4. Render footage.**

a. Verify that the work area bar extends over the entire movie on the Timeline; if necessary drag the start-of-movie marker and the end-of-movie marker to include the whole movie.
b. Render the work area.
c. Preview the rendered movie, then pause before you reach the end of the movie.
d. Move to the previous edit point.
e. Move to the beginning of the movie.
f. Save your changes to the project.

**5. Adjust clips for a slideshow.**

a. Open the PE B-2 project, then save it as **Clown Rough Cut 2**.
b. In the Media panel, switch to Icon view.
c. Enlarge the Media panel as much as possible.
d. Rearrange the thumbnails in the Movie Clips folder on the Media panel so they are in the following order: **Cam1_a.avi**, **Cam2_a.avi**, **Cam1_b.avi**, **Cam2_b.avi**, **Cam1_c.avi**, **Cam2_c.avi**, **Cam1_d.avi**, and **Cam2_d.avi**.
e. Delete the **Cam1_d.avi** clip, then compare your screen to Figure B-23.
f. Select the clips in the Media Panel, create a slideshow using the default settings, then render the work area.
g. Enlarge the Monitor panel, then preview the slideshow.
h. Save your changes to the project, then close it.

FIGURE B-23

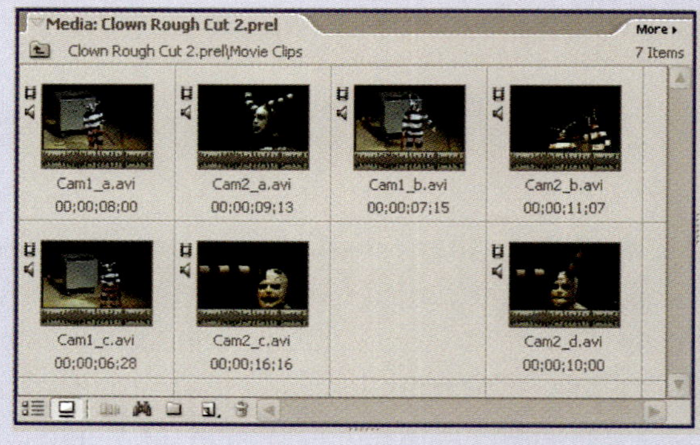


**6. Create a slideshow for stills.**

a. Open the PE B-2 project, then save it as **Clown Slideshow**.
b. Select the Photos folder.
c. Open the Create Slideshow dialog box.
d. Change the Image Duration to **80 Frames**.
e. Verify that a default transition will be applied, then change the Transition Duration to **20**.
f. Close the Create Slideshow dialog box, then play the slideshow.
g. Click Edit on the menu bar, then click Undo.

## ▼ SKILLS REVIEW (CONTINUED)

**7. Change the default transition.**

- **a.** Enlarge the Effects and Transitions panel so you can view its contents more easily.
- **b.** Expand the Video Transitions category.
- **c.** Expand the Page Peel subcategory.
- **d.** Preview the Page Turn transition.
- **e.** Collapse the Page Peel subcategory, then expand the Iris subcategory.
- **f.** Preview the Iris Box transition and the Iris Round transition, then set Iris Star as the default transition.
- **g.** Select the Photos folder, then open the Create Slideshow dialog box.
- **h.** Accept the default settings in the Create Slideshow dialog box, then create the slideshow.
- **i.** Save your changes to the project.

**8. Add a soundtrack to a slideshow.**

- **a.** Restore the Edit workspace.
- **b.** Open the Add Media dialog box, then open the Source Files folder.
- **c.** Add the **Fantastic Plastic.wav** file to the project.
- **d.** With the Fantastic Plastic clip selected in the Media Panel, open the Create Slideshow dialog box.
- **f.** Verify that the Media list box reads Take Audio only, then create the slideshow.
- **g.** Render the work area, then play only the part of the movie that contains the added soundtrack.
- **h.** Pause the movie, then drag the current-time indicator slowly over any transition to watch it in the Monitor.
- **i.** Save your changes to the project, then close it and exit Premiere Elements.

## ▼ INDEPENDENT CHALLENGE 1

You are continuing to work on a movie trailer for the film festival sponsored by your city's Department of Cultural Affairs. Your contact at the department has provided you with clips from several films premiering at the fest. You want to create a rough cut of the clip that you can show to city officials interested in seeing how marketing for the festival is coming along.

- **a.** Start Premiere Elements.
- **b.** Open the file PE B-3.prel from the drive and folder where your Data Files are located, then save it as **Film Fest Rough Cut** in the *YourName* folder where you are saving files for this book.
- **c.** Change the default transition to Fold Up. (*Hint*: This transition is located in the 3D Motion subcategory of the Transitions category on the Effects and Transitions panel.)
- **d.** Open the Movies folder, switch to Icon View, then arrange the clips in the following order: **Dress for Success.wmv**, **Tax Help.wmv**, **Muffin Control.wmv**, **Silent Breakfast.wmv**, and **Sad Song.wmv**.
- **e.** Create a slideshow in the order of your choice, using the clips in the Movies folder.
- **f.** Save your changes to the project.

**Advanced Challenge Exercise**

ACE

- Select the Stills folder.
- Use the Create Slideshow command to add the contents of the folder to the end of the Timeline.
- Save your changes to the project.

- **g.** Render the work area, preview the slideshow, then locate the transition at the beginning of the clip shown in Figure B-24; your frame number will differ.
- **h.** Close the project, then exit Premiere Elements.

FIGURE B-24

## ▼ INDEPENDENT CHALLENGE 2

You are continuing to work on your first original movie, a documentary that you are directing, shooting, and editing in Premiere Elements. This documentary can be on any topic of your choosing. Possible topics include a special event in your family, an interesting friend or person in your community, or a favorite hobby. The choice is up to you; however, you should make sure that everyone you record first agrees to appear in your film, and that you request permission to record in any location that is not a public place or your own private residence. For that reason, it's often easiest to work with friends and family. The final piece should be approximately three minutes long, so you don't need to shoot a lot of footage to create it.

- **a.** Shoot five to seven minutes worth of footage for your documentary, and include at least five separate scenes or shots.
- **b.** Start Premiere Elements, then click the Capture Video icon in the Welcome screen.
- **c.** Create a new project called **My Documentary** in the *YourName* folder where you are saving files for this book.
- **d.** Use the More button in the Capture panel to verify that Capture Audio and Video contains a check mark and that Scene Detect contains a check mark, and that Capture to Timeline does not contain a check mark.
- **e.** Capture the footage into your computer.
- **f.** When all the footage is captured, create a slideshow using the footage you captured.
- **g.** Save your changes to the project.
- **h.** Render the work area, then preview the rough cut.
- **i.** Close the project and exit Premiere Elements.

## ▼ INDEPENDENT CHALLENGE 3

You continue to work on the video you're creating for the internship program at Fig Media, the video production company where you work. Jim, president of the company, would like to see a rough cut of the footage you are thinking of including in the video. You want to create something that will give the best impression of your work so far, so you decide to make a few tweaks to the slideshow before presenting it to Jim.

- **a.** Open the file PE B-4.prel from the drive and folder where your Data Files are located, then save it as **Dream Job Rough Cut** in the *YourName* folder where you are saving files for this book.
- **b.** Create a slideshow using all the clips in the Media panel in the current Sort order and the default transition.
- **c.** Preview the slideshow. Use the current-time indicator and scrub pointer to replay to various parts of the slideshow to familiarize yourself with the clips.
- **d.** Undo the creation of the slideshow.
- **e.** Switch to Icon view in the media panel, then move the Jennifer clip so it is first and the Bill clip so it is last.
- **f.** Save your changes to the project.

**Advanced Challenge Exercise**

- Rearrange at least three other clips in the order of your choosing. Remember that you can open the Preview Area in the Media panel, then click any clip you wish to preview.
- Save your changes to the project.

- **g.** Browse through the Effects and Transitions panel to find a new transition that you like. When you find a transition you think suits the style of this project, set it as the default transition.
- **h.** Create the slideshow using the Transition Duration of your choosing.
- **i.** Render the work area, then preview the rough cut, as shown in Figure B-25. Your transition will vary.
- **j.** Save and close the project, then exit Premiere Elements.

FIGURE B-25

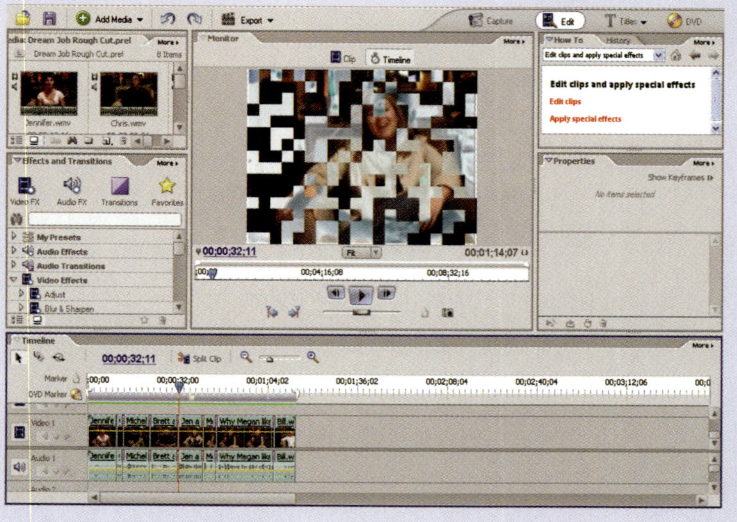

## ▼ INDEPENDENT CHALLENGE 4

In your quest to become a more knowledgeable filmmaker, you've formed a cinema club with some friends. Each month, the group gets together to discuss a selected filmmaker. The discussion covers the filmmaker's style and the dramatic impact of the filmmaker's production choices. At the end of each meeting, one person presents the filmmaker for the coming month. This month it's your turn to choose and introduce a filmmaker. You need to give a short presentation on your choice, in which you explain why you chose him or her, suggest films to view before the next discussion, and offer a few elements to look for in the chosen films. To enhance the presentation, you want to illustrate it with a slideshow.

**a.** Choose a film director you admire or want to learn more about.

**b.** Connect to the Internet, then use your favorite search engine to find information and images related to the filmmaker. Look for information on the filmmaker's production choices. For example, does the director you selected work with the same editor or cinematographer in each film? Does your director allow actors to improvise, or is the script set in stone? Does the director get involved in the screenwriting process, or leave that to someone else? Print at least two articles that reference your chosen filmmaker.

**c.** Find at least six images that illustrate the director and important films in his or her career. Sites such as *www.imdb.com* and *www.allmoviephoto.com* have large collections of such stills, but there are several other collections available on the Web. For each Web site that contains images you want to use, read the About page and/or Copyright pages on the site to learn whether you can legally download the images. Because you are using these images for editorial purposes (using work of the artist in context of an article, paper, and so on), downloading is often permissible, but the rules and guidelines vary by site.

**d.** When you have downloaded the images, close your browser program.

**e.** Start Premiere Elements, then create a new project called **Filmmaker Presentation** in the *YourName* folder where you are saving files for this book.

**f.** Add the image files you downloaded to the project, rearrange them if you wish in the Media panel, then use them to create a slideshow with the transition and image duration of your choosing.

**g.** Render the footage, then preview the slideshow with the new transition.

**h.** Save and close the project, then exit Premiere Elements.

## ▼ VISUAL WORKSHOP

Open the file PE B-5.prel in the drive and folder location where you are saving files for this book, then save it as **Butterfly Slideshow** in the *YourName* folder where you are saving files for this book. Arrange the workspace, move the clips, create a slideshow, render the work area, and navigate as needed so that your screen matches Figure B-26. Save your changes to the project. When you are finished, press [PrtScr], paste the image into your word-processing program, print a copy, then exit your word processor and Premiere Elements.

**FIGURE B-26**

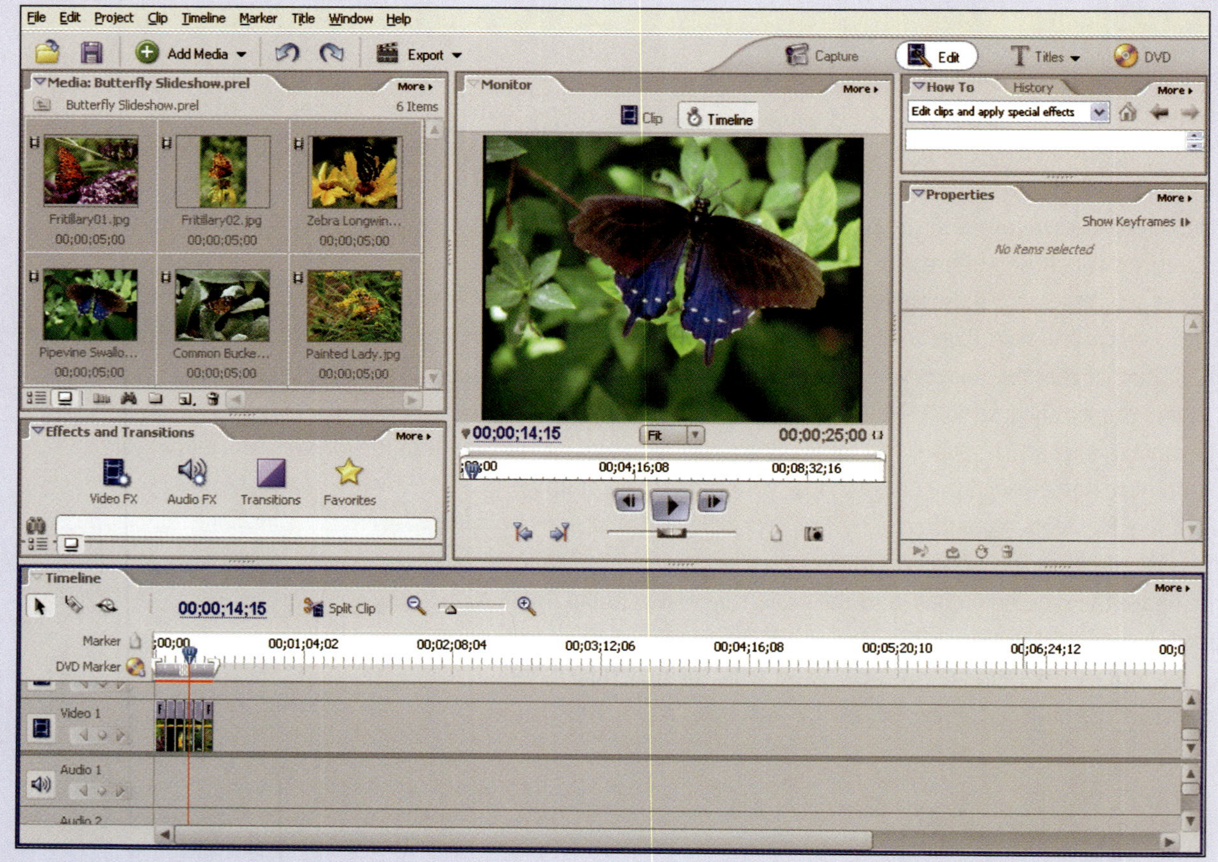

UNIT
C
Premiere Elements 2.0

# Editing Clips

## OBJECTIVES

- Add a clip from the Media panel
- Add a clip using the Monitor panel
- Delete a clip
- Move a clip
- Trim a clip
- Edit with the Snap feature
- Split a clip
- Use the Time Stretch Tool

The basic editing tools in Premiere Elements are simple yet powerful. In some ways, editing a movie is similar to editing a document in a word-processing program—you can add content, delete it, rearrange it, and extend or trim various sections. But because you are working with video instead of text, the creative possibilities are endless. The Timeline panel is where you edit clips, inserting them, rearranging them, shortening them, and so on. The Media panel and Monitor panel play key roles, too, helping you select and prepare clips for the Timeline and review your work. You're ready to create a promotional video for Genoa Stock & Training; you'll need to rearrange and trim the clips you want to use for this movie.

# Adding a Clip from the Media Panel

To edit clips, you first add them to the Timeline. To do so, you can drag a clip directly from the Media panel. You can add clips one at a time or as a group. For the Genoa Stock & Training video, you want to add several clips from the Media panel.

## STEPS

**QUICK TIP**

By default, the Snap command is turned on, but it's a good idea to verify that it is.

**TROUBLE**

If you accidentally drag the clip to the Video 2 track, press [Ctrl][Z] to undo the action, then repeat Step 3.

**QUICK TIP**

If you want to replace frames on the Timeline instead of shifting them, press and hold [Alt] when dragging a clip to the Timeline.

1. **Open the file PE C-1.prel from the drive and folder where your Data Files are located, then save it as Genoa Edit in the *YourName* folder where you are saving files for this book**
2. **Click Timeline on the menu bar, then verify that the Snap command contains a check mark**
   The **Snap** feature automatically aligns a clip or edit to the nearest positioning milestone—the start of the time ruler, the nearest marker or edge of another clip, or the current-time indicator.
3. **Click the Shannon1 clip in the Media panel, drag it to the Video 1 track on the Timeline, then, when the pointer changes to the insert pointer and a Snap icon appears at the beginning of the time ruler as shown in Figure C-1, release the mouse button**
   The video portion of the clip moves to the Video 1 track, and its audio portion moves to the Audio 1 track. When you drag a clip that contains video and audio to a video track, the audio automatically moves to the first available audio track, which is usually Audio 1. In most cases, you add video clips to the Video 1 track and use additional tracks only when you need to combine visual elements, such as titles and video images, or layer sounds, such as music and dialog.
4. **Select the Client8 clip in the Media panel, drag it to the right edge of the Shannon1 clip on the Timeline, then, when you see at the edge, release the mouse button**
   The clip you drag to the Timeline is actually a duplicate of the clip in the Media panel and is known as a clip instance when it is on the Timeline. You can insert multiple clip instances and modify them as you want without affecting the original. If you delete a clip in the Media panel, each instance of it is also deleted from the Timeline.
5. **Double-click the Action Clips folder, click the Sort icon to alphabetize the clips if necessary, click the ActionA clip, press and hold [Shift], then click the ActionG clip**
6. **Drag the selection to the beginning of the Timeline, then when you see , release the mouse button**
   As you position the selection on the Timeline, only the selected clips are visible. After releasing the mouse button, the selected clips are inserted at the beginning of the Timeline and the existing clips shift right, as shown in Figure C-2. By default, clips are **inserted** where you release the mouse button: frames to the left of an insertion do not move, but frames to the right move farther right to accommodate the insertion. The helps you position the insertion so you don't accidentally insert the selection in the middle of another clip.
7. **Click the ActionH clip in the Media panel, drag it to the left edge of the Client8 clip on the Timeline, then when you see , release the mouse button**
   The ActionH clip is inserted between the Shannon1 clip and the Client8 clip.
8. **Click the Save Project button on the toolbar, close the Action Clips folder, then render the work area**
   When rendering is complete, the movie plays automatically. See Figure C-3.

**FIGURE C-1: Adding a clip to the Timeline**

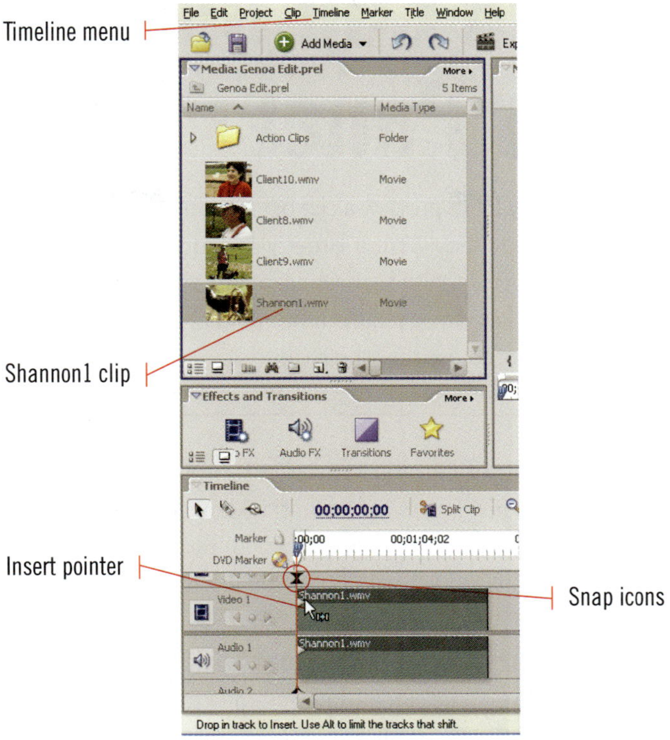


**FIGURE C-2: Multiple clips added to the Timeline**

**FIGURE C-3: Saved and rendered movie**

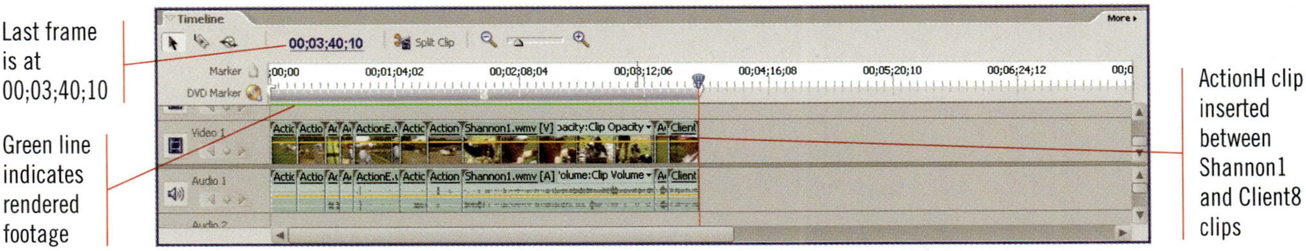

UNIT C
Premiere Elements 2.0

# Adding a Clip Using the Monitor Panel

There are times when you want to preview a clip before adding it to a movie. While you can open the Preview Area in the Media panel, you may want a larger view. You may also want to add just part of a clip to the Timeline instead of the entire clip. Although you can trim any clip once it's in the Timeline, using the Monitor panel for this purpose can save considerable time. You want to add another client interview to the Timeline, but you don't want to use the whole clip.

## STEPS

1. **Double-click the Client9 clip in the Media panel**
   The clip is selected, the first frame appears in the Monitor panel, and the Clip button Clip is selected, as shown in Figure C-4. The Monitor panel serves both the Media panel and the Timeline. You can preview a clip in the Monitor panel by double-clicking a clip in the Media panel or by dragging a clip from the Media panel to the Monitor panel.
2. **Click the Play button on the Monitor panel**
   As the clip plays, notice that the current-time indicator moves to show the progress of the clip, and the time display shows the current frame number of the clip. The gray time display at the right side of the Monitor panel shows the total duration of this clip.
3. **Drag the current-time indicator to 00;00;12;19**
   This is the first frame of the segment you want to use, or the **in point**.
4. **Click the Set In Point button In on the Monitor panel**
   Frame 00;00;12;19 is set as the in point.
5. **Click the time display, type 26;27, then click the Set Out Point button Out on the Monitor panel**
   The **out point** is the last frame you want to include. The set in and set out points are selected, as shown in Figure C-5. On the time ruler, the segment between the in and out point is highlighted in blue and bordered by brackets.
6. **Point to the In Point bracket on the time ruler, then when the pointer changes to the Trim In pointer, drag left to 00;00;06;25**
   You can set in and out points by using the In and Out buttons, by dragging the In Point and Out Point brackets, or by any combination of the two.
7. **Click anywhere in the preview area of the Monitor window, then drag the clip to the Timeline and align it with the right edge of the Client8 clip**
   The partial clip is added to the end of the Timeline.
8. **Click the Add Media button Add Media on the toolbar, navigate to the Source Files folder in the drive and folder where your Data Files are located, then add Client5.wmv, Client6.wmv., and Client7.wmv to the Media panel**
9. **Preview each clip you added in the Monitor panel, add them in numerical order to the end of the Timeline as shown in Figure C-6, then save your changes**

**QUICK TIP**
You can switch between clips in the Media panel and the Timeline panel by clicking Clip or Timeline on the Monitor panel.

**QUICK TIP**
You can drag the shuttle on the highlighted area of the time display to select a different part of the clip while maintaining the same segment duration.

**TROUBLE**
Zoom in or out of the Timeline as desired.

FIGURE C-4: Previewing a clip in the Monitor panel

FIGURE C-5: Setting in and out points

FIGURE C-6: Clips added to Timeline

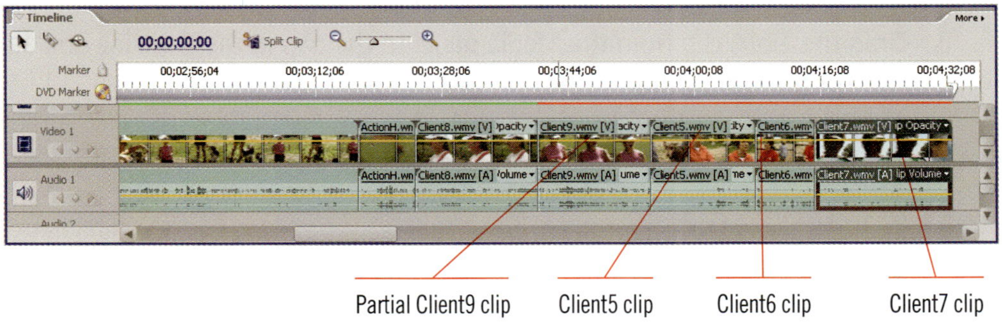

UNIT
C
Premiere Elements 2.0

# Deleting a Clip

You can remove any clip from the Timeline if you no longer want to include it in a movie. If you want to remove the clip and close the gap created by the deletion, you use the Delete command. If you want to remove the clip but don't want to close the gap, you use the Clear command. Both commands remove the clip from the Timeline and leave the clip in the Media panel. To remove a clip, you must first select it. You decide to remove a few clips from the movie that aren't essential to the action.

## STEPS

**QUICK TIP**
It's helpful to zoom in enough to see the clip names on the Timeline. Work at a zoom level that's comfortable for you.

1. **If necessary, click the Zoom In button on the Timeline so that you can see the names of the clips on the Timeline, then scroll if necessary to see the beginning of the time ruler**

2. **Drag the current-time indicator to the start of the ActionD clip (frame 00;00;35;14), press [Spacebar], watch the clip, then press [Spacebar] again**
   The ActionD clip is interesting, but since the movie does not include an interview with the client shown, you decide the clip is not serving the action.

**QUICK TIP**
To delete a selected clip and close the gap, you can also press [Delete].

3. **Click the Selection Tool on the Timeline, then right-click the ActionD clip**
   A selection border surrounds the clip, information about the clip appears in the Properties panel, and a shortcut menu opens, as shown in Figure C-7. The Properties panel displays the poster frame of the clip, along with its filename, duration, and media type. The shortcut menu offers a **Clear** command, which removes the clip without closing up the gap left by the deletion, a **Delete and Close Gap** command, a **Delete Audio** command, which removes just the audio track from the selected clip, and a **Delete Video** command, which removes just the video portion of the clip.

4. **Click Delete and Close Gap**
   The clip is deleted from the Timeline, and the clip to its right moves left to close the gap. In video editing parlance, this type of deletion is also known as a **ripple deletion**, because no gap remains in the movie.

5. **Zoom out until you can see the end of the movie on the Timeline, right-click the Client5 clip, then click Clear**
   The clip is cleared from the Timeline, but the gap left by its deletion remains.

6. **Drag to approximately 00;03;47;00, press [Spacebar], play the movie until it reaches approximately 00;04;10;00, then press [Spacebar] again**
   When the current-time indicator passes over the blank portion of the Timeline, the Monitor is black and silent until you reach the next clip.

7. **Click the Add Media button Add Media on the toolbar, navigate to the Source Files folder if necessary, then add Tibbs.bmp to the project**

8. **Drag the Tibbs clip from the Media panel to the gap in the Timeline and align it to the right of the Client9 clip**
   Adding a still image to the Timeline is similar to adding a video clip. The default duration of a still image is five seconds, as indicated on the Properties panel. The audio track is blank because still images do not contain sound.

**QUICK TIP**
You can also press [Backspace] when a gap is selected to close it.

9. **Right-click anywhere in the gap, click Delete and Close Gap, as shown in Figure C-8, then save your changes**
   The gap between the Tibbs clip and the Client6 clip closes.

FIGURE C-7: Clip shortcut menu

FIGURE C-8: Closing a gap on Timeline

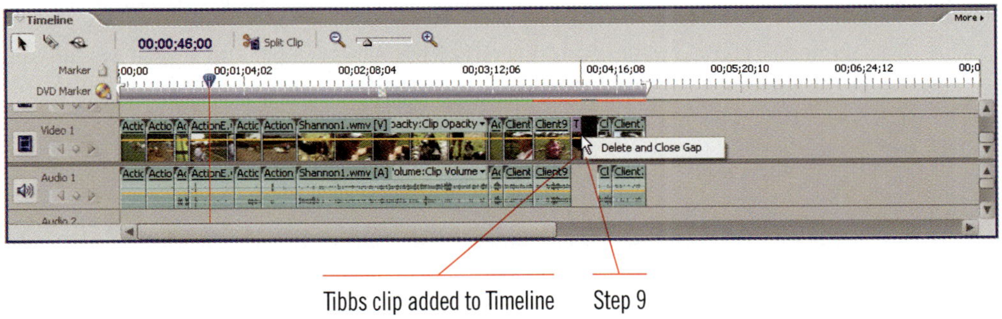


## Production Matters

### Understanding scenes, shots, and takes

As an editor, you often have to piece together various shots to create a finished scene. A **scene** is one related sequence of action. For example, a movie about a young woman's first year at college might include a scene of her moving into her new dorm room. The scene can consist of one or more **shots**, or smaller units of action. Our sample scene might contain one shot of the woman walking into the room, and another shot of her setting down her backpack. Shots are generally categorized into types. The size of the subject in relation to the frame determines the type of shot. If the frame shows the subject's entire body, it's a **long shot**. If the frame shows only the head and shoulders, it's a **close-up**. Between a long shot and a close-up is a **medium shot**, a three-quarter-length shot where we see the subject's waist up to the face. For each shot, there might be several **takes**, or instances of the camera recording the same action, so you might have to choose from different takes to find the best one. Many editors try to vary the types of shots when piecing them together. So, if you use a long shot of the woman entering the room, you would likely cut to a medium shot of her setting down the backpack rather than another long shot. However, there are no hard and fast rules. An **establishing shot**, which is a shot at the beginning of a scene that tells the viewer where a scene is taking place, is often a long shot, but it doesn't have to be. Take note the next time you watch a movie or TV show. To develop a sense of when to use what type of shot to create the effect you want, observe the types of shots and how they are pieced together.

UNIT C

Premiere Elements 2.0

# Moving a Clip

You can move clips anywhere on the Timeline. Moving a clip is just like inserting one: by default, all the clips to its right shift to make room for it. You can also choose to replace existing frames on the Timeline with the new frames. When you move a clip, the video and audio remain linked, so the sound travels with the video. See Table C-1 for a description of move options. To move a clip, you must first select it. You want to rearrange some clips in the Timeline to change the flow of the action. First, you want to move the Shannon1 clip so it comes right before the ActionG clip.

## STEPS

1. **Click the ActionG clip on the Timeline, then read the Properties panel**
   Information about the clip appears on the Properties panel because the Selection Tool is still active; it remains active until you select a different toll on the Timeline panel. This clip, exactly 18 seconds long, is the **target clip**—the destination location of the clip you plan to move.

2. **Select the Shannon1 clip on the Timeline, then drag it to the beginning of the ActionG clip until you see the Snap icon, as shown in Figure C-9, but do not release the mouse button**
   As you drag, a solid placeholder appears on the Timeline where the selected clip will be inserted. The mouse pointer changes to the Insert pointer, indicating that the clip will be inserted in its new location, and a pop-up window informs you that the clip is moving a negative distance of 18 seconds, which is the duration of the clip it's replacing.

**QUICK TIP**

Negative numbers indicate you are moving backward in a movie, and positive numbers indicate you are moving forward.

3. **Release the mouse button**
   The Shannon1 clip is positioned to the left of the ActionG clip, and a large gap appears on the Timeline where the Shannon1 clip was originally.

4. **Click the gap to the right of the ActionG clip, then press [Backspace]**

5. **Click the ActionG clip, drag the clip to the beginning of the Client9 clip, press and hold [Alt], then release the mouse button**
   The **Rearrange pointer** appears when you press and hold [Alt] before releasing the mouse button; this edit **rearranges** a clip by shifting clips to the right. The gap left by the moved clip closes automatically.

**TROUBLE**

If you accidentally press [Alt] before you begin dragging the clip, only the video track of the clip is selected and moved. If this happens, release the mouse button, undo the action, then repeat Step 5.

6. **Select the Client10 clip in the Media panel, then drag it to the end of the movie**
   The Client10 clip is aligned with the right edge of the Client7 clip. You move a clip to overlap this clip.

7. **Click the Tibbs clip on the Timeline, press and hold [Ctrl], then drag it to the beginning of the Client10 clip**
   The **Overlay pointer** appears when you press and hold [Ctrl] while dragging the clip to its new location. Pressing and holding [Ctrl] **overlays** a clip by replacing the frames on the target clip with the frames of the moved clip. The first 150 frames of the video portion of the Client10 clip are replaced with the Tibbs clip, which is 150 frames long. Because the Tibbs clip doesn't contain any audio, the first 150 frames of the audio portion of Client10 are not replaced.

8. **Save your changes to the project, if necessary, drag the end-of-movie marker on the time ruler to align with the end of the Client10 clip, as shown in Figure C-10, then render the work area**
   The Render work area command renders only the area of a movie bounded by the start-of-movie and end-of-movie markers on the time ruler. Sometimes you need to manually resize the work area when you add clips to and remove them from the Timeline.

**FIGURE C-9: Moving and inserting a clip**

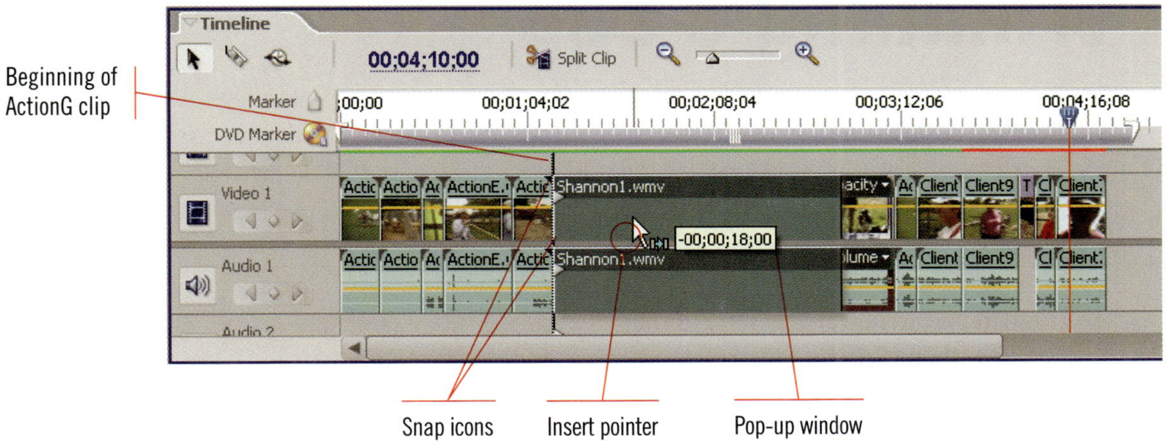


**FIGURE C-10: Rearranged and overlaid clips**

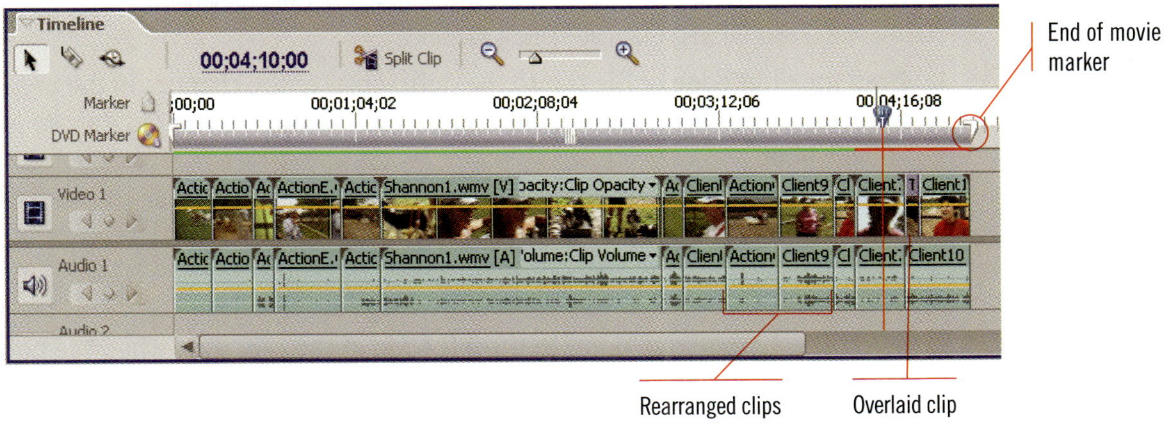


**TABLE C-1: Move pointers and options**

| pointer or command | use to | to activate |
|---|---|---|
| | Move and insert a clip | Select clip, then drag |
| | Rearrange a clip | Select clip, drag, then press [Alt] before releasing mouse button |
| | Rearrange only the video or audio track of a clip | Select the audio or video track of a clip, then drag while pressing [Alt] |
| | Move and overlay a clip | Select clip, then drag while pressing [Ctrl] |
| Cut command | Move and insert a clip without dragging | Right-click a clip, click Cut, click in new location, right-click, then click Paste |
| Copy command | Move a copy of a clip | Right-click a clip, click Copy, click in new location, right-click, then click Paste |

UNIT
C
Premiere Elements 2.0

# Trimming a Clip

**Trimming** removes frames at the beginning or end of a clip; you can trim as much or as little of a clip as you like. Trimming the left edge removes frames at the in point, and trimming the right edge removes frames at the out point. If any clips follow or **trail** the clip you are trimming, they shift on the Timeline to prevent any gaps. You want to trim a few clips in the movie to move the action along more energetically.

## STEPS

1. **Zoom in and scroll, if necessary, so that you can see the ActionE and ActionF clips on the Timeline, then click the time ruler at the beginning of the ActionE clip (frame 00;00;35;14)**
   Clicking the time ruler moves the current-time indicator to the frame you clicked.
2. **Click the Play button on the Monitor panel, then press [Spacebar] when you reach the end of the ActionF clip**
3. **Select the ActionE clip, point to the right edge of the clip, then when the pointer changes to the Trim Out Point pointer, drag left as shown in Figure C-11, but do not release the mouse button**
   As you drag, the Monitor panel displays a preview of the selected clip's new out point on the left, and the next clip's in point on the right. If there were no clip trailing this clip, the Monitor would display only the selected clip. The farther left you drag, the more frames you trim.

**TROUBLE**

If you can't drag exactly to –00;00;14;00, release the mouse button, undo the action, then zoom in on the Timeline. The more you zoom in, the greater your degree of control when trimming clips.

4. **Drag the right edge of the clip to the right, observe the changes in the preview and in the time display on the Monitor panel and pop-up window, then drag the clip left to –00;00;14;00**
   The pop-up window and the time display on the Monitor panel display the amount of the clip you are trimming. The number is negative when you drag to an earlier point in the clip, or farther back on the timeline. The ActionE clip is 14 seconds shorter. This action is also known as a **ripple-trim**, because frames trailing the clip automatically adjust so there is no gap in the Timeline.

**QUICK TIP**

You can trim just the video or audio track of a clip by pressing and holding [Alt] while dragging the track with the Trim pointer.

5. **Select the ActionF clip, point to the left edge of the clip, then when the pointer changes to the Trim In Pointer, drag right until the time display in the Monitor reads +00;00;05;00, as shown in Figure C-12**
   The removes frames from the beginning, and the Monitor window shows the in point. Because you are setting an in point that is later in the clip than the previous point, the number in the time display and pop-up window is positive. You trimmed five seconds from the beginning of this clip.
6. **Select the ActionE clip, point to the right edge of the clip, then when the pointer changes to, drag right until the pop-up window reads +00;00;06;22, as shown in Figure C-13**
   You regained 6 seconds and 22 frames at the end of this clip. You can restore or **regain** trimmed frames at any point in the editing process if you change your mind about an edit. As with trimming, any clips trailing the clip shift on the Timeline to make room for the added frames.
7. **Save your changes**
   Notice that the end of the ActionE clip and the beginning of the ActionF clip that you just trimmed do not display small triangles at their upper corners. The absence of a triangle at the in or out point indicates that the clip has been trimmed; you can regain those frames if you like. The presence of a triangle indicates that the edge has not been trimmed.

FIGURE C-11: Trimming the out point of a clip

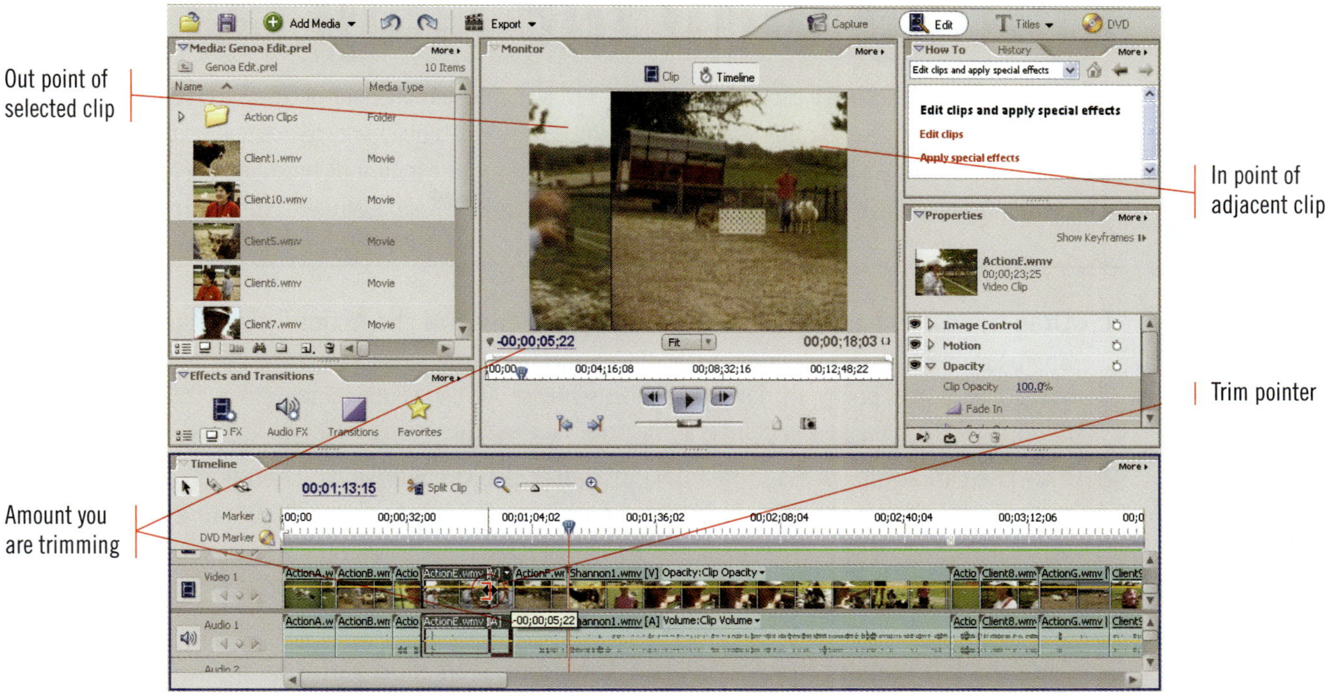


FIGURE C-12: Trimming the in point of a clip

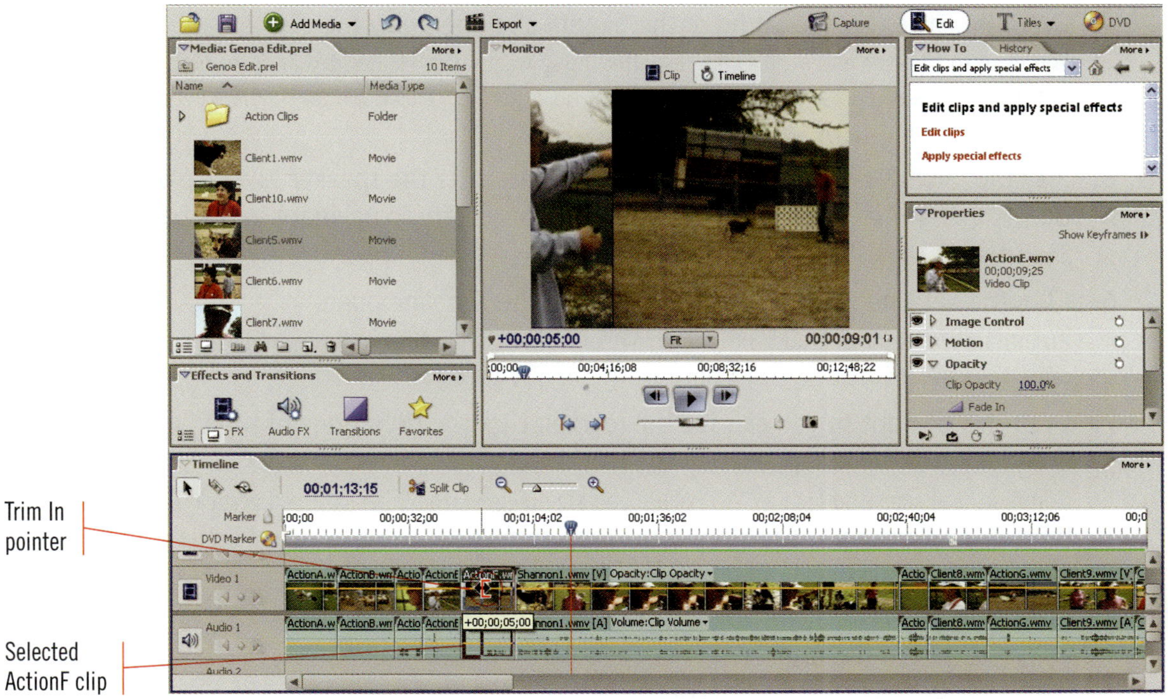


FIGURE C-13: Regaining frames at the out point of a clip

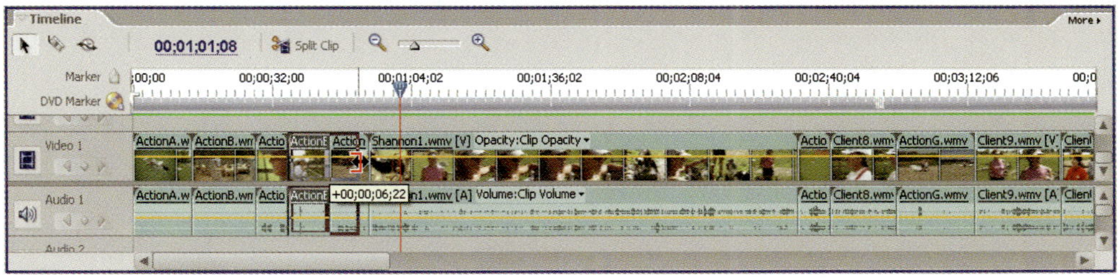

UNIT
C
Premiere Elements 2.0

# Editing with the Snap Feature

Dragging to trim or lengthen a clip is easy, but sometimes you need more control. The Snap feature in combination with the current-time indicator or a marker on the time ruler is a quick way to position edits right where you want them. **Markers** are icons that you can place anywhere in the Monitor or Timeline time ruler. You want to trim a few more clips in the Timeline and decide to use the Snap feature to work more efficiently.

## STEPS

1. **Drag the current-time indicator to the beginning of the ActionE clip, then play the clip**
   Approximately four seconds into the clip, the speaker in the video says, "Then you can move out around the sheep." She pauses briefly, then begins another sentence, "When you're standing here like this…" You want to trim the clip so the new in point is at the pause between those two sentences.
2. **Play the clip again, press [Spacebar] just after the speaker says "Then you can move out…", then press ← or → as many times as necessary to reach 00;00;39;21**
   When navigating to a precise edit point, you may not reach it just by starting and stopping the clip. Pressing ← or → moves the current-time indicator back or forward one frame at a time. This degree of precision is usually what you need to locate a specific edit point.
3. **Click the left edge of the ActionE clip, then drag it to align with the , as shown in Figure C-14**
   The in point of the clip is trimmed to the location of the current-time indicator. The Snap feature aligns the edit to the current-time indicator because this is the nearest editing milestone.
4. **Drag the to the beginning of the Client8 clip, then play the clip**
   You want to trim the end of this clip, just after the speaker says, "He decided to do something that's kind of not usual in his breed," and before he says, "but he enjoys it." This is a more challenging edit, because you need to trim in the middle of a very brief pause.
5. **Play the Client8 clip again, press [Spacebar] just after the speaker says "He decided to do…", then press ← or → as many times as necessary to navigate to the pause before the speaker says, "but he enjoys it"**
6. **Click the Set Unnumbered Marker icon on the Timeline panel**
   An unnumbered marker is added to the time ruler, although it is difficult to see behind the current-time indicator. You can set a marker when a clip is playing or is stopped.
7. **Drag the right so you can see the marker, click the right edge of the Client8 clip, then drag left until the appears on the marker**
   Compare your screen to Figure C-15. While you are dragging, the Snap icon and vertical line that appear at the marker indicate where the edit will occur. This is useful if the Timeline contains several markers or if you are dragging near the current-time indicator, another positioning milestone.
8. **Click Marker on the menu bar, point to Clear Timeline Marker, click All Markers, then save your changes to the project**
   Markers remain in a project until you clear them.

**QUICK TIP**
When trimming a clip that cuts off a speaker mid-sentence, use the arrow keys to navigate to a point when the speaker's mouth is closed, before it opens again to form the next word.

**QUICK TIP**
You can also clear or set markers by right-clicking a marker, and then clicking a command in the list.

**FIGURE C-14: Trimming to the current-time indicator**

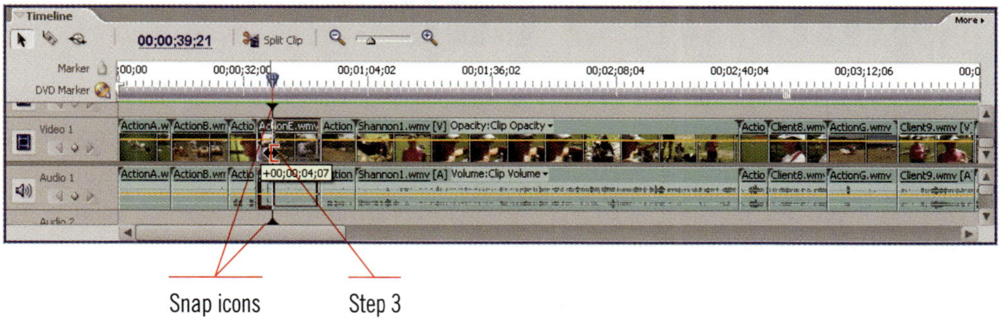


**FIGURE C-15: Trimming to a marker**

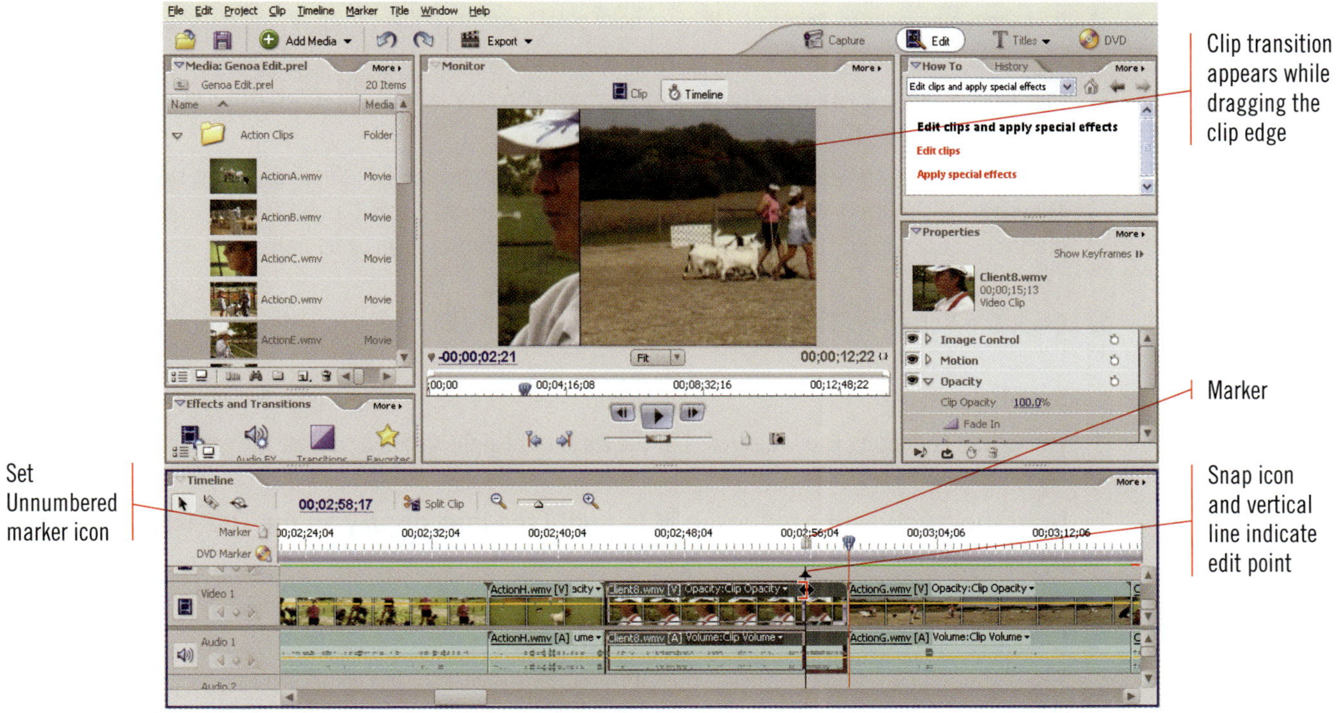


## Clues to Use

### Working with markers

You can add and clear markers as you work, or you can save them with the project and use them in a future editing session. If you are working on a complex edit or simply want to keep track of your markers, you can set numbered markers. To do so, navigate to the position on the Timeline where you want to position the marker. Click Marker on the menu bar, point to Set Timeline Marker, then click Next Available Numbered or Other Numbered. If you choose the Next Available Numbered command, Premiere Elements numbers the markers automatically as you set them. If you choose Other Numbered, you can set the numbers manually. You can also drag markers anywhere on the Timeline, so if you add a marker, then change your mind about where you want it, you don't need to remove it and start again.

UNIT
C
Premiere Elements 2.0

# Splitting a Clip

You can **split** a clip to divide it into two or more separate clips on the Timeline. Once the clip is split, you can move, delete, or apply effects to the clips independently. Both clips can be lengthened to the original duration of the clip, just as if you had trimmed them. To split a clip, you can use either the Split Clip Tool or the Razor Tool on the Timeline panel. You want to split the Shannon1 clip so that you can move some of the interview later in the movie.

## STEPS

**QUICK TIP**
You can zoom in by pressing [+] or zoom out by pressing [–].

1. **Zoom if necessary until you see the 00;01;36;02 and the 00;02;08;04 marks on the time ruler with no numbered marks between them**

2. **Click the Razor Tool on the Timeline panel, then move the Razor pointer anywhere on the Shannon1 clip**
   The indicates that anywhere you click, the clip will be split. You do not need to select a clip before splitting it. If the mouse pointer changes to , you have positioned the pointer over a blank track instead of a clip.

**QUICK TIP**
You can also press [C] to select the Razor Tool.

3. **Position at approximately two hash marks to the left of the 00;02;08;04 mark on the time ruler, then click the mouse**
   See Figure C-16. The clip is split at the point you clicked, creating two Shannon1 clips side by side on the Timeline. Your split point may not match the figure exactly; the Razor Tool is easy to use, but it's not always precise because you are pointing and clicking rather than choosing an exact frame.

4. **Click the Selection Tool on the Timeline, then click the second Shannon1 clip**

5. **Press [Delete]**
   The second Shannon1 clip is deleted, and the clips to the right shift left to close the gap.

6. **Drag the current-time indicator left until the time display on the Timeline reads 00;01;28;02**

7. **Click the Split Clip Tool Split Clip on the Timeline**
   The Shannon1 clip is split at the location of the current-time indicator, as shown in Figure C-17. This tool is more precise than the Razor Tool because you can move to the exact frame you want before splitting the clip.

**QUICK TIP**
To avoid a gap, remember that when moving a clip, you can press [Alt] just before releasing the mouse button.

8. **Zoom if necessary to see the Client9 clip, then drag the second Shannon1 clip so it aligns with the right edge of the Client9 clip, as shown in Figure C-18**
   The second part of the Shannon1 clip now comes after the Client9 clip in the movie. A gap remains on the Timeline where the second Shannon1 clip was moved.

9. **Right-click the gap, click Delete and Close Gap, then save your changes to the project**

**FIGURE C-16: Splitting a clip with the Razor Tool**

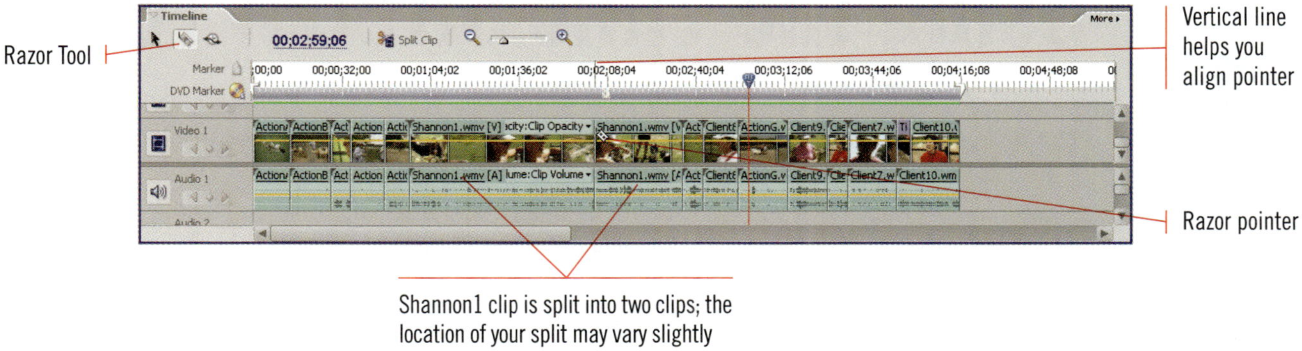


**FIGURE C-17: Using the Split Clip Tool**

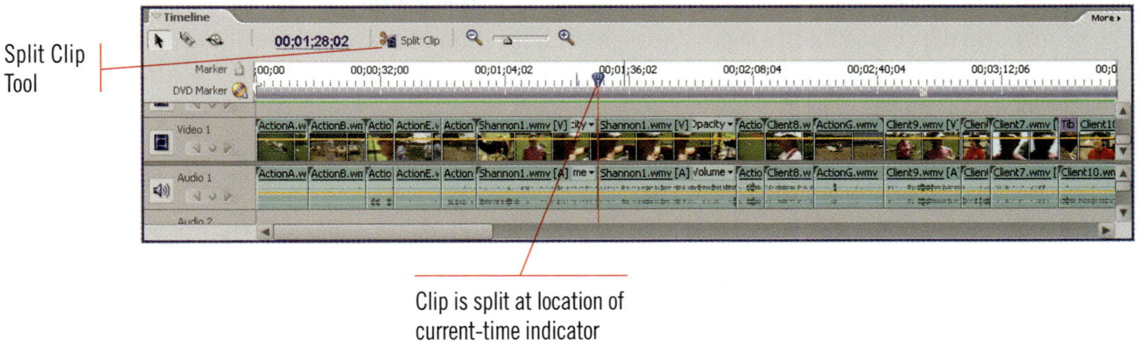


**FIGURE C-18: Moving the split clip**

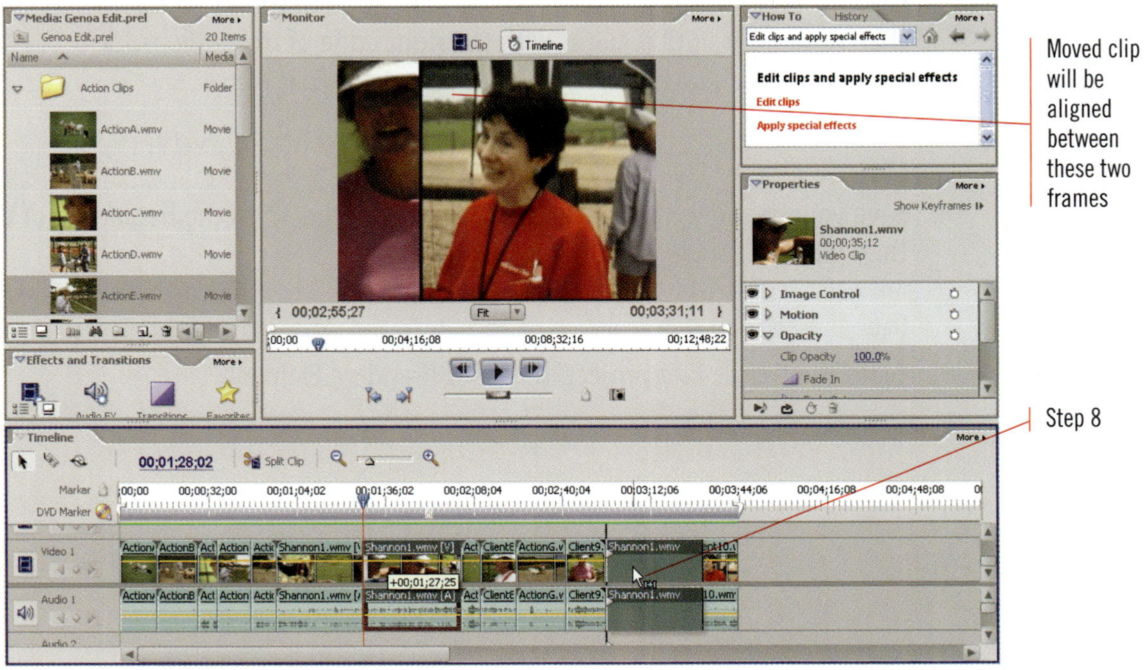

UNIT C

Premiere Elements 2.0

# Using the Time Stretch Tool

The Time Stretch Tool lets you slow down or speed up a clip or the audio or video portion of a clip to create a variety of effects. You can speed up or slow down a clip as much as you want, although the quality of the sound or visual component varies depending on the file type and the amount of the stretch. You can also use this tool when you want to use all of an audio track, but only part of the video track. The Time Stretch Tool lets you stretch just the video portion of the clip so it's the same length as the audio clip. You want to add one final clip of Shannon to the movie, and you want to create a slow motion effect that highlights the theme of teamwork discussed in the interviews.

## STEPS

1. **Expand the Action Clips folder in the Media panel, then drag the ActionK clip to the end of the movie on the Timeline, so it aligns with the right edge of the Client10 clip**

2. **Click the Time Stretch Tool on the Timeline, point to the right edge of the ActionK clip, then when the pointer changes to the Time Stretch pointer, drag the pointer approximately 45 seconds to the right, as shown in Figure C-19**

   The clip stretches so that the right edge aligns with the point where you release the mouse button. Dragging right with the slows down a clip; dragging left speeds it up. The clip name on the Timeline displays the amount of stretch applied.

3. **Press [V] to activate the Selection Tool, drag the current-time indicator to the beginning of the ActionK clip, then play it**

   Slowing down the clip creates a more dramatic visual effect, but the slowed audio changes the tone so that the words are hard to understand.

4. **Press [Ctrl][Z] to undo your changes**

   You want to slow down the visual part of the clip, but keep the audio at normal speed, so you undo your changes and try a different approach.

5. **Move to frame 00:04;00;10 on the Timeline, press and hold [Alt], then drag the right edge of the video track of the ActionK clip to align it with the**

   Pressing and holding [Alt] selects just one track of a clip, so that you can edit it independently. The video track is now shorter than the audio track, as shown in Figure C-20.

6. **Click on the Timeline, point to the right edge of the video track of the ActionK clip, then drag right until it aligns with the right edge of the audio track**

   The video portion stretches so it is the same length as the audio portion. See Figure C-21.

7. **Drag the to the beginning of the clip, then play it**

   The audio plays at normal speed, but the video portion slows down.

8. **Save your changes, render the work area, drag the to the beginning of the movie, then play the movie**

   As a result of your edits, you've created a movie that introduces viewers to the value of herding lessons, illustrates Shannon's expertise as owner of Genoa Stock, and moves at a brisk pace.

9. **Close the Genoa Edit project, then exit Premiere Elements**

**QUICK TIP**

You can also press [X] to select the Time Stretch Tool.

**TROUBLE**

If you accidentally drag the audio track instead of the video track, press [Ctrl][Z], then repeat Step 5, making sure to click the video track and not the audio track.

**QUICK TIP**

You can change the speed of a clip or reverse its speed by using the Time Stretch dialog box. To open it, select the clip in the Timeline, click Clip on the menu bar, then click Time Stretch.

FIGURE C-19: Stretching a clip

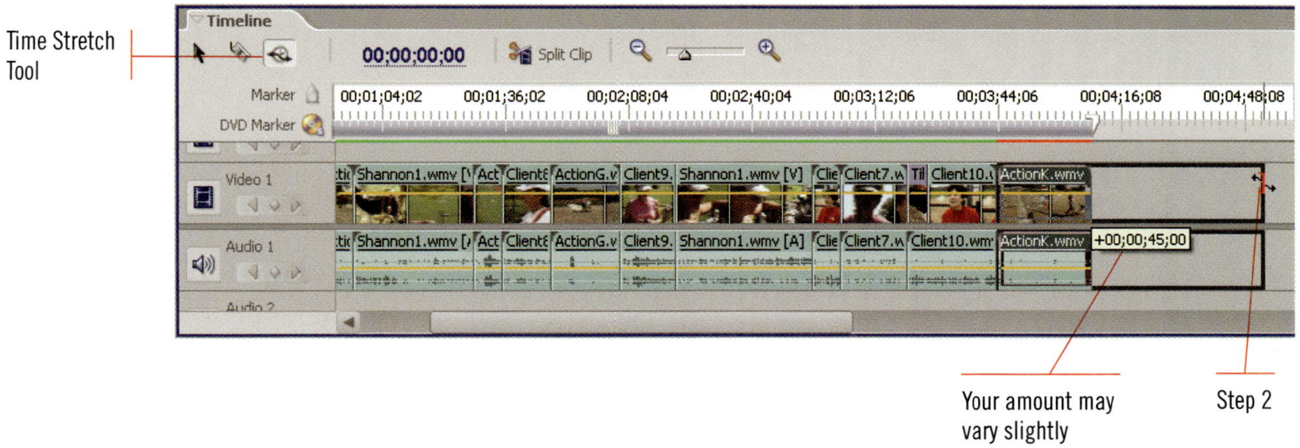


FIGURE C-20: Trimming the video track of a clip

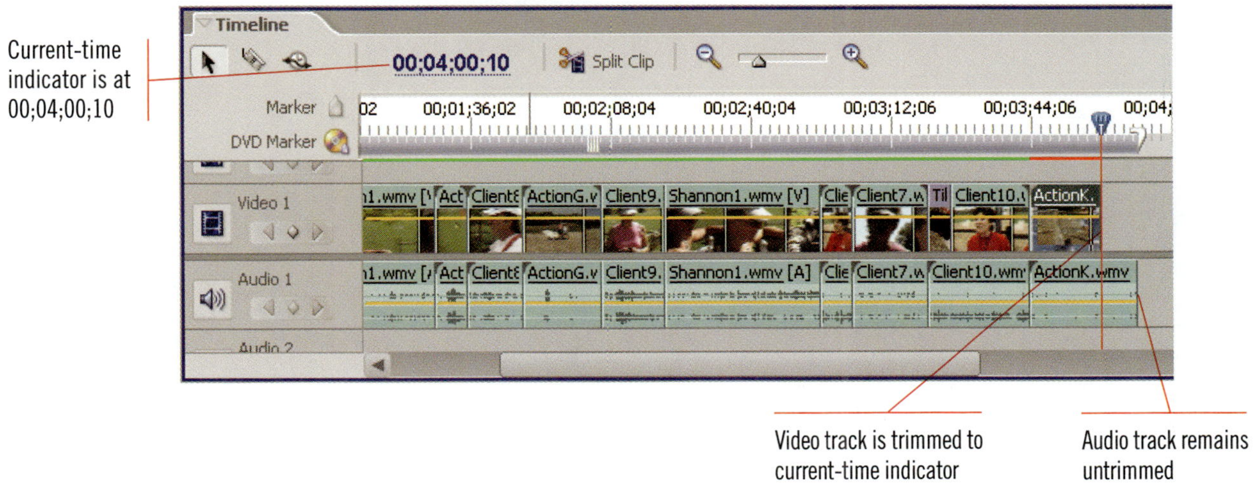


FIGURE C-21: Time Stretch Tool applied to video track

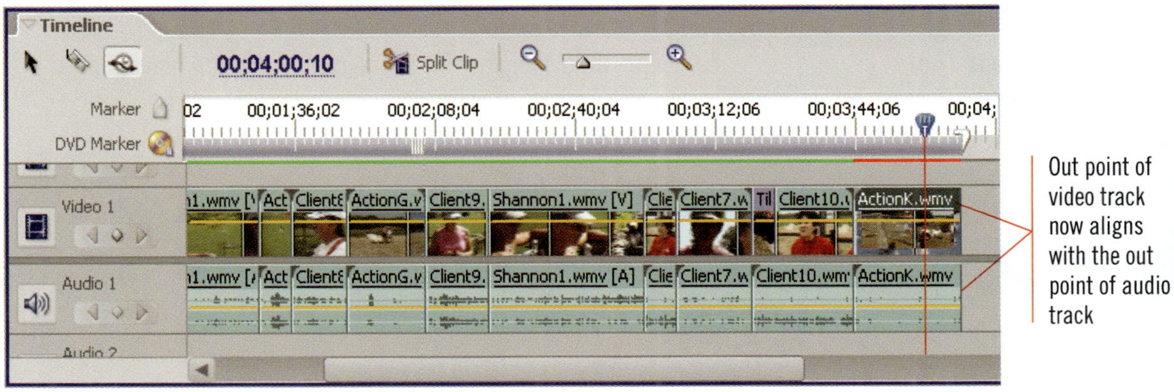


Premiere Elements 2.0

# Practice

## ▼ CONCEPTS REVIEW

**Label the elements of the Premiere Elements program window shown in Figure C-22.**

FIGURE C-22

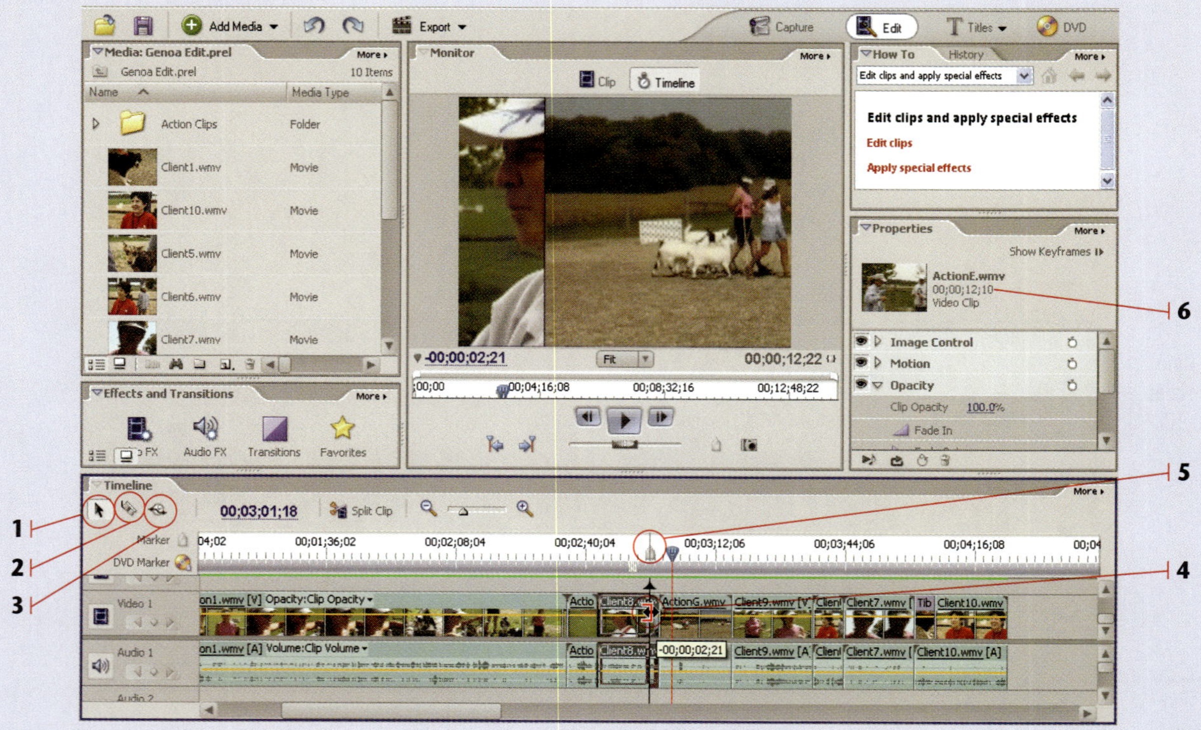


**Match each term with the statement that best describes it.**

7. **Timeline**
8. **Monitor window**
9. **In point**
10. **Out point**
11. **Split Clip Tool**
12. **Time Stretch Tool**
13. **Razor Tool**
14. **Snap Tool**

**a.** Use to split a clip at location of current-time indicator
**b.** Drag clips here to combine with other clips in movie
**c.** Use to split a clip at location you click with mouse pointer
**d.** Drag clips here to change in point or out point before combining with other clips
**e.** First frame of a clip
**f.** Use to align a clip or edit to the nearest editing milestone
**g.** Use to speed up or slow down a clip or track of a clip
**h.** Last frame of a clip

**Select the best answer from the list of choices.**

**15. When you drag a video clip from the Media panel to the Timeline, the audio track:**
   **a.** Moves to a hidden area of the video track.
   **b.** Moves to the first available audio track on the Timeline.
   **c.** Does not move to the Timeline unless you press and hold [Shift].
   **d.** Moves to the Properties panel.

**16. When you insert a clip between two clips on the Timeline:**
   **a.** The clip on the right is replaced by the inserted clip.
   **b.** The clip on the left is replaced by the inserted clip.
   **c.** The clip on the right shifts right to make room.
   **d.** The clip on the left shifts left to make room.

**17. If you want to add only part of a clip in the Media panel to the Timeline:**
   **a.** You can use the Split Clip Tool in the Monitor panel.
   **b.** You can set in and out points in the Monitor panel.
   **c.** You can delete part of the clip by pressing [Delete].
   **d.** You can set in and out points in the Media panel.

**18. If you want to remove a clip on the Timeline and leave a gap in place of the clip:**
   **a.** Press [Delete].
   **b.** Right-click the clip, then click Delete and Close Gap.
   **c.** Right-click the clip, then click Clear.
   **d.** Press and hold [Ctrl] while deleting the clip.

**19. A clip instance is:**
   **a.** A copy of the clip on the Timeline.
   **b.** A copy of the clip in the Media panel.
   **c.** The original source file for the clip.
   **d.** One frame of a clip.

**20. To overlay a target clip with the clip you are moving:**
   **a.** Press and hold [Alt] while dragging the clip you want to move.
   **b.** Press and hold [Shift] while dragging the clip you want to move.
   **c.** Click the Time Stretch Tool before dragging the clip you want to move.
   **d.** Press and hold [Ctrl] while dragging the clip you want to move.

## ▼ SKILLS REVIEW

**1. Add a clip from the Media panel.**
   **a.** Start Premiere Elements.
   **b.** Open the file PE C-2.prel from the drive and folder where your Data Files are located.
   **c.** Save the file as **Clown Edit** in the *YourName* folder where you are saving files for this book.
   **d.** Verify that the Snap command on the Timeline menu is activated, then drag the Cam1_a clip from the Media panel to the beginning of the Timeline.
   **e.** Drag the Kapoot6 clip so it aligns with the end of the Cam1_a clip on the Timeline, then drag the Kapoot7 clip so it aligns with the end of the Kapoot6 clip on the Timeline.
   **f.** Select the clips Cam1_b, Cam1_c, Cam1_d, and Cam1_e.
   **g.** Drag the selected clips to the Timeline so the selection aligns with the end of the Kapoot7 clip.
   **h.** Expand the Camera 2 Clips folder, then drag the Cam2_b clip to the Timeline and insert it between the Cam1_b clip and the Cam1_c clip. (*Hint*: The order of clips should be Cam1_a, Kapoot6, Kapoot7, Cam1_b, Cam2_b, Cam1_c, Cam1_d, and Cam1_e.)
   **i.** Save your changes to the project, render the work area, then watch the movie.

## ▼ SKILLS REVIEW (CONTINUED)

2. **Add a clip using the Monitor panel.**
   a. Double-click the Cam2_c clip in the Media panel.
   b. Play the clip on the Monitor panel.
   c. Set the in point of the clip to 00;00;04;25 on the time display.
   d. Set the out point of the clip to 00;00;08;14 on the time display.
   e. Change the in point of the clip to 00;00;02;28 by dragging the In Point bracket.
   f. Drag the clip from the Monitor to the end of the movie, so it follows the Cam1_e clip.
   g. Play the Cam2_d clip in the Monitor panel, then drag it to the end of the movie on the Timeline.
   h. Open the Cam2_e clip in the Monitor panel, leave its in point at the beginning of the clip, change its out point to 00;00;05;08, then drag it to the end of the movie.
   i. Save your changes to the project.
3. **Delete a clip.**
   a. If necessary, zoom in on the Timeline so you can see the names of the clips on the Timeline (you don't need to see the file extensions).
   b. Activate the Selection Tool if necessary, then select the Kapoot6 clip.
   c. Perform a ripple delete of the clip (closing the gap caused by the deletion).
   d. Select the Kapoot7 clip, then clear it from the Timeline.
   e. Play the movie from a few seconds before the gap through a few seconds after it.
   f. Drag the Cam2_a clip from the Media panel to the beginning of the gap on the Timeline.
   g. Save your changes to the project.
4. **Move a clip.**
   a. Select the Cam2_c clip on the Timeline, then read the Properties panel, noting the current duration of the clip.
   b. Drag the Cam2_c clip to the beginning of the Cam1_d clip.
   c. Close the gap caused by the move.
   d. Rearrange clips Cam1_e and Cam2_d, with no gap between any clips.
   e. Save your changes to the project.
5. **Trim a clip.**
   a. Play the Cam2_d clip on the Timeline, then pause when you reach the end of the clip.
   b. Point to the end of the clip until you see the Trim pointer.
   c. Drag the end point of the clip left and right, observing the change in the Monitor panel.
   d. Use the Trim pointer to trim the out point of the clip by –00;00;02;26 frames.
   e. Save your changes to the project.
6. **Edit using the Snap feature.**
   a. Play the Cam1_b clip on the Timeline, pausing when you reach the end of the clip.
   b. Move the current-time indicator to 00;00;19;20.
   c. Trim the in point of the clip to the location of the current-time indicator.
   d. Add a marker at the 00;00;16;20 point on the time ruler.
   e. Trim the out point of the Cam2_a clip to the location of the marker.
   f. Save your changes to the project, then clear the marker.
7. **Split a clip.**
   a. Play the Cam2_b clip on the Timeline, then pause the movie.
   b. Use the Razor Tool to split the Cam2_b clip in half (approximately five and a half seconds into the clip; the split does not need to be exact).
   c. Activate the Selection Tool.
   d. Use the Split Clip Tool to split the Cam1_c clip in half (approximately three seconds into the clip).
   e. Ripple-delete the second Cam1_c clip.

# ▼ SKILLS REVIEW (CONTINUED)

- **f.** Overlay the remaining Cam1_c clip at the beginning of the second Cam2_b clip, then delete the resulting gap. (*Hint*: Press and hold [Ctrl] while moving the Cam1_c clip to the in point of the second Cam2_b clip.)
- **g.** Save your changes to the project. (*Hint*: The order of clips should be Cam1_b, Cam2_b, Cam1_c, Cam2_b, and Cam2_c.)

**8. Use the Time Stretch Tool.**

- **a.** Drag the Cam1_f clip from the Media panel to the end of the movie.
- **b.** Activate the Time Stretch Tool, then slow down the Cam1_f clip by approximately five seconds or 50%, then play the clip.
- **c.** Undo the edit.
- **d.** Use the Trim pointer to trim the out point of the previous clip, Cam2_e, by approximately three seconds (to the point where the clown grabs his ears).
- **e.** Use the [Alt] key to trim the in point of the video track of the Cam1_f clip by approximately two seconds (to the point where the clown has grabbed his ears).
- **f.** Activate the Time Stretch Tool, then stretch the video track of the Cam1_f clip so it aligns with the end of the audio track.
- **g.** Compare your screen to Figure C-23, save your changes, render the work area, then watch the movie. (*Note:* The duration of your final movie may differ slightly.)
- **h.** Close the Clown Edit project, then exit Premiere Elements.

**FIGURE C-23**

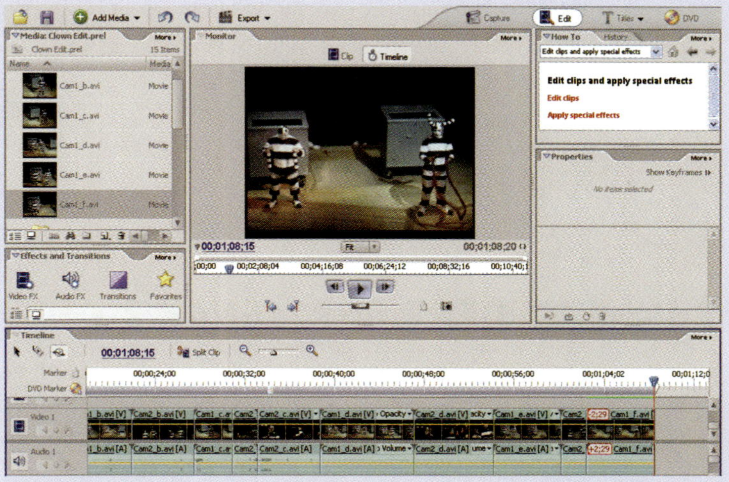

# ▼ INDEPENDENT CHALLENGE 1

You are ready to edit the movie trailer for the film festival sponsored by your city's Department of Cultural Affairs. You want to combine the clips in a way that emphasizes the comic spirit of the festival and sparks the viewer's interest in seeing the complete program. The movie will be posted to the city's Web site, so you want to keep it short and fast-paced.

- **a.** Start Premiere Elements.
- **b.** Open the file PE C-3.prel from the drive and folder where your Data Files are located, then save it as **Film Fest Edit** in the *YourName* folder where you are saving files for this book.
- **c.** Add the Dress for Success clip to the beginning of the Timeline.
- **d.** Select the clips Muffin Control, Sad Song, and Silent Breakfast, then add the selection to the end of the Timeline. (*Hint*: Remember, you can press and hold [Ctrl] while clicking to select noncontiguous clips.) The order of clips should be: Dress for Success, Muffin Control, Sad Song, and Silent Breakfast.
- **e.** Add the Tax Help clip to the Timeline, inserting it between the Sad Song clip and the Silent Breakfast clip.
- **f.** Trim the in point and out point of the Dress for Success clip so that it begins with the man starting to put on his wig and ends just before we see the couple walking up the street.
- **g.** Use the current-time indicator or markers to trim the in point and out point of the Muffin Control clip slightly, to remove the partial sentence at the beginning and end of the clip. (*Hint*: The clip should begin with the line, "You want a muffin?" and end with the line, "What if I want it heated?")
- **h.** Open the Really Hot Coffee clip in the Monitor, watch the clip, set an in point just before the man opens the microwave (approximately 23 seconds into the clip) and an out point just after the screen fades to black on the two coffee cups (approximately 38 seconds into the clip), then insert the adjusted clip between the Tax Help clip and the Silent Breakfast clip.

## ▼ INDEPENDENT CHALLENGE 1 (CONTINUED)

i. Delete the Silent Breakfast clip in the Timeline, then save your changes to the project. Compare your Timeline to Figure C-24.

FIGURE C-24

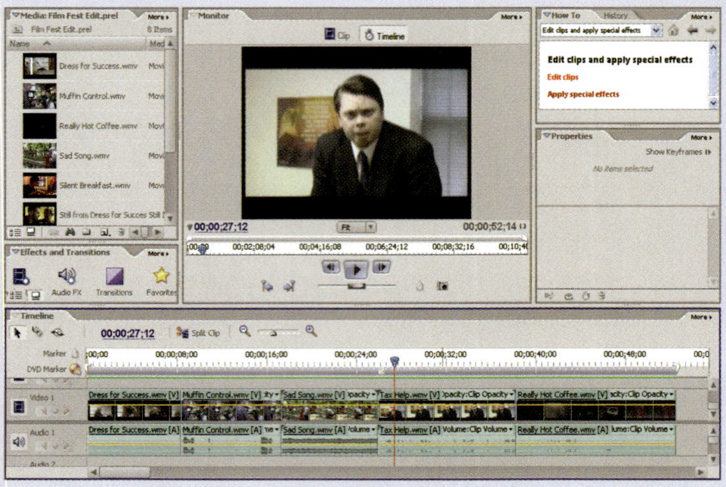

**Advanced Challenge Exercise**

- Use the Time Stretch dialog box to speed up the Sad Song clip to 115%. (*Hint*: Right-click the clip, then click Time Stretch in the shortcut menu.)
- Delete the gap caused by the previous edit.
- Reverse the action of the Dress for Success clip. (*Hint*: Use a command in the Time Stretch dialog box.)

j. Render the work area, save your changes to the project, watch the movie, then close the project.

## ▼ INDEPENDENT CHALLENGE 2

You are ready to edit the documentary you making. By this point, you have recorded some footage and captured it into Premiere Elements. You also created a rough cut of all the clips you captured, and the clips are on the Timeline. In this Independent Challenge, you need to rearrange and trim the clips to create a movie that is approximately three minutes long. If you plan to make this into a longer documentary, think of this movie as Part 1. You can create a fast-paced movie, using short clips, or a slower-paced one, using fewer clips. The choice is up to you.

a. Start Premiere Elements if necessary, open the file My Documentary.prel from the drive and folder location where you are saving files for this book, then save it as **My Documentary Edit** in the *YourName* folder where you are saving files for this book. (*Note*: If you did not record and capture this movie, consult your instructor.)
b. Rearrange the clips so that they convey the information you want, in the order you want. Remember that you can insert, rearrange, and overlay clips to achieve the final arrangement of clips.
c. If you want to use any additional video or still images that are not part of the project, add them, then use the Monitor panel to add just the parts you want to the Timeline.
d. Delete any clips you think are unnecessary.
e. Trim clips as needed to remove extraneous footage and bring the final duration of the movie to approximately three minutes.
f. Use the Time Stretch Tool if you want to slow down, speed up, or reverse a clip or a track on a clip.
g. Render the work area, then save your changes to the project.
h. Close the project and exit Premiere Elements.

## ▼ INDEPENDENT CHALLENGE 3

You need to edit the video you're creating for the internship program at Fig Media, the video production company where you work. Jim, the owner, wants a movie that introduces viewers to the fun and supportive atmosphere at the company. He has a few suggestions for the final edit.

a. Open the file PE C-4.prel from the drive and folder where your your Data Files are located, then save it as **Dream Job Edit** in the *YourName* folder where you are saving files for this book. The project contains two folders. One clip has already been added to the Timeline.
b. Review the contents of each folder and preview any clips to familiarize yourself with all your resources. The Staff Clips folder contains eight clips of staffers talking about the company. The New Clips folder contains two exterior shots of the company offices and two interior shots of the staff at work.

## ▼ INDEPENDENT CHALLENGE 3 (CONTINUED)

**c.** Trim the Jennifer clip on the Timeline using the two markers on the time ruler as in and out points. Jim wants clips to move smoothly from one to another, without false starts or pauses at the beginning or end.

**d.** Add at least seven additional clips from the Media panel to the Timeline. Jim asks that you use at least five more clips from the Staff Clips folder and at least two clips from the New Clips folder. These can be used as establishing shots at the beginning of the movie, as closing shots, or in any way you choose.

**e.** Trim, split, and rearrange the clips in the order you choose.

**f.** Save your changes to the project.

**Advanced Challenge Exercise**

ACE

- Experiment with editing just the video or audio track of two contiguous clips. For example, trim only the video track of one clip at its end point, and only the video track of the next clip at its in point, so that the sound from the next clip begins before the video from the current clip ends. See Figure C-25.

**g.** Trim clips of staff members used to remove pauses at the beginning or end of each clip.

**h.** Create a final movie that is under one minute long.

**i.** Save your changes, render the work area, watch the movie, then close the project and exit Premiere Elements.

FIGURE C-25

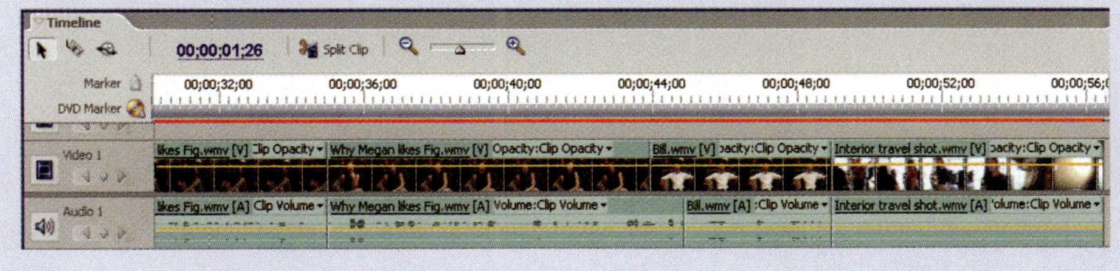


E-QUEST

## ▼ INDEPENDENT CHALLENGE 4

The local university has asked your cinema club to speak at an upcoming conference called Cinema and Education. The conference is intended to encourage teachers in all disciplines to take advantage of the Internet's vast resources of public domain film and video footage. Other members in the cinema club are speaking on the use of public domain footage in filmmaking and film history classes, but you have been asked to address the needs of instructors in non-film-related classes, such as science and marketing. Your goal is to encourage them to use film footage in the classroom to engage student interest and provide historical perspective. You decide to show a movie that contains excerpts of public domain films.

**a.** Connect to the Internet if necessary, then use your favorite search engine to search for sites that offer public domain film footage. Popular sites include the Library of Congress (*www.loc.gov*) and the Internet Archive (*www.archive.org*). For each Web site you visit, read the Terms of Use page and/or Copyright pages on the site to learn whether you can legally download video files. Because you are using these images for educational purposes, using them is often permissible, but the rules and guidelines vary by site.

**b.** Browse the Web site to find and download three examples of films related to science or marketing. When downloading, several formats are often available. Choose a format that is compatible with Premiere Elements, such as AVI, WMV, or MPEG4, with a file size that is manageable for your system.

**c.** Create a new project called **Internet Education** in the *YourName* folder where you are saving files for this book.

**d.** Add the files you downloaded to the project, then add them to the Timeline. If you downloaded a lower-quality format, such as 64 KB MPEG4, the quality of the clips may be low. That's acceptable, because you are using the footage for reference purposes.

**e.** Trim the clips to show a representative excerpt from each movie that is approximately one minute long. The total running time should be under four minutes.

**f.** Render the work areas, save your changes to the project, then watch the movie.

**g.** When you are finished, close the project and exit Premiere Elements.

# ▼ VISUAL WORKSHOP

Open the file PE C-5.prel in the drive and folder location where you are saving files for this book, then save it as **Butterfly Edit** in the *YourName* folder where you are saving files for this book. Add clips from the Media panel, then trim and rearrange them to match the Timeline shown in Figure C-26. (*Hint*: Use the markers shown to help figure out where to trim clips as needed.) Save your changes to the project. When you are finished, press [PrtScr], paste the image into your word-processing program, print a copy, then exit your word processor and Premiere Elements.

FIGURE C-26

UNIT
D
Premiere Elements 2.0

# Adding Effects and Transitions

## OBJECTIVES

- Apply a standard effect
- Adjust an effect and create a preset
- Adjust a fixed effect
- Animate with keyframes in the Properties panel
- Keyframe in the Timeline panel
- Use Preset Effects
- Add and adjust a double-sided transition
- Add and adjust a single-sided transition
- Remove an effect or transition

Premiere Elements includes a variety of effects and transitions you can apply to clips to improve their appearance, suggest a mood, create an illusion, and smooth the progression from one clip to the next. Effects can help correct a technical problem such as an underexposed clip, or they can serve a creative purpose, such as reducing the number of colors in a clip or changing it from color to black-and-white. Transitions can be as simple as a dissolve from one clip to another, or as dramatic as a swirl of images. You can adjust various properties of almost all effects and transitions, including effects that are automatically applied when you add a clip to the Timeline. Now that the basic edit of the Genoa Stock video is complete, you're ready to fine-tune it with effects and transitions.

UNIT
D
Premiere Elements 2.0

# Applying a Standard Effect

**Standard effects** are special video and audio alterations you can apply to a clip to change the way it looks or sounds. (You work with audio effects in a later unit.) To apply a standard video effect, you drag it from the Effects and Transitions panel to the clip on the Timeline. By default, the effect is applied to the duration of the clip. You can apply more than one effect to a clip, and you can delete an effect if you decide not to use it. You want to apply an effect to the opening clip in the Genoa Stock video to enhance it.

## STEPS

**TROUBLE**

If you don't want the movie to play automatically when you render the work area, click Edit on the menu bar, point to Preferences, click General, then remove the check mark in the Play work area after rendering the previews check box.

1. **Open the file PE D-1.prel from the drive and folder where your Data Files are located, save it as Genoa Effects and Transitions in the *YourName* folder where you are saving files for this book, then render the work area**

   The clips for the promotional video for Genoa Stock are arranged on the Timeline. You need to render most effects you apply, so starting with the movie rendered can save time.

2. **Increase the size of the Effects and Transitions panel, but make sure that the Video 1 track is still visible on the Timeline**

   You want room to work comfortably in both these panels and preview your work in the Monitor.

3. **Click the Video FX button on the Effects and Transitions panel, then click the Video Effects Expand icon**

   The list of Video Effects categories appears, as shown in Figure D-1. Premiere Elements includes more than 70 video effects, organized into categories to make them easier to browse and preview. See Table D-1 for a description of the available video effects.

4. **Click the Image Control Expand icon**

   This category contains effects you can apply to change the color properties of a clip. Each effect contains thumbnail images that illustrate the result of the effect.

**QUICK TIP**

To apply an effect to part of a clip, split the clip and then apply the effect to the desired clip segment.

5. **Drag the Black & White effect to the ActionA clip at the beginning of the Timeline**

   The Black & White effect is applied to the clip. You can also add an effect by selecting the clip and then dragging the effect to the Properties panel.

6. **Drag the current-time indicator to the beginning of the ActionA clip, then play the clip**

   You can preview most effects without rendering them, although they may not play smoothly.

**QUICK TIP**

To learn more about applying effects, click the Apply special effects link in the How To panel.

7. **Press [Ctrl][Z] to undo your edit, then click the Image Control collapse icon in the Effects and Transitions panel**

   You want to try a different effect for this first clip.

8. **Click the Stylize expand icon in the Effects and Transitions panel, scroll to see the Stylize effects, then drag the Find Edges effect to the ActionA clip on the Timeline**

   This effect emphasizes the edges within the frame and de-emphasizes colors between the edges, as shown in Figure D-2. The Properties panel lists the effect in the properties for this clip, and the poster frame shows the effect applied.

9. **Render the work area, play the first clip, then save your changes**

FIGURE D-1: Video Effects categories

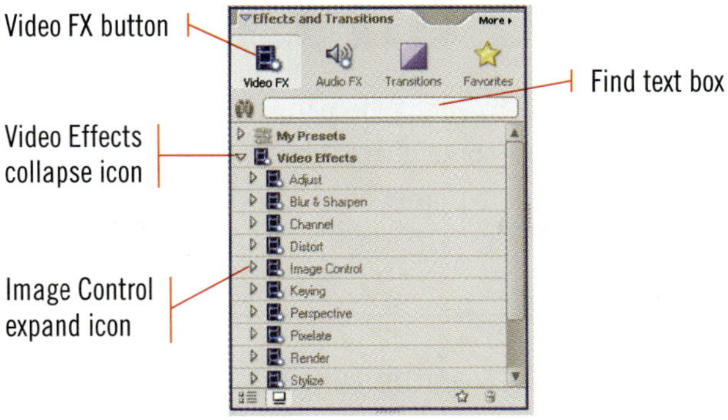


FIGURE D-2: Find Edges effect applied to a clip

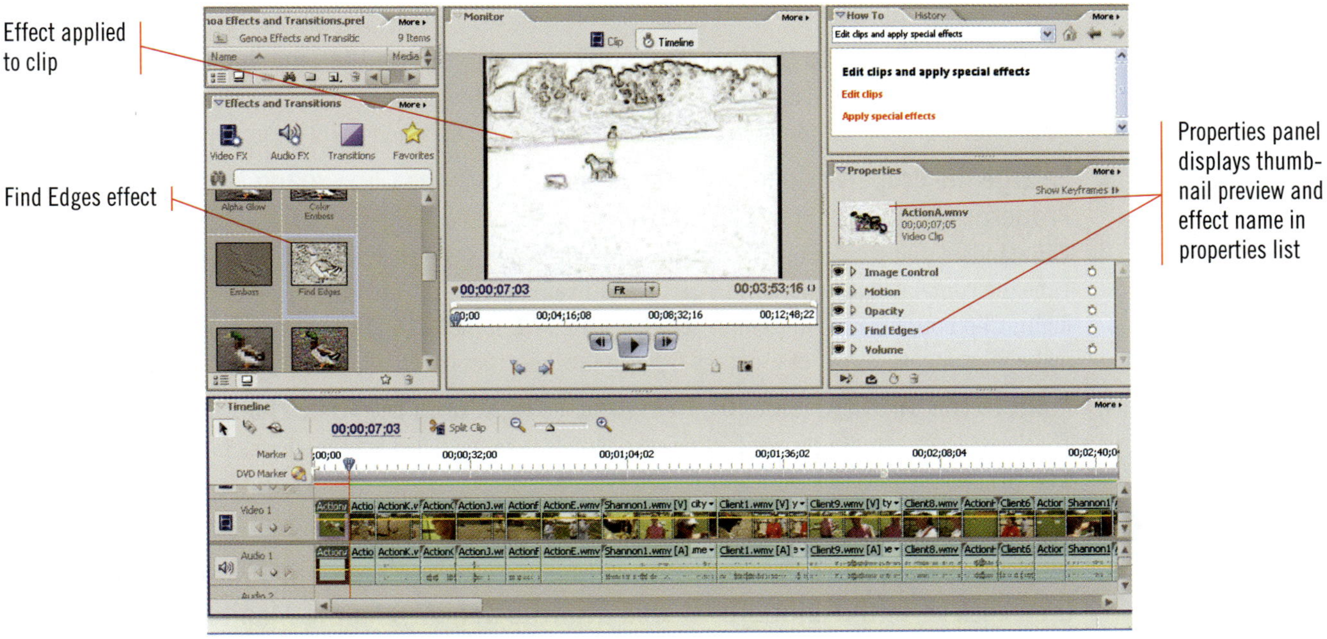


TABLE D-1: Video Effects categories

| category | use to |
|---|---|
| Adjust | Adjust aspects of color in a clip, such as brightness, contrast, hue, saturation, luminance, tonal levels, and shadows |
| Blur & Sharpen | Increase or decrease sharpness in a clip to smooth jagged edges, create a ghosted effect, or compensate for blurriness |
| Channel | Invert one or more of the color channels (such as the red, green, and blue channels in an RGB color system) in a clip |
| Distort | Distort a clip in a variety of ways to create illusions such as a mirror effect, a bend in the frame, or a rippled or twirled surface |
| Image Control | Change a clip from color to black and white, adjust specific color properties, replace one color with another, and perform manual color corrections |
| Keying | Create mattes to mask unwanted parts of the frame in a clip |
| Perspective | Add visual perspective to a clip, such as rotating it around a horizontal or vertical axis, or adding beveled edges |
| Pixelate | Create an oil-painting effect by grouping pixels of similar colors together, reducing the amount of detail in the image |
| Render | Create effects such as a lens refraction, lightning bolt, or color gradient in a clip |
| Stylize | Produce artistic effects such as a mosaic or embossed surface, a strobe light effect, or replicating tiles |
| Time | Create sequence-related effects where the moving subject in a clip appears blurred or trailed, or where the frame rate is locked to create special effects by rendering at a different frame rate |
| Transform | Manipulate a clip in a variety of ways, such as cropping part of the frame, flipping it vertically or horizontally, feathering its edges, or simulating a different camera angle |

UNIT
D
Premiere Elements 2.0

# Adjusting an Effect

You can use the Properties panel to adjust the **properties**, or attributes, of a selected effect. Not all effects have editable properties, and for some effects you must adjust the properties before you see a change in the clip. You want to add a border around a clip of Shannon, owner of Genoa Stock, to set off the clip from the other clips.

## STEPS

1. **Move to frame 00;00;59;16 on the Timeline, click the Stylize collapse icon in the Effects and Transitions panel, then expand the Transform category**
   Transform effects include simulating a different camera angle to distort the look of a clip, cropping a clip, flipping a clip, and other dramatic transformations.
2. **Drag the Clip effect to the first Shannon1 clip segment on the Timeline (00;01;04;02)**
   The effect is applied and its name appears in the Properties panel, although no change is visible in the Monitor panel or in the Properties thumbnail. Some effects are neutral until you adjust their properties.
3. **Enlarge the Properties panel, if necessary, then click the Clip expand icon in the Properties panel**
   The standard and fixed properties for the Clip effect are listed, as shown in Figure D-3. Each clip on the Timeline contains fixed effects. You can adjust five properties for the Clip effect: Clip Left, Clip Top, Clip Right, Clip Bottom, and Fill Color. The Setup icon indicates that you can open a Setup dialog box to make adjustments instead of using the fields in the Properties panel.
4. **Point to the Clip Left value (0), then drag right until the value changes to 10**
   The frame in the Monitor panel is clipped so that 10% of the left side of the frame is clipped and replaced with the background color, which by default is black.

> **QUICK TIP**
> Not every effect has properties you can adjust; if you apply an effect and it does not display an Expand icon next to it in the Properties panel, the effect cannot be adjusted.

5. **Click the remaining clip values, then change each value to 10**
6. **Click the Eyedropper Tool next to the Fill Color option in the Properties panel, then click in the light brown area near the dog's eye in the Monitor panel, as shown in Figure D-4**
   The matte changes to the color you clicked. You can use the Eyedropper Tool to **sample**, or pull a color from anywhere on the screen, or you can click the Color Picker box to open the Color Picker dialog box and choose a color from a palette.
7. **Select the clip, click Edit on the menu bar, click Copy, select the second Shannon1 clip segment (00;02;33;23), click Edit on the menu bar, then click Paste Attributes**
   The adjusted effect is copied to the second Shannon1 clip segment. Copying the attributes of a clip is a quick way to copy any effects added to the clip to another clip.
8. **Right-click the second Shannon1 clip segment, click Copy, right-click the third Shannon1 clip segment (00;03;07;04), then click Paste Attributes**
   All the attributes of the second Shannon1 clip are applied to the third Shannon1 clip.
9. **Save your changes to the project**
   The effect is applied to and adjusted in all three clip segments, as shown in Figure D-5. The light-colored line beneath the clip name indicates that an effect has been applied.

FIGURE D-3: Properties for Clip effect

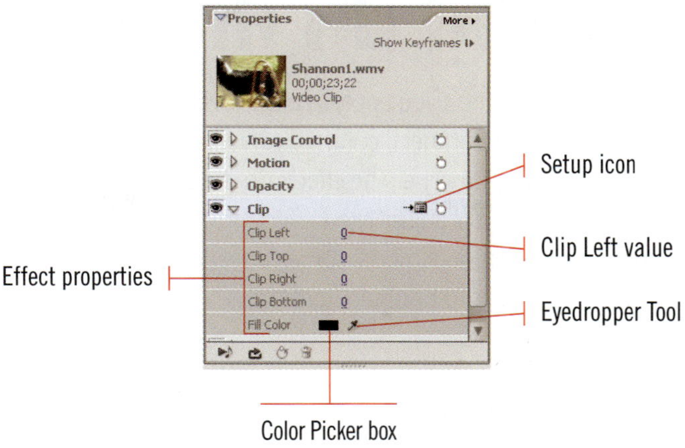


FIGURE D-4: Sampling a color

FIGURE D-5: Adjusted effect applied to three clips

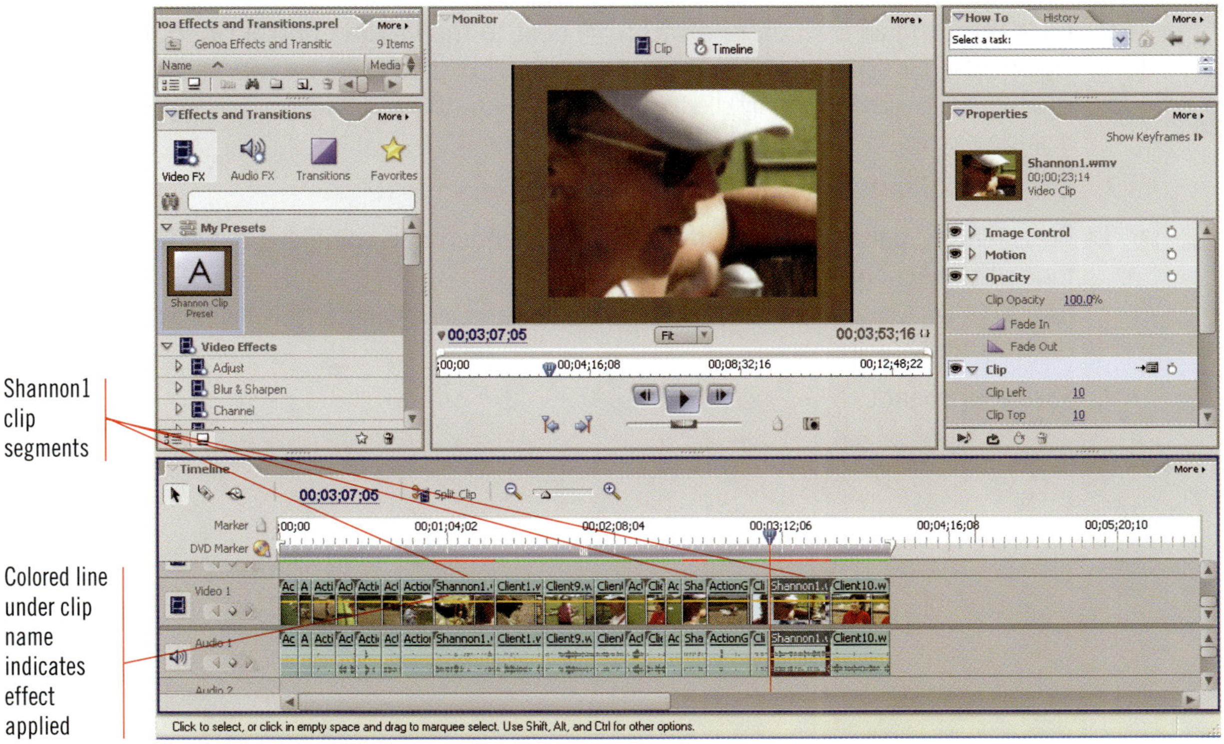


Premiere Elements 2.0

UNIT D

Premiere Elements 2.0

# Adjusting a Fixed Effect

In addition to any standard effects you apply to a clip, every clip in the Timeline has fixed effects. **Fixed effects** are basic properties, such as brightness, contrast, rotation, and audio volume, that Premiere Elements applies to a clip when you add it to the Timeline. The effects do not change the look or sound of the clip unless you adjust them. Like standard effects, you adjust fixed effects in the Properties panel. The ActionE clip, which shows Shannon talking to a student, needs some correction. The video was recorded on a cloudy day, and both faces are hard to see. You want to brighten up the clip.

## STEPS

**QUICK TIP**

You cannot change the order of fixed effects or remove a fixed effect in the Properties panel.

**QUICK TIP**

You can also adjust fixed effects by clicking the list arrow on a clip on the Timeline and then clicking the Fixed Effect category you want to change; by default, the Clip Opacity effect is displayed.

**QUICK TIP**

If the work area is already rendered when you press [Enter], the movie plays from the beginning.

1. **Select the ActionE clip on the Timeline, then drag the current-time indicator to the beginning of the clip**

   The Properties panel lists four fixed effect categories for the ActionE clip: Image Control, Motion, Opacity, and Volume. See Table D-2 for a description of each category.

2. **Click the Image Control expand icon in the Properties panel**

   The Image Control category contains four settings: Brightness, Contrast, Hue, and Saturation. The default Brightness and Hue settings are currently 0.0, and the Contrast and Saturation settings are 100. The **Brightness** setting changes the relative exposure in a clip, **Contrast** affects the distinctions between light and dark colors, **Hue** affects the relative color of pixels, and **Saturation** increases or decreases the strength of the colors.

3. **Point to the Brightness setting, then drag the scrub pointer to 18, as shown in Figure D-6**

   The clip lightens, and the faces of the subjects become more visible.

4. **Click the Contrast setting, type 110, then press [Enter]**

   The distinctions between highlights, shadows, and midtones become more pronounced, helping to make the image look sharper. You can change a value by dragging or typing a value. Dragging allows you to watch the results in the Monitor panel, while typing is faster when you know how much you want to change.

5. **Change the Saturation value to 140**

   Increasing the saturation gives the colors a more vivid appearance.

6. **Click the Toggle effect on or off icon next to the Image Control category**

   The results of the new settings are hidden, and the icon changes to a gray rectangle. You can hide or show effects in the Properties panel by clicking , which is especially useful when you're experimenting with multiple effects.

7. **Click to display the Image Control effects**

8. **Press [Enter], pause the movie if it plays after rendering is complete, move to the beginning of the ActionE clip, then play the clip**

   Pressing [Enter] when the Timeline is active renders the work area. Compare your results to Figure D-7. The clip looks brighter and more vivid.

9. **Save your changes**

FIGURE D-6: Adjusting a fixed effect

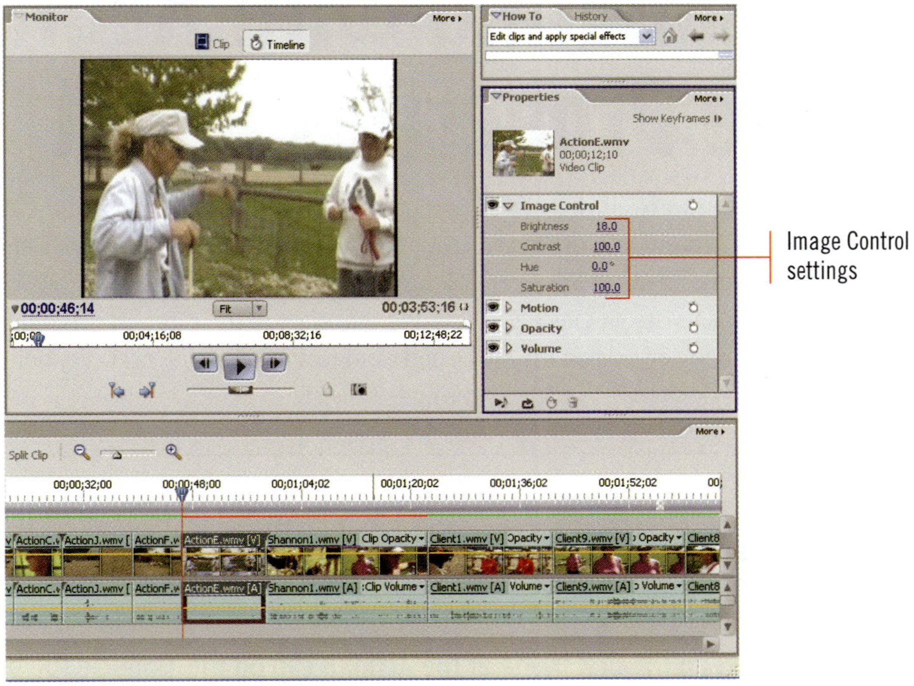


FIGURE D-7: Adjusted and rendered clip

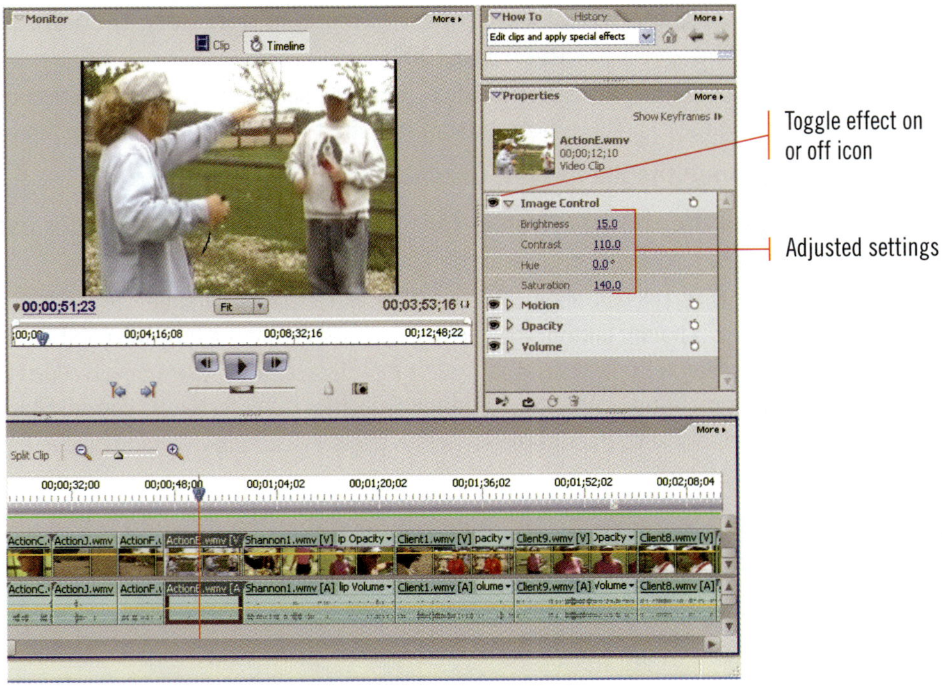


TABLE D-2: Fixed Effects categories

| category | description |
|---|---|
| Image Control | Increases or decreases a clip's brightness, contrast, hue (pixel colors), and saturation (purity of color) |
| Motion | Changes the rotation, position, or scale of a clip, all relative to its anchor point, which can also be adjusted |
| Opacity | Makes a clip appear more transparent in order to fade it or superimpose it with other clips |
| Volume | Increases or decreases the volume of an audio clip or of a video clip's audio track |

UNIT
D
Premiere Elements 2.0

# Animating with Keyframes in the Properties Panel

You can **animate** an effect by adjusting where it starts and stops so that the effect is applied to only part of the clip. To do so, you use **keyframes**, frames within a clip that Premiere Elements uses to control the path of an animation at the time you select. You can work with keyframes in the Timeline panel or the Properties panel. To animate an effect, you first add the effect to the clip. You like the Find Edges effect you applied to the first clip in the movie and want to apply it to the next clip, but you want the effect to diminish gradually so that it's gone by the end of the clip.

## STEPS

**QUICK TIP**

The Favorites category on the Effects and Transitions panel lists your favorite effects and transitions so you don't have to drill through several categories to find them; to add one, select it and then click the Add to Favorites button.

1. **Type find in the Search text box in the Effects and Transitions panel, then when the Find Edges effect appears in the list, drag it to the ActionB clip**

   If you know the name of the effect you want to apply, you can begin typing it in the Find text box; all effects that contain the text you type appear in the list.

2. **Move to the first frame of the ActionB clip on the Timeline (00;00;07;05), then click the Find Edges Expand icon in the Properties panel**

   The settings for this effect are Invert and Blend With Original. The Invert check box reverses the light and dark colors in the image. The Blend With Original setting increases or decreases the intensity of the effect.

3. **Increase the size of the Properties panel, if necessary, then drag the Blend With Original setting scrub pointer to 100%**

   A 100% setting increasingly blends in the original clip pixels with the effect until the effect is no longer visible in the clip. This is how you want the effect to look at the end of the clip.

4. **Change the Blend With Original setting to 0**

5. **Click the Show Keyframes button at the top of the Properties panel, then click the Toggle animation button for the Find Edges effect**

   See Figure D-8. The Show Keyframes button opens the Keyframes area of the Properties panel; it toggles to the Hide Keyframes button when active. This area contains a time ruler and zoom controls so that you move to different points in the clip and adjust the effect settings. A keyframe is added automatically at the location of the current-time indicator in the Properties panel each time you adjust an effect. You can manually add or remove keyframes in the Properties panel by clicking the Add/Remove Keyframe button next to the effect setting.

6. **Zoom in the Properties panel as needed, then move to frame 00;00;11;00**

   You can drag on the Timeline or in the Properties panel.

**QUICK TIP**

To animate an effect, you must use a clip that contains at least two keyframes: one for the beginning and another for the end of the animation.

7. **Change the Blend With Original setting to 100%**

   The setting changes to 100%, and the effect is no longer visible. Because you changed an effect setting, Premiere Elements adds a keyframe at this location, as shown in Figure D-9.

8. **Render the work area, save your changes, then play the ActionB clip**

   The Find Edges effect starts at full intensity at the beginning of the clip, then diminishes completely by frame 00;00;11;00. Premiere Elements creates the animation effect by **interpolating** the values between two keyframes. It calculates the difference between a 0% Blend With Original setting at 00;00;07;05 and a 100% setting at 00;00;11;00, and adjusts the setting to the frames between the keyframes to create a smooth transition.

9. **Move to frame 00;00;09;00 on the Timeline**

   This frame is halfway between the two keyframes you set, so the Properties panel displays a Blend Edges setting of approximately 50% and the effect is partially visible, as shown in Figure D-10.

**FIGURE D-8: Keyframe area of Properties panel**

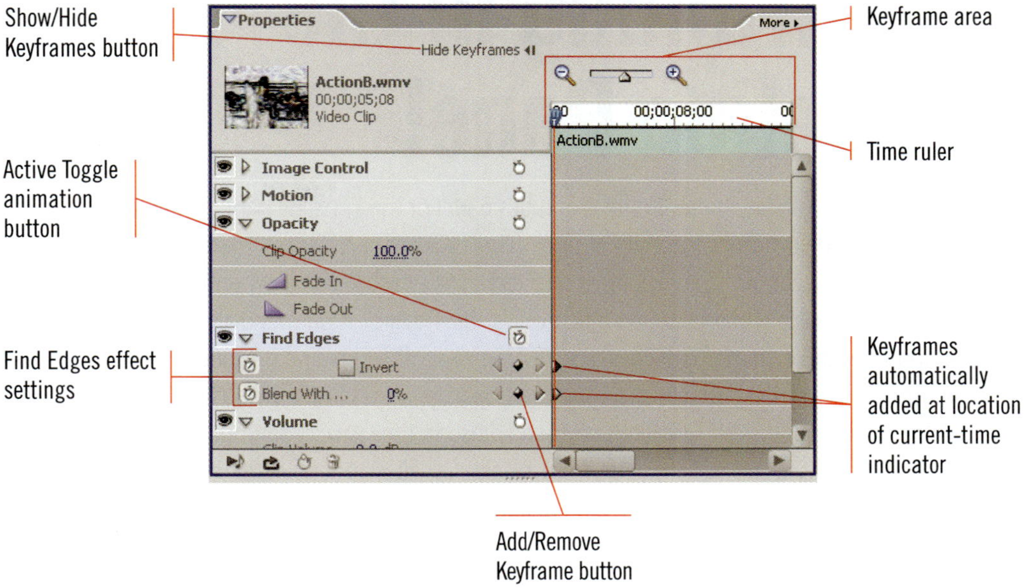


**FIGURE D-9: Adding a keyframe for the adjusted effect setting**

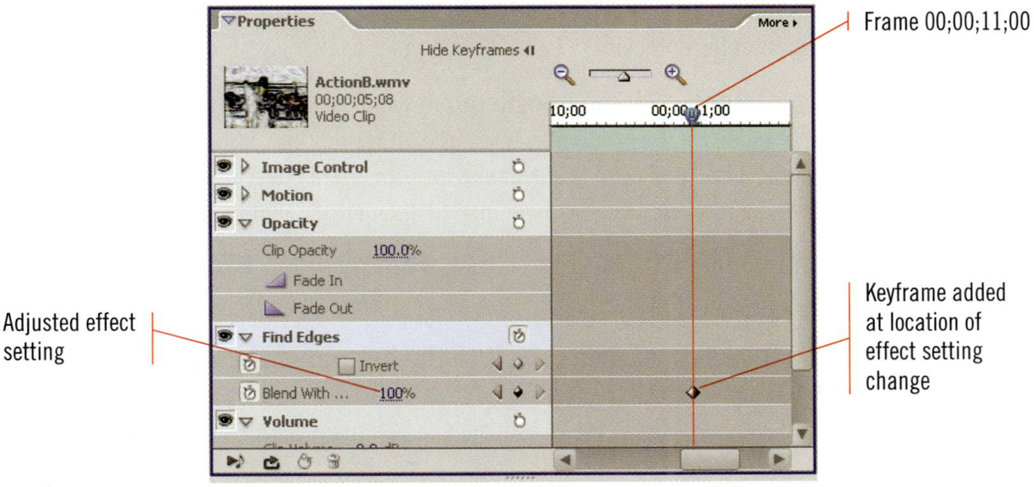


**FIGURE D-10: Viewing an animated effect in the Properties panel**

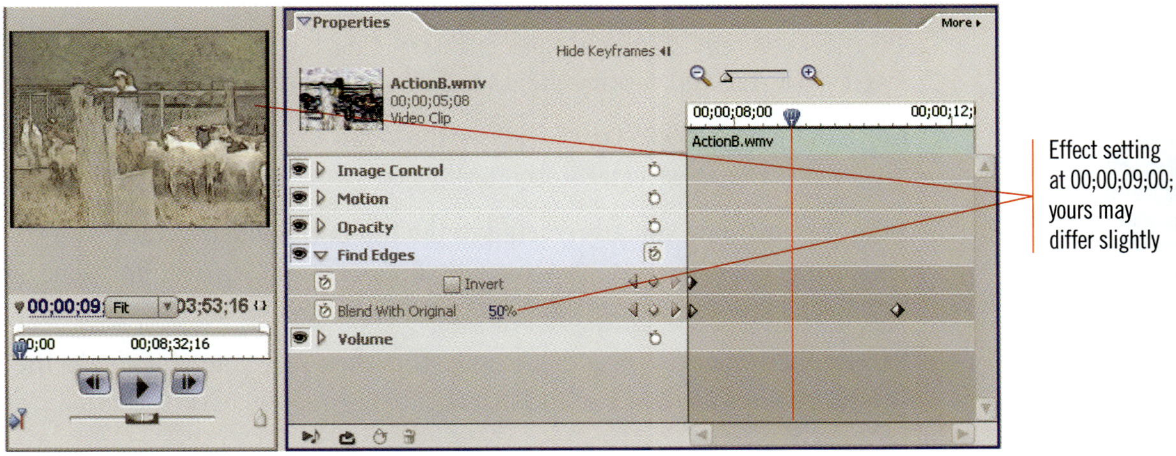

UNIT
D
Premiere Elements 2.0

# Keyframing in the Timeline Panel

You can work with keyframes in the Properties panel or the Timeline panel. The Properties panel displays all the properties and keyframes for a clip at once. The Timeline can display keyframes for only one effect or property at a time, but it can do so for multiple selected clips, which is useful when you're working with the same effect across several clips. To animate an effect using the Timeline, you manually add keyframes and then adjust the setting at each keyframe. Working with keyframes on the Timeline is especially convenient when you want to adjust a simple setting such as clip volume or opacity. For example, you can quickly fade a clip up or down by adding keyframes on the Timeline and then adjusting the Opacity setting at each keyframe. You want the first clip of the movie to fade in from black. You also want to scale the clip so the subject appears to get closer at the end of the clip. You decide to add keyframes on the Timeline to achieve these results.

## STEPS

**QUICK TIP**
You can also fade in or out of a clip by adjusting the Clip Opacity property in the Opacity fixed effect category in the Properties panel.

1. **Zoom in closely on the beginning of the Timeline, then select the ActionA clip**
   Familiarize yourself with the elements shown in Figure D-11. The **effect properties menu icon** is located next to the clip name, and it displays the current property, Clip: Clip Opacity. You can click the menu icon to change the current property. Each track on the Timeline has an Add/Remove Keyframe button, along with buttons for moving to the previous and next keyframe. When you add keyframes on the Timeline, they affect the current effect property only, so it's important to change this setting before adding any keyframes.

2. **Press [Home], then click the Add/Remove Keyframe button on the Video 1 track**
   A keyframe is added on the property graph at the location of the current-time indicator. The **property graph** is a yellow line that displays keyframes for the current effect and that allows you to manipulate properties by dragging plot points up or down instead of entering values in the Properties panel.

3. **Move to frame 00;00;02;00, then click on the Video 1 track**
   A keyframe is added to this frame.

**QUICK TIP**
To adjust the path of an animated effect, you can drag a keyframe earlier or later on the Timeline or higher or lower on the property graph.

4. **Click the first keyframe, then drag it to the bottom of the Video 1 track, as shown in Figure D-12**
   The path of the property graph rises gradually between the first and second keyframes, and the Monitor displays the altered frame.

5. **Drag between the two keyframes to preview the effect**
   The clip fades in from black over a period of two seconds.

6. **Click the Effect properties menu icon on the ActionA clip, point to Motion, then click Scale**
   The current property changes to Motion: Scale, and the keyframes for the Clip Opacity property are no longer visible. The effect properties menu lists all effects for the current clip.

**TROUBLE**
If you add a keyframe at the wrong location, click it and then click the Add/Remove Keyframe button; this button functions as a toggle, so clicking it when a keyframe is selected removes the keyframe.

7. **Move to frame 00;00;05;00, click on the Video 1 track, move to 00;00;07;00, then click**
   Two keyframes are added for the Motion: Scale property.

8. **Drag the keyframe you just created to the top of the Video 1 track**
   The property graph rises gradually between the first and second keyframe, illustrating the path of the animated effect, as shown in Figure D-13.

9. **Render the work area, play the ActionA clip, then save your changes to the project**
   The clip fades in slowly from black, and the outlined sheep appear to get closer to the camera.

**FIGURE D-11: Keyframe controls on the Timeline**

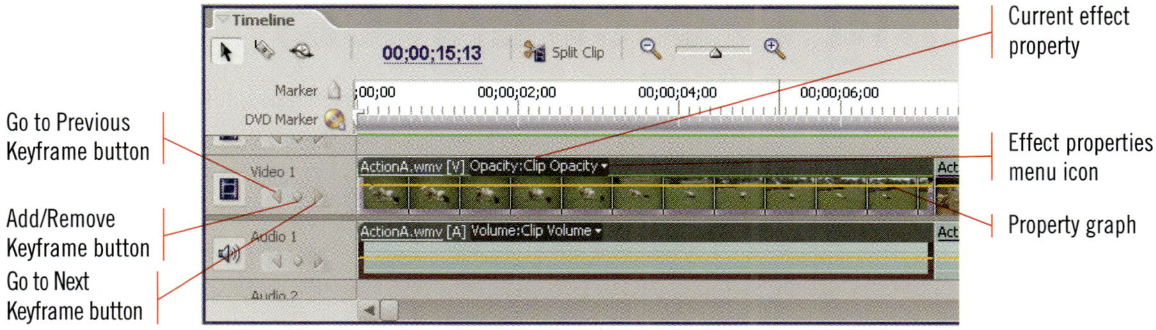


**FIGURE D-12: Adjusting keyframes for Opacity: Clip Opacity effect**

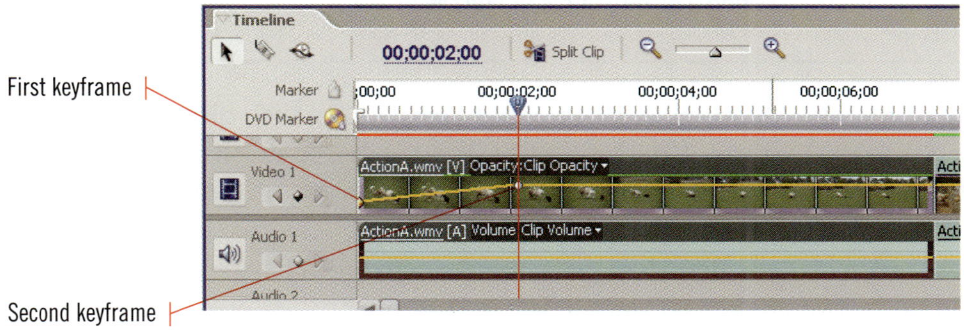


**FIGURE D-13: Adjusted keyframes for Motion: Scale effect**

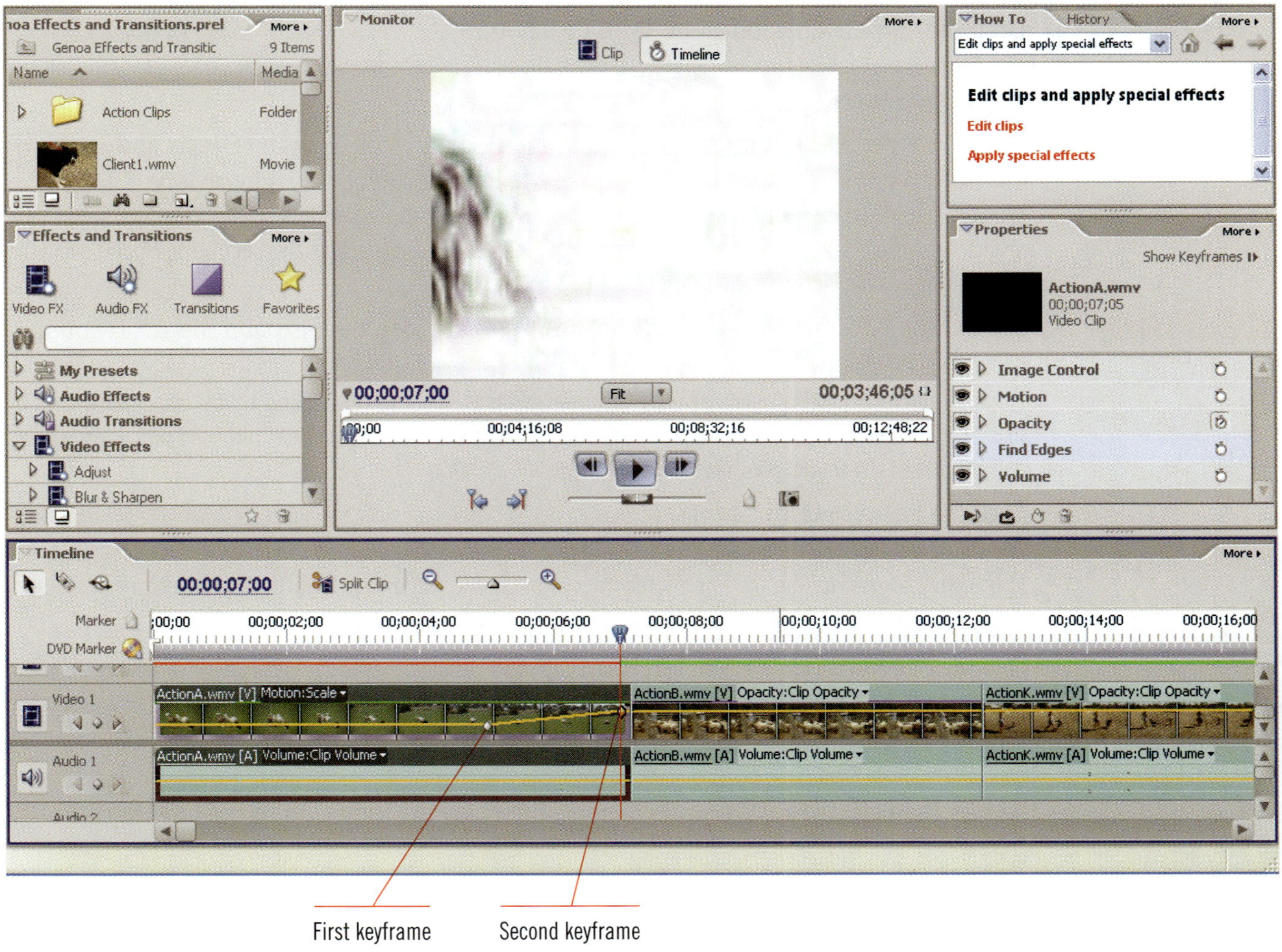

UNIT
D
Premiere Elements 2.0

# Using Preset Effects

**Preset effects** are preconfigured effects you can apply to clips to create sophisticated results quickly. Some presets are static, like those found in the Standard Video Effect categories, with settings customized for popular uses. For example, you can use the Hyper Tint Red preset to colorize a clip in red, a result you could also achieve by applying the Tint standard effect and changing the settings. Many presets are animated, allowing you to create sophisticated effects that automatically add keyframes to a clip—all you have to do is drag the effect to the clip. For example, **picture-in-picture** presets superimpose one clip playing in a frame on top of another, and many are animated to move within the frame. Like standard effects, you can usually adjust a preset (and any resulting keyframes) once you've applied it to a clip, and you can use the adjusted effect to create a new preset in the My Presets category. You want to superimpose the ActionH clip on top of the Client8 clip using a picture-in-picture preset.

## STEPS

**QUICK TIP**
You can expand the height of the Timeline as needed; you can also change the track size by clicking the More button More ▸ on the Timeline, pointing to Track Size, and then clicking a different size.

1. **Right-click the ActionH clip (which starts at 00;02;12;21), then click Delete Audio**
   The audio track of the ActionH clip is deleted. You want to superimpose only the video portion of the clip; you don't need the audio. The clips to the right do not shift to close the gap because you did not delete the entire clip.
2. **Press and hold [Ctrl], then drag the ActionH clip to the Video 2 track and align it with the start of the Client8 clip, as shown in Figure D-14**
   The ActionH clip is positioned at the same location on the Timeline as the Client8 clip, but on the Video2 track, and the clips shift to remove the gap left by the ActionH clip. You use additional tracks when you want to create layered effects, such as superimposing one clip over another.
3. **Drag the current-time indicator to 00;02;00;14**
   The ActionH clip appears in the monitor. Clips on the uppermost video track appear on top of, or in front of, clips on lower tracks.
4. **Click the Video FX button, click the Presets Expand icon in the Effects and Transitions panel, then scroll down to see the Presets categories, if necessary**
   Presets are organized into 12 categories, such as Drop Shadows, Blurs, and PiPs. **Drop Shadow** presets add a static or animated drop shadow to the frame of a clip, **Blur** presets blur the beginning or end of a clip, and **PiP** stands for Picture in Picture.

**QUICK TIP**
To expand a category, you can double-click a category name instead of clicking the Expand icon.

5. **Expand the PiPs category, expand the 40% PiPs category, then expand the 40% Motion category**
   Picture-in-picture presets are organized by position (such as LL for lower left and UR for upper right) and by size. The 25% presets create a small picture that is 25% of the size of the frame, while 40% presets are almost half the size of the frame. Four presets exist for the 40% Motion category.
6. **Click the PiP 40% LL to LR preset**
   The thumbnail previews the size, position, and motion path of the selected preset, as shown in Figure D-15. This picture moves in from the lower-left corner of the frame and moves to the lower-right corner.

**QUICK TIP**
A Summary Keyframe icon appears in the Properties panel to indicate that one or more keyframes exist in a collapsed category.

7. **Click the PiP 40% LR to LL preset, then drag it to the ActionH clip**
   Compare your workspace to Figure D-16. The Properties panel shows the preset added to the selected clip, and the Monitor shows the effect for both clips at the current frame location. The Keyframe area on the Properties panel displays a Keyframe Summary icon in the Motion category because the PiP effect affects this fixed effect category.
8. **Render the work area, save your changes, then play the movie up to the Client6 clip**

FIGURE D-14: Video clip on Video 2 track

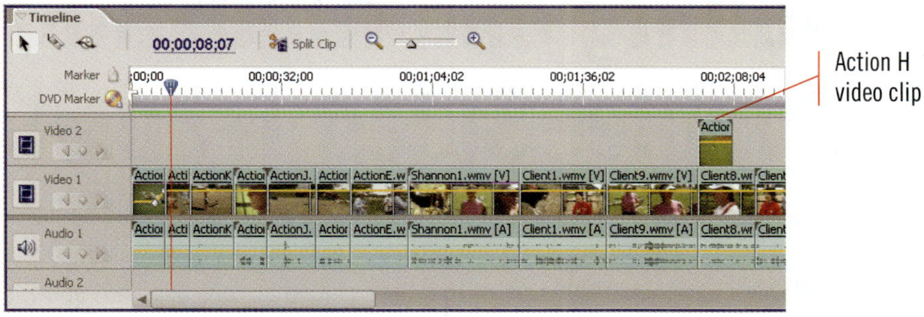


FIGURE D-15: 40% Motion category of PiPs category

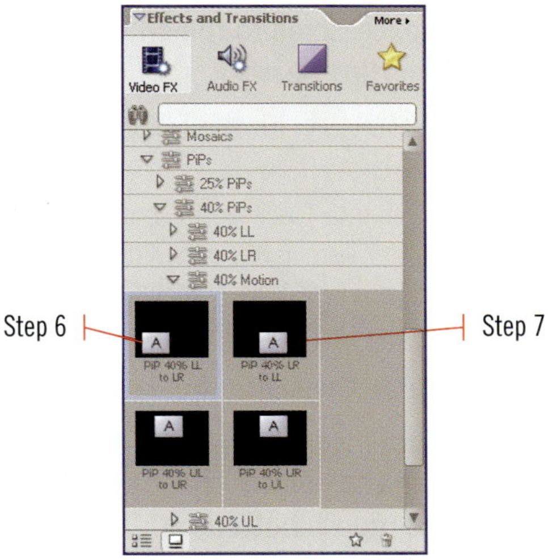


FIGURE D-16: Preset added to clip

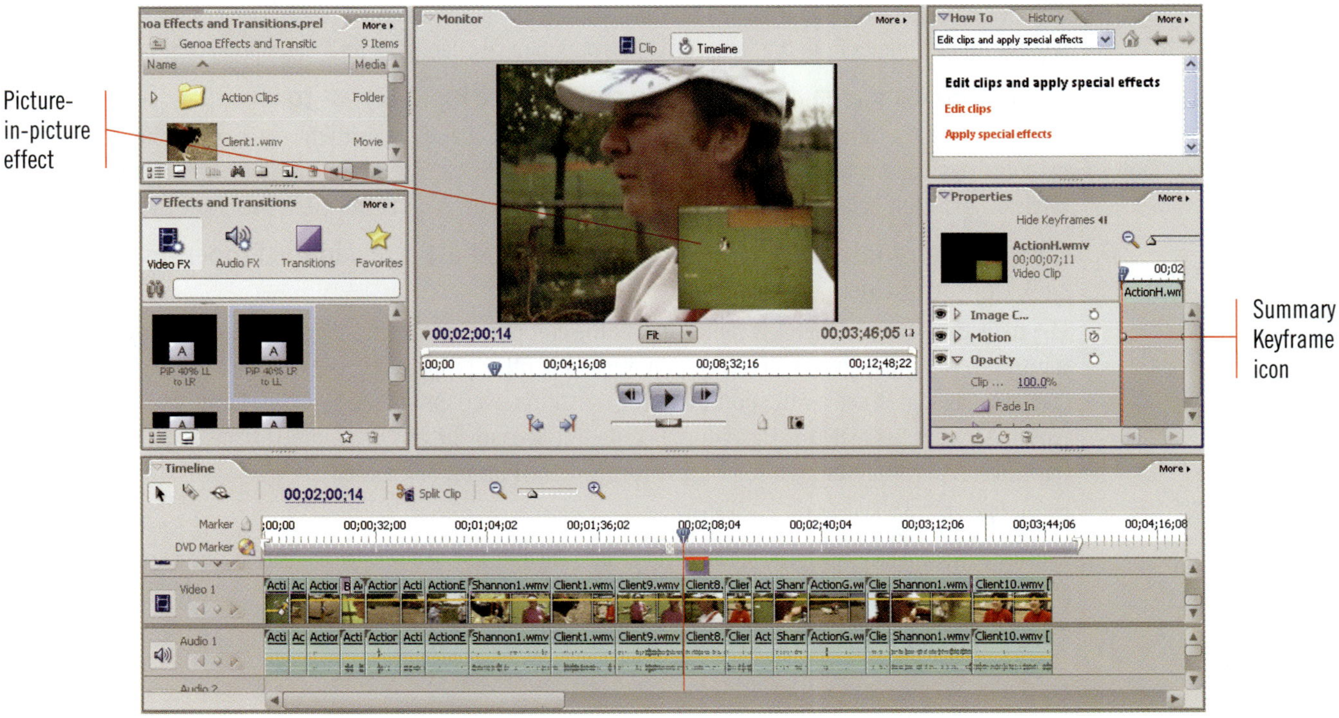

# Adding and Adjusting a Double-Sided Transition

Premiere Elements includes dozens of transitions you can apply to the beginning and end of clips to control how scenes change from one to the next. A **double-sided transition** overlaps frames from two clips to blend them together at the **edit point**, the point where one clip ends and the next starts. It can be as subtle as one clip dissolving into the next, or more dramatic, such as a paint-like splash of the new clip splattering over the old clip. You add a transition by dragging it between two clips on the Timeline. You want to add a transition between the second-to-last clip in the movie and the last clip.

## STEPS

**QUICK TIP**

When previewing a transition thumbnail, the letter A represents the first clip in the transition, and the letter B represents the second clip.

**QUICK TIP**

A small gray triangle appears at the edge of a clip if the edge has *not* been trimmed; if the edge has been trimmed, the edge is empty.

1. **Restore the Edit workspace, scroll to the end of the movie if necessary, then zoom in so you can see the last two clips clearly**
2. **Click the Transitions button on the Effects and Transitions panel, then expand the Video Transitions category**

   Video transitions are organized into 10 categories, including 3D Motion and Dissolve. 3D Motion transitions create three-dimensional effects, such as one clip folding up and disappearing as the new clip fills the screen, or one clip flipping on its side to reveal the other clip on the other side. Dissolve transitions create illusions where pixels from one clip seem to dissolve into pixels from the next.
3. **Expand the Slide category, then click the Band Slide transition**
4. **Preview the Center Merge transition, drag it to the beginning of the Client10 clip on the Timeline, then when the pointer changes to the Start at Cut icon as shown in Figure D-17, release the mouse button**

   The transition aligns at the start of the last clip, and the Properties panel displays the settings for the selected transition. When you drag a transition to the Timeline, the pointer displays an icon to show how the transition will be aligned. The presence or absence of trimmed frames at the edit point affects alignment. Transitions use trimmed frames, if they exist, or repeat frames if necessary, that blend together to create the transition. In this case, the Shannon1 clip contains trimmed frames at its out point, while the Client10 clip does not contain trimmed frames at its in point. Therefore, you can align the transition only at the in point of the second clip, and it uses trimmed frames from the Shannon1 clip's out point. See Table D-3 for a description of alignment options.
5. **Render the work area, then drag the current-time indicator to 00;03;23;13**

   See Figure D-18. Transitions are displayed on the Timeline in a colored bar with the name of the transition and one or more diagonal lines to indicate the frames used in the transition. The default transition time is one second. The single diagonal line across the transition indicates that no frames have been repeated to create the transition.
6. **Click the transition to select it, click the Alignment list arrow in the Properties panel, then click Center at Cut**

   The transition shifts so that it is centered over the edit point, as shown in Figure D-19. Once you've added a transition, you can adjust its alignment, duration, and other properties in the Properties panel. The transition displays diagonal bars over the portion of the transition overlapping the first clip, indicating that it is using repeated frames to create the transition. Because the second clip has no trimmed frames at the in point, the transition repeats frames from second clip to create the illusion of the merge.
7. **Drag slowly over the transition**

   Repeating the first frame of the second clip creates the illusion of a merge, but the second clip does not actually begin to move until the edit point.
8. **Save your changes to the project**

**FIGURE D-17: Adding a transition**

**FIGURE D-18: Transition left-aligned at beginning of second clip**

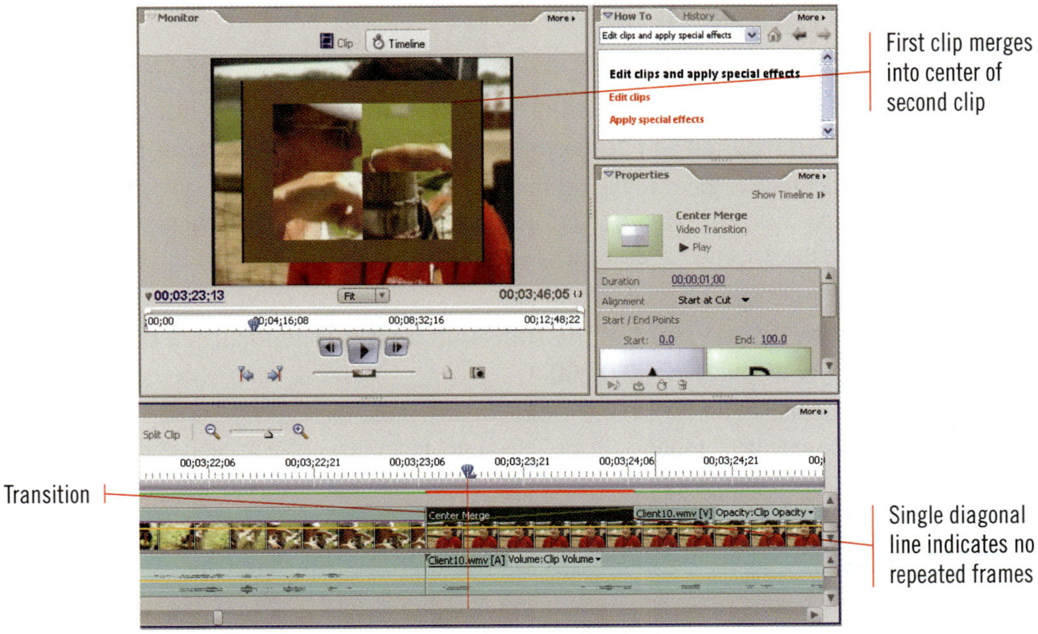


**FIGURE D-19: Adjusted transition**

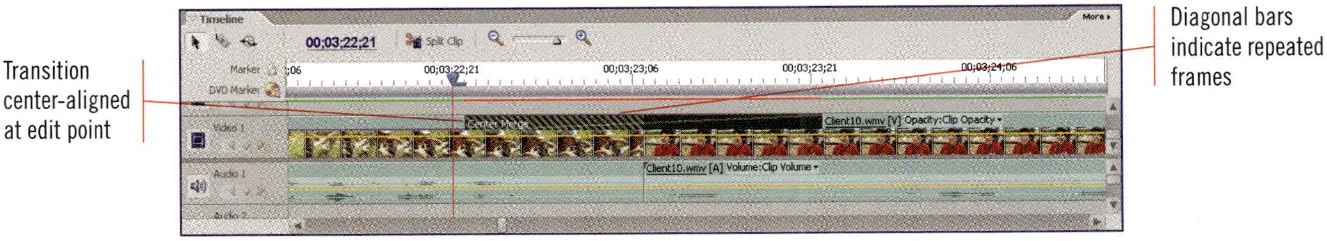


**TABLE D-3: Transition alignment options**

| icon | indicates... | available when |
|---|---|---|
| | Transition will left-align at in point of second clip | Both clips or neither clip contains trimmed frames; first clip contains trimmed frames and second clip does not |
| | Transition will center-align at edit point between clips | Both clips or neither clip contain trimmed frames |
| | Transition will right-align at out point of first clip | Both clips or neither clip contain trimmed frames; second clip contains trimmed frames and first clip does not |

UNIT D
Premiere Elements 2.0

# Adding and Adjusting a Single-Sided Transition

By default, transitions in Premiere Elements are double-sided, meaning they use frames from two clips to create the illusion of one clip blending into the next. However, you can also apply a transition to a single clip. The transition uses transparent frames instead of frames from the previous or next clip to create the effect. You want to add a transition to the ActionC clip, which is the first time Shannon is shown coaching a client. You don't want the transition to overlap with the previous clip, so you create a single-sided transition.

## STEPS

1. **Drag the current-time indicator to 00;00;22;24**
   A frame near the beginning of the ActionC clip appears in the Monitor.
2. **In the Effects and Transitions panel, collapse the Slide category, then expand the Wipe category**
   Transitions in this category include a variety of designs that wipe across the screen to reveal the next clip.
3. **Drag the Barn Doors transition to the beginning of the ActionC clip, press and hold [Ctrl], then when the pointer changes to , release the mouse button**
   The transition is added to the beginning of the ActionC clip, and the properties for this transition appear in the Properties panel. Pressing [Ctrl] after you position the transition but before you release the mouse button applies the transition to the current clip only. If you had not pressed [Ctrl], the transparent area of the screen would display the previous clip.
4. **Point to the out point of the transition on the Timeline, then drag until the pop-up window displays 00;00;02;00**
   The duration of the transition increases by 30 frames. You can drag the in point or out point of many transitions to lengthen or shorten them. You cannot reposition the in or out point of every transition, however. For example, because you added a single-sided transition to this clip, its in point cannot be extended before the clip's in point.
5. **Click the North to South icon in the Properties panel, as shown in Figure D-20**
   The orientation of the Barn Door transition changes from horizontal to vertical.
6. **Point to the right edge of the transition on the Properties panel timeline, then drag until the time display on the Monitor panel displays 00;00;03;00**
   The duration of the transition is extended by an additional second, as shown in Figure D-21. Sometimes it's easier to work in the Properties panel than on the Timeline panel when you need to adjust a transition. Adjusting a transition on the Timeline panel often requires you to zoom in extensively, whereas you can zoom in on the timeline in the Properties panel and leave the Timeline panel zoom level at a more comfortable level for other tasks.
7. **Restore the Edit workspace, render the work area, click the Timeline just before the ActionC clip, then play the Action C clip**
   If you don't want to watch the entire movie once you're rendered the work area, you can click anywhere on the Timeline to move the current-time indicator to that location and pause the playback. The ActionC clip fills the screen slowly from blackness, revealing the subject.
8. **Save your changes to the project**

**QUICK TIP**
If you apply a one-sided transition to a part of the Timeline that contains a clip on two or more video tracks, the clip on the lower track appears in the transparent area.

**QUICK TIP**
You can also change the duration of a transition in the Properties panel by entering a new Duration setting.

FIGURE D-20: Adding a single-sided transition

FIGURE D-21: Adjusted transition

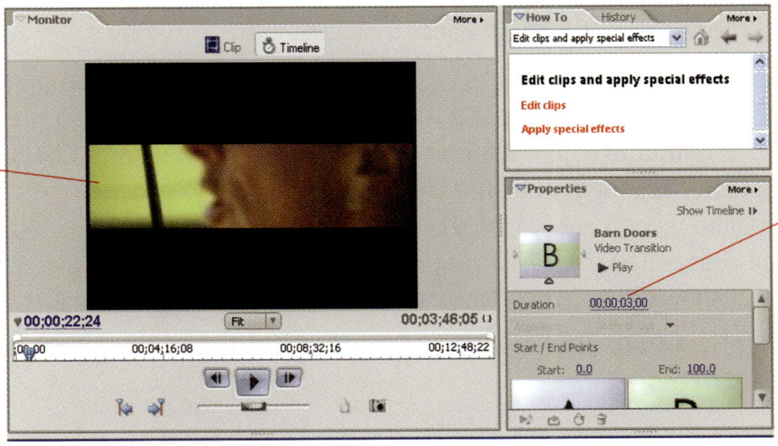


## Clues to Use

### Creating an image mask transition

The more you experiment with the Effects and Transitions panel, the more creative possibilities you'll discover. For example, you can create an image mask transition and customize it with an image of your choice. A **mask** or **matte** is an image with a distinct shape you can use to create overlapping effects. You use the shape to cover, or mask, part of a clip with color or another clip. An **image mask transition** uses an image to define two areas on a clip—the shape of the image and its background—and then fills the shape with one clip and the background with the other. The result is an interesting overlap of two clips, customized by the image you chose. To create an image mask transition, expand the Special Effects category in the Effects and Transitions panel, then drag the Image Mask transition to the edit point between two clips. The Image Mask Settings dialog box opens. Click Select Image, navigate to an image file on your computer to use as the mask, click Open, then click OK. Premiere Elements fills the black pixels in the image with the first clip and the white pixels in the image with the second clip. If you have Adobe Photoshop Elements installed on your computer, you can use the Cookie Cutter tool to create a simple graphic to use as a mask. You can use any image for an image mask, but it's best to use a black and white image with a clearly defined outline. Premiere Elements converts grayscale or color images to black and white if necessary, but these complex pictures can be hard to recognize as masks. Of course, this might be just the effect you're looking for, so experiment to find the results you want.

UNIT
D
Premiere Elements 2.0

# Removing an Effect or Transition

You can easily remove an effect or transition you've added to a clip by deleting it in the Properties panel. You can also delete a transition by selecting it on the Timeline or by replacing it with another transition. When you're experimenting with adding and removing several effects and transitions, you can use the Undo commands and the History panel to undo or redo your changes. You want to experiment with a few more effects and transitions in the movie. You also want to try a different transition between the Shannon1 and Client10 clips as an alternative to the Center Merge transition.

## STEPS

**QUICK TIP**

You cannot keyframe the Facet effect; this effect can only be applied evenly to an entire clip.

**QUICK TIP**

You cannot delete a fixed effect.

1. **Scroll if necessary until you see the ActionG clip, expand the Video Effects category on the Effects and Transitions panel, expand the Pixelate category, then drag the Facet effect to the ActionG clip**
2. **Play the clip to see the effect**

   The clip takes on the look of an oil painting, with color values simplified so there are fewer gradations in color.
3. **Click Facet in the Properties panel, as shown in Figure D-22, then press Delete**

   The effect is removed from the clip. Because you haven't made any other edits, you could also have deleted this effect by pressing [Ctrl][Z] to undo the action.
4. **Click the Transitions button on the Effects and Properties panel, expand the Video Transitions category, expand the Dissolve category, then drag the Dither Dissolve on top of the Center Merge transition between the Shannon1 and Client10 clips on the Timeline, as shown in Figure D-23**

   The Dither Dissolve transition replaces the Center Merge transition. When you replace a transition, it takes on the same alignment and duration as the transition it replaces. Therefore, even though the second clip does not contain trimmed frames, the new transition is centered over the edit point instead of left-aligning at the edit point.
5. **Drag the Dip to Black transition from the Effects and Transitions panel to the end of the Client10 clip**
6. **Render the work area, then play the last two clips**

   The Dither Dissolve transition creates a pixilated effect, where pixel colors alternate with adjacent pixels and then blend into the new clip. The Dip to Black transition fades out more quickly than the fade from black effect you keyframed at the beginning of the movie.
7. **Select the Dip to Black transition on the Client10 clip, then press [Delete]**
8. **Press [Ctrl][Z], then change the Dip to Black Duration value on the Properties panel to 00;00;02;00, as shown in Figure D-24**
9. **Render the work area, play the adjusted transition, save your changes, then exit Premiere Elements**

FIGURE D-22: Deleting an effect

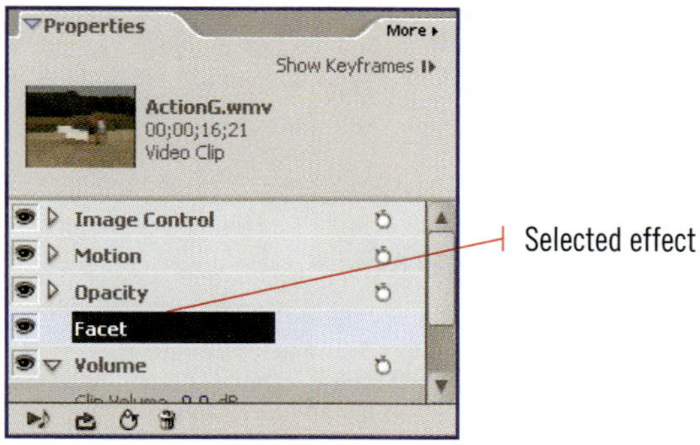


FIGURE D-23: Replacing a transition

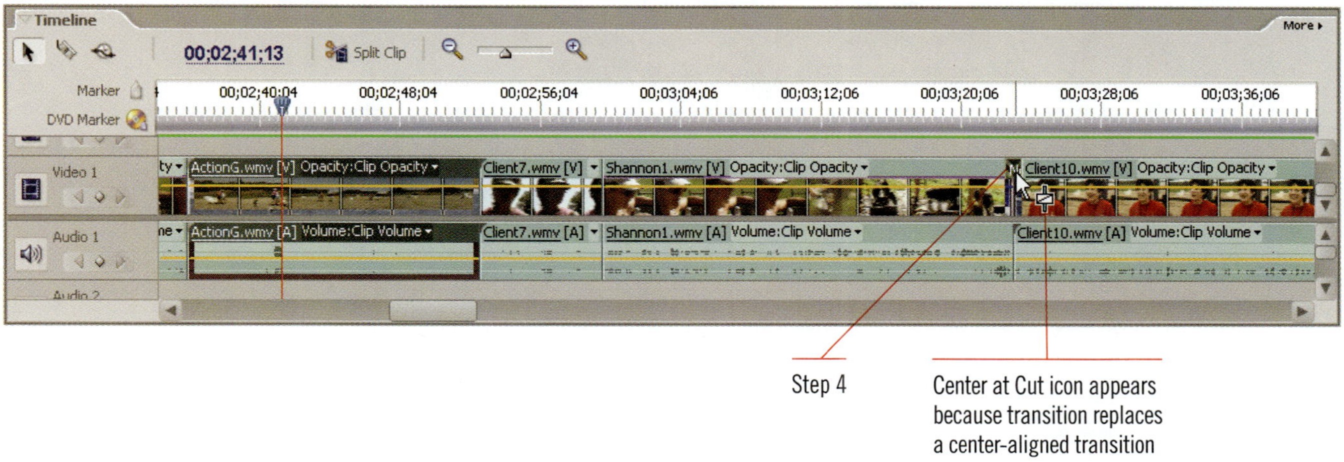


FIGURE D-24: Adjusted transition duration

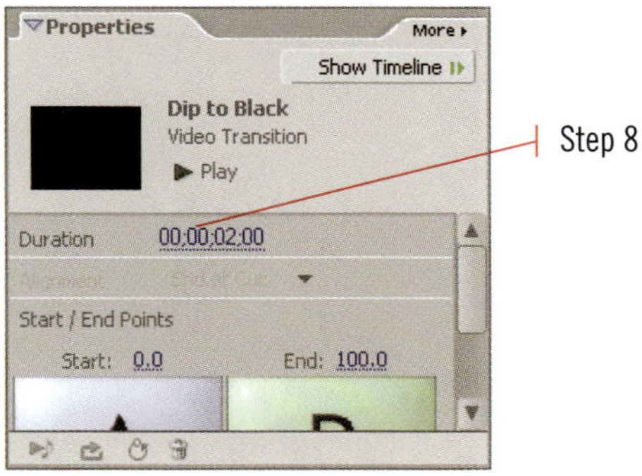


## Clues to Use

### Using the History panel

When you want to undo or restore more than the last edit—for example, you want to restore a clip you deleted a few minutes ago—you can use the History panel. This panel lists most edits you've made to a project, from the time you open it until the time you close it, so you can step back through a project to find the edit you want to reverse. To open the History panel, click Window on the menu bar, then click History, or click the History tab in the How To window. You can delete any step to restore the project to the state it was in before the step. Reversing an edit reverses any edits made after that point, so you can think of it as restoring your project to a certain point in history rather than selectively reversing old edits. The History panel lists the following types of edits: adding, moving, cutting or deleting a clip; adding or deleting a transition or effect (called a filter on the History panel); and trimming a clip, stretching a clip, or adding a marker. It does not list program-wide changes, such as changing the default transition, nor does it list some detailed settings, such as filter names or changing a transition duration in the Properties panel. When you close a project, the History panel is cleared automatically; to clear it without closing a project, click the More button on the History panel, then click Clear History.

# Practice

## ▼ CONCEPTS REVIEW

**Label the elements of the Premiere Elements program window shown in Figure D-26.**

FIGURE D-25

**Match each term with the statement that best describes it.**

| | |
|---|---|
| **7. Effects and Transitions panel** | **a.** Preconfigured effect you can apply to a clip to achieve complex results quickly |
| **8. Transition** | **b.** Panel that can display keyframes for multiple clips at once, but only one effect |
| **9. Properties panel** | **c.** Alteration you can apply to a clip to change the way it looks |
| **10. Fixed effect** | **d.** Frame of a clip that Premiere Elements uses to control the path of an animated effect |
| **11. Timeline panel** | **e.** Panel that can display keyframes for multiple effects at once, but only one clip |
| **12. Preset effect** | **f.** Basic properties of a clip that you can change but not remove |
| **13. Keyframe** | **g.** Panel that contains a Search text box for all transitions and effects |
| **14. Standard effect** | **h.** Alteration you can apply to the beginning or end of a clip to blend with the previous or next clip |

**Select the best answer from the list of choices.**

**15. Dragging a standard video effect to a clip applies the effect to:**
- **a.** The frame at the location of the current-time indicator.
- **b.** All clips on the Timeline.
- **c.** The entire clip.
- **d.** The entire work area.

**16. Which category of video effects includes artistic effects such as mosaic and embossed surfaces?**
- **a.** Stylize
- **b.** Perspective
- **c.** Transform
- **d.** Keying

**17. Animating an effect:**
- **a.** Adjusts where it starts and stops within a clip.
- **b.** Moves the clip up and down on the Timeline.
- **c.** Is necessary to change the properties of an effect.
- **d.** Removes the effect.

**18. The  icon indicates:**
- **a.** The transition will right-align at the beginning of the first clip.
- **b.** The transition cannot be inserted at this location.
- **c.** The transition will center-align at the edit point.
- **d.** The transition will left-align at the edit point.

**19. A Keyframe Summary icon appears on the Properties panel to indicate:**
- **a.** You have added too many keyframes to a clip.
- **b.** An effect in a selected clip contains a keyframe and the Keyframes area is collapsed.
- **c.** More than one standard effect has been applied to a clip.
- **d.** The clip contains trimmed frames.

**20. Which of the following is *not* a fixed effect category?**
- **a.** Opacity
- **b.** Render
- **c.** Motion
- **d.** Image Control

## ▼ SKILLS REVIEW

**1. Apply a standard video effect.**
- **a.** Start Premiere Elements.
- **b.** Open the file PE D-2.prel from the drive and folder where your Data Files are located.
- **c.** Save the file as **Clown Effects and Transitions** in the *YourName* folder where you are saving files for this book.
- **d.** Expand the Video Effects category on the Effects and Transitions panel.
- **e.** Expand the Stylize category.
- **f.** Drag the Emboss transition to the Cam1_a clip.
- **g.** Play the Cam1_a clip.
- **h.** Undo the transition, then collapse the Stylize category.

## ▼ SKILLS REVIEW (CONTINUED)

i. Expand the Adjust category, then drag the Posterize effect to the Cam1_a clip.
j. Render the work area, play the clip to which you added the effect, then save your changes to the project.

**2. Adjusting an effect and creating a preset.**

a. Drag the current-time indicator to 00;00;10;10.
b. Expand the Image Control category on the Effects and Transitions panel, then add the Color Replace effect to the Cam2_a clip.
c. Expand the Color Replace effect on the Properties panel.
d. Click the Eyedropper pointer for the Target Color property, then click a bright area of the clown's hat.
e. Click the Eyedropper pointer for the Replace Color property, then click anywhere in the dark purple half of the Transitions button on the Effects and Transitions panel.
f. Change the Similarity property to **12**.
g. Repeat Steps b–f to add the Color Replace effect to the Cam1_b and Cam1_c clips and adjust the Replace Color and Similarity properties.
h. Render the work area, then save your changes to the project.

**3. Adjust a fixed effect.**

a. Select the Cam1_f clip at the end of the movie.
b. Expand the Opacity effect on the Properties panel.
c. Click the Fade Out button.
d. Drag the current-time indicator in the Properties panel to 00;01;07;00.
e. Click the Toggle effect on or off icon for the Opacity effect on the Properties panel to hide the effect, then click again to show the effect.
f. Render the work area, then play the Cam1_f clip.
g. Save your changes to the project.

**4. Animate with keyframes on the Properties panel.**

a. Use the Search text box to find the Camera View effect, then drag it to the Cam1_a clip on the Timeline.
b. Move the current-time indicator to the first frame of the Cam1_a clip.
c. Open the Keyframes area on the Properties panel, then click the Toggle Animation button for the Camera View setting. (*Hint*: Expand the panel if necessary.)
d. Drag the current-time indicator to the first frame of the clip, change the Longitude value to **75**, change the Roll value to **100**, and change the Fill Color to **black**.
e. Drag the current-time indicator to the last frame of the clip, change the Longitude value to **0**, then change the Roll value to **0**. (*Hint*: You do not need to change the Fill Color.)
f. Render the work area, save your changes, then play the first clip.
g. Drag the current-time indicator to 00;00;04;00, then verify that the Longitude value in the Properties panel reads 37 and the Roll value reads 50; your values may vary slightly.

**5. Keyframe in the Timeline.**

a. Select the Cam2_d clip that begins at 00;00;50;15.
b. Zoom in so you can see the effect properties menu icon, click the icon, point to Motion, then click Scale.
c. Drag the current-time indicator to 00;00;53;00, then click the Add/Remove Keyframe button on the Video 1 track.
d. Add a second keyframe at 00;00;56;12 (the last frame in the clip).
e. Drag the second keyframe down to the bottom of the Video 1 track.
f. Render the work area, play the Cam2_d clip, then save your changes to the project.

## ▼ SKILLS REVIEW (CONTINUED)

**6. Use Effect Presets.**

**a.** Expand the Presets category on the Effects and Transitions panel, then expand the Horizontal Image Pans category.

**b.** Preview the 1024×768 Image Pan L-R preset.

**c.** Drag the 1024×768 Image Pan L-R effect to the Cam1_e clip that begins at frame 00;00;56;14.

**d.** Drag the 1024×768 Image Pan R-L effect to the Cam2_e clip that follows the Cam1_e clip.

**e.** Render the work areas, then play the two clips.

**f.** Save your changes to the project.

**7. Add and adjust a double-sided transition.**

**a.** Expand the Video Transitions category on the Effects and Transitions panel, then expand the Iris category.

**b.** Preview the Iris Star transition.

**c.** Add the Iris Star transition between the last two clips on the Timeline, then center–align it.

**d.** Play the transition.

**e.** Adjust the transition's Alignment setting in the Properties panel to **Start at Cut**.

**f.** Render the work area, then play the transition.

**8. Add and adjust a single-sided transition.**

**a.** Expand the Slide option in the Transition category on the Effects and Transitions panel.

**b.** Drag the Slide transition to the Timeline, press and hold [Ctrl], then release the transition at the beginning of the Cam1_b clip.

**c.** On the Timeline, drag the out point of the transition to extend its duration by one second (30 frames).

**d.** In the Properties panel, change the Border Width property to **5.0**, then use the Eyedropper pointer for the Border Color to change the value to the dark purple on the Transitions button.

**e.** Render the work area, play the clip, then save your changes to the project.

**9. Remove an effect or transition.**

**a.** Remove the Color Replace effect from the Cam1_c clip.

**b.** Replace the Slide transition on the Cam1_b clip with the Push transition. (*Hint*: The Push transition is located in the Slide category.)

**c.** Remove the Color Replace effect from the Cam1_b clip.

**d.** Undo the deletion, then change the Similarity value for the restored effect to **2**. Move to frame 00;00;22;10, then compare your screen to Figure D-26.

**e.** Render the work area, then play the clip.

**f.** Save your changes to the project, then close it and exit Premiere Elements.

**FIGURE D-26**

## ▼ INDEPENDENT CHALLENGE 1

You've made a lot of progress on the movie trailer for the film festival. You're ready to add effects and transitions to further refine the edit. You want to add and adjust some effects to correct lighting and focus problems in the clips. In keeping with the brisk pace and comic spirit of the trailer, you also want to add transitions that are unexpected and fun.

**a.** Start Premiere Elements.

**b.** Open the file PE- D-4.prel from the drive and folder where your Data Files are located, then save it as **Film Fest Effects and Transitions** in the *YourName* folder where you are saving files for this book.

**c.** Add the Sharpen effect to the Tax Help clip, and change the Sharpen Amount to 25.

**d.** Adjust the fixed effects of the Really Hot Coffee clip to increase the clip's Brightness to 20.0 and the Contrast to 110.0. See Figure D-27.

FIGURE D-27

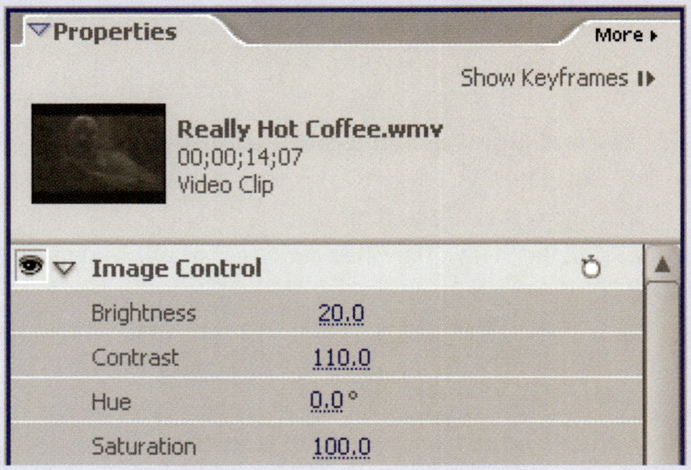


**e.** Add the Zoom transition to all five internal edit points in the movie, starting with the edit point between Dress for Success and Muffin Control and ending with the edit point between Tax Help and Really Hot Coffee. Adjust each transition as necessary so it center-aligns at the cut.

**f.** Add any transition from the Iris category to the beginning of the Dress for Success clip and the end of the Really Hot Coffee clip so that the movie opens and closes with the same transition. Adjust the transitions so the duration of each is 3 seconds.

### Advanced Challenge Exercise

ACE

- Apply a standard effect of your choice to the Muffin Control clip and the Sad Song clip. You can choose two different effects or the same effect.
- Animate at least one of the effects you added.

**g.** Render the work area, save your changes to the project, watch the movie, then close the project and exit Premiere Elements.

## ▼ INDEPENDENT CHALLENGE 2

You've edited the clips for your documentary, and now you're ready to add some effects and transitions. Based on your vision and goals for this movie, use the skills you've learned in this unit to improve the look of your clips, add visual interest, and smooth or accentuate the transitions from scene to scene.

**a.** Start Premiere Elements, open the file My Documentary.prel from the drive and folder where you are saving files for this book, then save it as **My Documentary Effects and Transitions**. (*Note*: If you did not create and edit this movie, consult your instructor.)

**b.** Add a standard effect to at least one clip in the movie.

**c.** Adjust the fixed effects of at least one clip in the movie.

**d.** Add at least one preset effect.

**e.** Add at least one double-sided or single-sided transition.

**f.** Adjust the duration of at least one transition or animate the effect for at least one clip.

**g.** Render the work area, then save your changes to the project.

**h.** Close the project and exit Premiere Elements.

## ▼ INDEPENDENT CHALLENGE 3

You're ready to add effects and transitions to the video you're creating for the internship program at Fig Media, the video production company where you work. Jim, the owner, wants you to use your creativity to improve and enhance the movie with the skills you've learned.

**a.** Open the Dream Job Edit project you created from the drive and folder where you are saving files for this book, then save it as **Dream Job Effects and Transitions**. (*Note*: If you did not create and edit this movie, consult your instructor.)
**b.** Add standard or preset effects to at least three clips in the movie.
**c.** Add a transition of your choice to at least three edits points.
**d.** Use keyframes in the first and last clip to animate the Opacity so the movie fades up at the start and down at the end.
**e.** Animate at least one effect using the Properties panel.
**f.** Save your changes to the project.

**Advanced Challenge Exercise**

- Add the Clip effect to at least three adjacent clips in the movie.
- Adjust the settings in each clip effect to mask a different part of the screen.

**g.** Save your changes, render the work area, then preview the movie.
**h.** Save and close the project, then exit Premiere Elements.

E-QUEST

## ▼ INDEPENDENT CHALLENGE 4

You are continuing to work on the Internet Education video that will accompany your talk at the upcoming conference on Cinema and Education. You want to add transitions to the movie so it looks more polished. In particular, you want to add an Image Mask transition to create a special effect.

**a.** Connect to the Internet if necessary, then use your favorite search engine to search for Web sites that offer public domain clip art, such as www.openclipart.org. For each Web site you visit, read the About page and/or Copyright pages on the site to learn whether you can legally download their clip art. Because you are using these images for editorial purposes, downloading is often permissible, but the rules and guidelines vary by site.
**b.** Download a clip art image to use as an image mask. It can be any image file you like, though simple, black-and-white images with clear outlines tend to work best for an image mask.
**c.** Open the file Internet Education.prel in the *YourName* folder where you are saving files for this book, then save it as **Internet Education Transitions**.
**d.** Add the Image Mask transition between the first and second clip and between the second and third clip, using the image you downloaded. (*Hint*: This transition is located in the Special Effects category.)
**e.** Add and adjust any additional transitions or effects you think enhance the movie.
**f.** Render the work area, save your changes to the project, then preview the movie.
**g.** When you are finished, close the project and exit Premiere Elements.

## ▼ VISUAL WORKSHOP

Open the file PE D-4.prel in the drive and folder where your Data Files are located, then save it as **Butterfly Transitions** in the *YourName* folder where you are saving files for this book. Navigate to the frame shown in Figure D-28, then find and add a transition so that your screen matches the one shown in the figure. When you are finished, save your changes to the project, press [PrtScr], paste the image into your word-processing program, print a copy, then exit your word processor and Premiere Elements.

FIGURE D-28

UNIT
**E**
Premiere Elements 2.0

# Working with Sound

## OBJECTIVES

- Adjust gain in a clip
- Adjust clip volume
- View an audio waveform
- Perform a J-cut or an L-cut
- Apply an audio transition
- Apply an audio effect
- Add a sound clip
- Mix audio tracks

Premiere Elements provides rich audio capabilities that let you adjust volume levels, add a soundtrack, fix problems, and mix multiple sounds together. An audio clip can be an audio-only file, such as a .wav or .mp3 file, or it can be the audio track of a video clip. In either case, the way you work with audio clips is similar to the way you work with video and still image clips. You can add them to the Timeline, rearrange and trim them, adjust their properties on the Properties panel or the Timeline, and add effects and transitions. Some clips in the Genoa Stock video require audio adjustment. You also want to add additional sound to parts of the movie.

UNIT
E
Premiere Elements 2.0

# Adjusting Gain in a Clip

When editing a movie, you often need to adjust the volume of a clip so it is louder or softer, or so that it matches the volume of clips before and after it on the Timeline. Before adjusting volume, you should monitor the overall sound levels in a clip and consider adjusting the **gain**, or input level of the clip. If the overall levels are too low or too high, adjusting the gain optimizes **sound amplitude**, or loudness, without increasing **noise**, extraneous or unintended sound such as hiss or distortion. Adjusting the gain often boosts volume enough that you don't need to make further adjustments. You want to monitor the volume of a clip where the dialogue is difficult to hear.

## STEPS

1. **Open the file PE E-1.prel from the drive and folder where your Data Files are located, then save it as Genoa Audio Adjustments in the *YourName* folder where you are saving files for this book**

   The latest edit of the video for Genoa Stock & Training appears on the Timeline.

> **QUICK TIP**
> The term decibel was named for Alexander Graham Bell, inventor of the telephone; *deci* means one-tenth, and *bel* is short for Bell.

2. **Click Window on the menu bar, then click Audio Meters**

   The Audio Meters window opens, where you can monitor the overall audio level of a clip on the Timeline. The left meter represents the left audio channel and the right one represents the right audio channel. The meters measure volume in **decibels (dB)**, a relative measuring system that describes signal drop-off over distance. Decibels originally measured drop-off in telephone signals; one decibel equaled one-tenth of a bel, the decrease in signal level over one mile of telephone wire.

> **QUICK TIP**
> If there are multiple audio clips at the location of the current-time indicator, such as a dialog track and a musical soundtrack, the meters measure the combined sound.

3. **Play the movie for a few moments**

   As the clip plays, the meters in the Audio Meters window display current and peak audio levels. See Figure E-1. The solid colors move up and down according to loudness at the location of the current-time indicator. The single-color lines indicate **peaking**, or the highest level that has played so far. In Premiere Elements, it's recommended that audio levels **peak**, or reach their highest point, in the range between –6 and 0. The meters turn amber at levels between 0 and –6, and turn green at levels below –6. The meters display a red **clipping indicator** to warn you when levels exceed 0. **Clipping** is a type of distortion that occurs when the audio signal is above the recommended range for output.

4. **Pause the playback**

   The Audio Meters window no longer displays information. It displays audio levels only when a clip is playing.

5. **Play the ActionK clip, observing the Audio Meters windows as the clip plays, then pause the playback**

   The input levels of this clip are too low. The loudest levels occur when Shannon speaks to her dog, and they peak between –12 and –18, too low for her dialogue to be clearly audible.

6. **Select the ActionK clip, click Clip on the menu bar, point to Audio Options, then click Audio Gain**

   The Clip Gain dialog box opens. The starting input level of an audio clip on the Timeline is 0.0; this setting does not indicate silence. Because a decibel is a relative measurement (it represents the ratio between two variables instead of a set amount), there is no absolute method by which to measure the gain. The original level of 0.0 serves as a reference point from which you can adjust the gain up (positive numbers) or down (negative numbers).

> **QUICK TIP**
> If you normalize a clip that contains a wide range of audio levels, some clipping might occur. You can always adjust levels within a clip if they are still too loud or too soft.

7. **Click Normalize**

   The gain changes to 12.9 dB, as shown in Figure E-2. **Normalizing** automatically adjusts the levels to optimize the overall volume without peaking over the recommended range. You can also adjust the gain value manually, but the Normalize command usually calculates the best settings.

8. **Click OK, then play the ActionK clip, observing the Audio Meters window as the clip plays**

   The meters now peak between –6 and 0, as shown in Figure E-3.

9. **Save your changes to the project**

FIGURE E-1: Monitoring audio levels of a clip

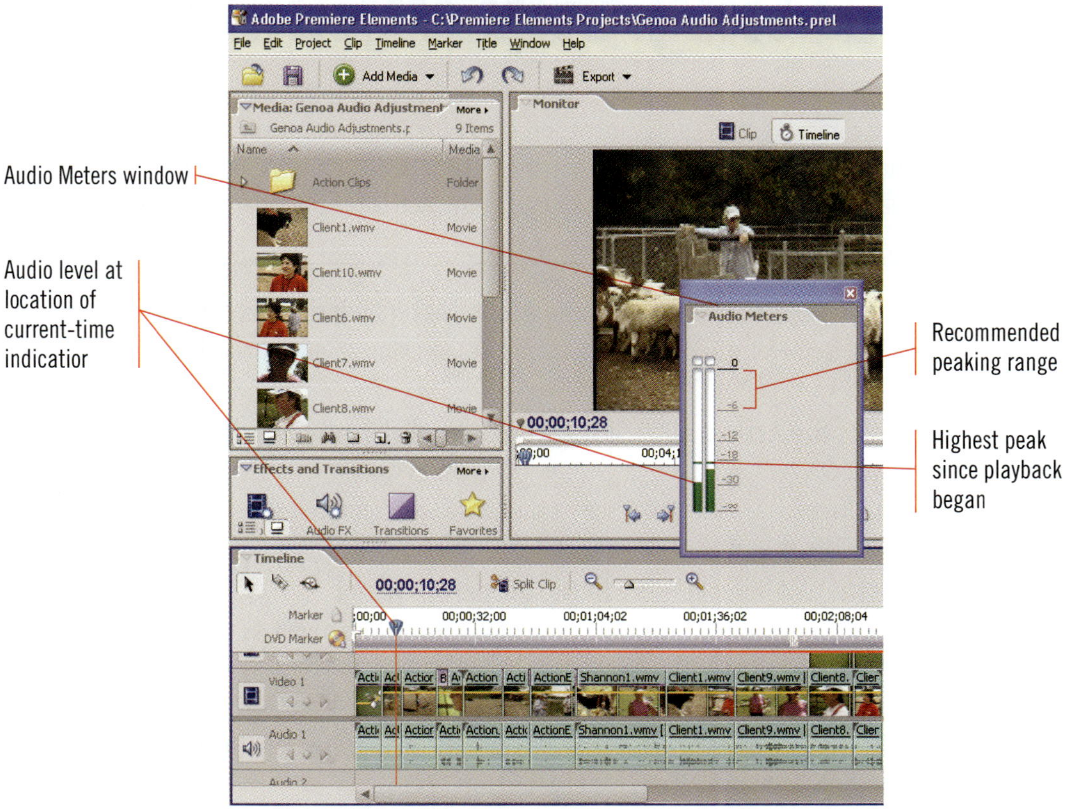


FIGURE E-2: Adjusting the gain

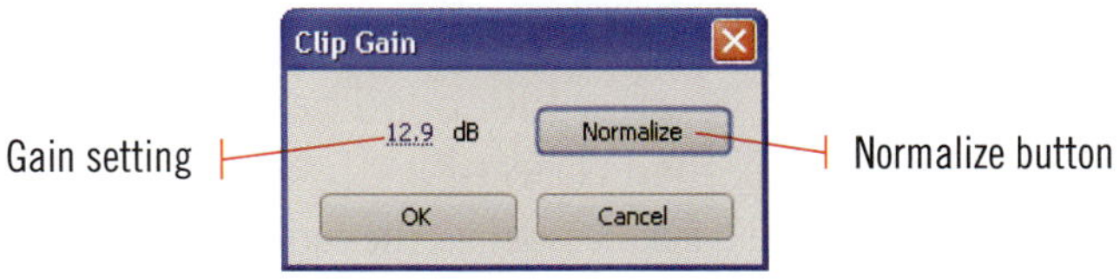


FIGURE E-3: Monitoring levels of adjusted clip

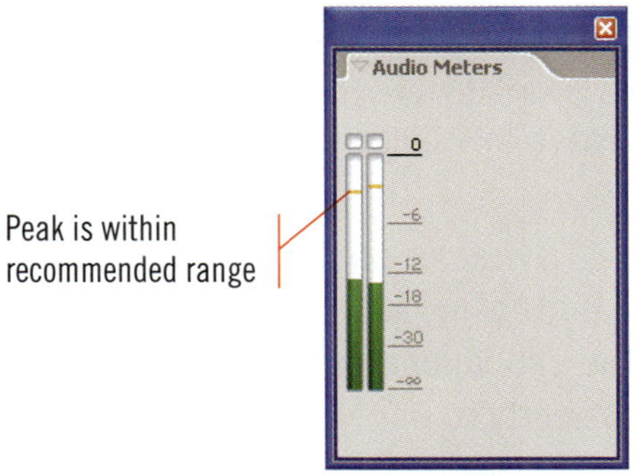


## Production Matters

### Improving sound before you edit

You can adjust levels and other aspects of sound in editing, but your results ultimately depend on the quality of the original sound recording. If the input levels are too low, adjusting the gain can only boost them to a certain point without introducing an unacceptable level of noise. If they're too high, you have to contend with clipping and distortion. For best results, you should record source audio at the best possible quality. Professional videographers often use separate audio equipment, including a microphone, sound mixer, and headphones instead of relying on the camera's built-in microphone. If you must use the built-in microphone, wearing headphones while shooting increases your chances of success. You can hear exactly what the camera is recording, which often differs from what you'd think, and you can adjust your position or try to adapt to the situation accordingly.

UNIT

E

Premiere Elements 2.0

# Adjusting Clip Volume

You can adjust the volume of an entire audio clip or just part of the clip. Because volume is a fixed effect of a clip, you can make these adjustments on either the Properties panel or on the Timeline. You can also animate the path of the property, so that the volume is louder in some parts of the clip and softer in others. You want to adjust the volume of the ActionJ clip so that it is more audible.

## STEPS

1. **Play the ActionJ clip, observing the Audio Meters window as the clip plays**

   The overall levels for this clip remain around –12, peaking at approximately frame 00;00;32;18, when the dog barks.

2. **Right-click the ActionJ clip, click Audio Gain, click Normalize in the Clip Gain dialog box, then click OK**

   The gain increases to .3 dB. This is the greatest increase recommended to avoid causing the sound of the dog barking to **clip**, or peak at an unacceptable range. However, you want the dialogue to be louder.

QUICK TIP

To fade volume in at the beginning of a selected clip, click the Fade In button on the Properties panel; to fade it down at the end, click the Fade Out button .

3. **Expand the Volume category in the Properties panel**

   The Properties panel contains several controls for working with sound, as shown in Figure E-4. You can adjust the overall volume of a clip by changing the Volume setting. You can use keyframes to control the path of the volume property by clicking Show Keyframes and the Toggle animation button .

4. **Click the Toggle looping audio playback button on the Properties panel, then click the Play only the audio for this clip button**

   The Toggle looping audio playback feature causes the playback to **loop**, or play continuously from the beginning when it reaches the end. The Play only the audio feature causes the audio to play without the linked video track.

5. **Click the Stop button after the sound has played through once, change the Clip Volume property to 3.0, then click**

   When the Play only the audio feature is active, the current-time indicator on the Timeline doesn't move, and the Audio Meters window doesn't display levels.

6. **Press [Page Up] to move to the first frame of the clip, then play the clip, observing the Audio Meters window**

   The overall volume of the clip is louder. However, the levels now clip at around frame 00;00;31;18, where the dog barks. When the range of levels within a clip is wide, you often need to adjust parts of it, raising some levels and lowering others.

QUICK TIP

Resize the Properties panel as necessary.

7. **Press [Page Up], click Show Keyframes on the Properties panel if necessary, click the Volume Toggle animation button , move to frame 00;00;31;00, click the Add/Remove Keyframe button for the Clip Volume property, move to frame 00;00;31;10, then change the Clip Volume property to 0.0**

   You added keyframes to maintain the clip volume of 3.0 dB through frame 00;00;31;00, and then to fade it to 0.0 by frame 00;00;31;10. Keyframes were added at frames 00;00;28;00 and 00;00;31;10 even though you didn't click the Add/Remove Keyframes button. Activating the Toggle animation button or changing a property when the button is active automatically adds a keyframe for that property at the current frame.

8. **Move to frame 00;00;31;20, click , move to frame 00;00;32;15, then change the Clip Volume property to 3.0**

   You added keyframes to maintain the clip volume of 0.0 dB through frame 00;00;31;20, then fade up to 3.0 by frame 00;00;32;15. See Figure E-5.

9. **Save your changes, then play the clip**

   When you reach frame 00;00;31;18, the levels do not clip, but the sound in the rest of the clip is more audible. See Figure E-6.

**FIGURE E-4: Audio controls on Properties panel**

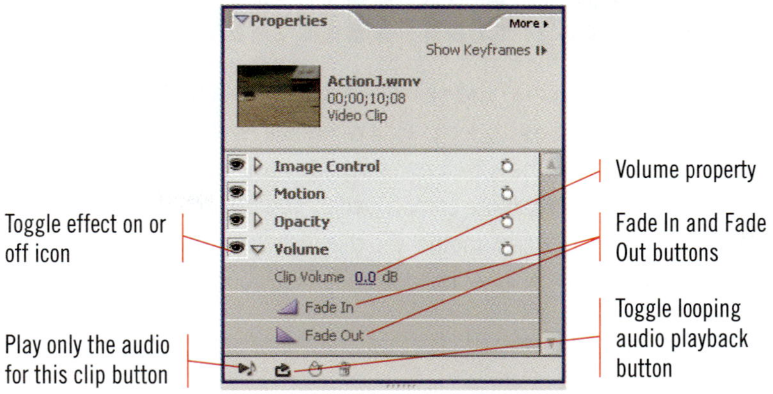


**FIGURE E-5: Keyframing the Clip Volume property**

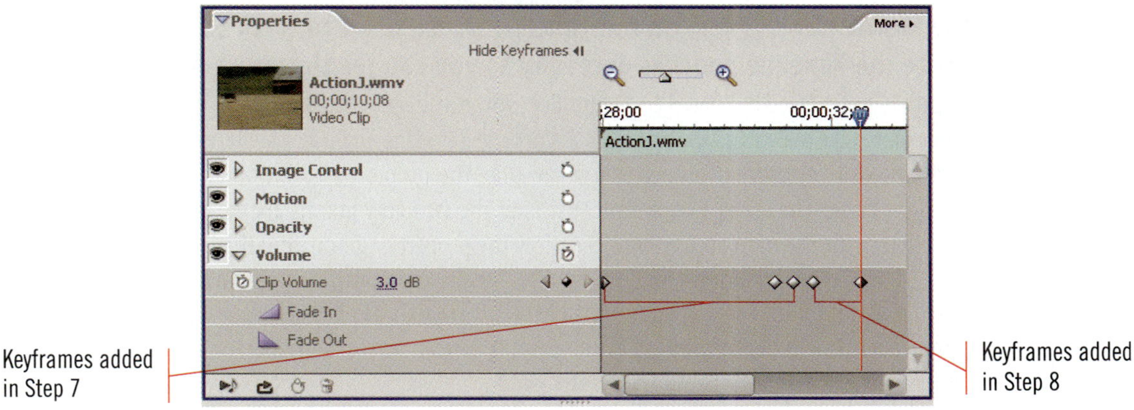


**FIGURE E-6: Adjusted clip volume**

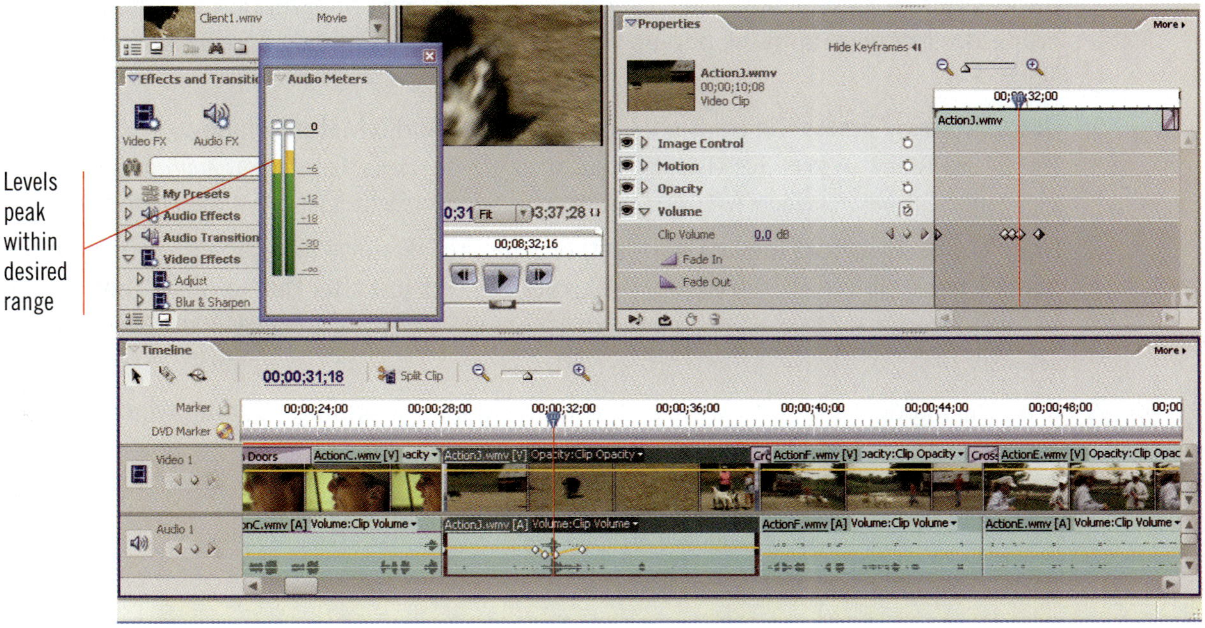

UNIT
E
Premiere Elements 2.0

# Viewing an Audio Waveform

By default, the audio tracks in the Timeline panel display a clip's **audio waveform**, a graphical representation of the audio signal that you can use to see exactly where the levels change. If you work directly on the Timeline to adjust properties, you can use the waveform as a guide in making detailed adjustments to properties, transitions, and effects, and for performing more complex edits. You can adjust your view to see the waveform in greater detail. You decide to adjust another clip that includes a dog barking; you need to increase the overall volume but avoid clipping at the point of the dog bark. First, you want to take a closer look at the audio waveform.

## STEPS

**TROUBLE**

If clicking dis-plays the properties graph, do not re-click the button.

**QUICK TIP**

To increase the height of a track, point to the header area between the Audio 1 track and the Video 1 track, drag the Split Track pointer, then scroll up or down to see more of the desired track.

**TROUBLE**

Be careful not to move the mouse from side to side as you drag, or you will change the frame location of the keyframe.

1. **Click the Set Audio Track Display Style button on the Audio 1 track, observe the result, then click to restore the display style**

   You can choose to hide the properties graph and the waveform if you are working on the video portion of a clip and want the rest of the workspace as uncluttered as possible. When working with audio, leave these elements displayed.

2. **Select the ActionJ clip, zoom in until the whole clip is visible and as large as possible, click the More button More ▸ on the Timeline panel, point to Track Size, click Large, then resize the Timeline panel as necessary so you can see the entire Audio 1 track**

   Compare your Timeline panel to Figure E-7. You can display tracks on the Timeline in Small, Medium, or Large size. Like video tracks, audio tracks on the Timeline include a yellow properties graph that displays keyframes for the current property. You can drag the properties graph on an audio clip to adjust the fixed effect, volume. The audio waveform consists of the two gray graphs above and below the properties graph; these represent the right audio channel (below the properties graph) and the left channel (above it). The thinner regions of the waveform represent weaker signals, and the thicker regions represent stronger signals. The thick, roughly triangular-shaped regions are called **transients** because they represent short, strong bursts of sound, such as a door slamming, a drumbeat in a song, a person laughing, or, in this case, a dog barking. The widest part of a transient is the **transient peak**.

3. **Move to frame 00;02;29;34, then drag the current-time indicator slowly across the ActionG clip, observing the Audio Meters window as passes over the waveform**

   This clip consists of little dialogue and an extended dog bark, represented by the two transients that begin at approximately 00;02;34;18. In this clip, the left channel is louder than the right channel.

4. **Zoom out and scroll in the Timeline panel so you can see the full Video 1 and Audio 1 tracks, right-click the ActionG clip, click Audio Gain, click Normalize, click OK, then drag the properties graph up until the pop-up window reads approximately 2.5 dB, as shown in Figure E-8**

5. **Drag slowly across the transients, observing the Audio Meters window**

   The volume is now so loud that clipping occurs when the dog barks, but the waveform does not change appearance. The waveform does not reflect volume, only signal strength relative to the rest of the signal.

6. **Drag directly before the first transient, click the Add/Remove Keyframe button on the Audio 1 track, click the first transient peak, click , click just after the transient, then click**

   You added keyframes before, during, and after the dog bark. A precise positioning of the keyframes is not necessary.

7. **Drag the middle keyframe down, as shown in Figure E-9, until the pop-up window reads approximately –2.66 dB**

8. **Save your changes, then play the clip**

   The overall volume is louder, but the sound of the dog barking does not cause clipping.

FIGURE E-7: Viewing an audio waveform

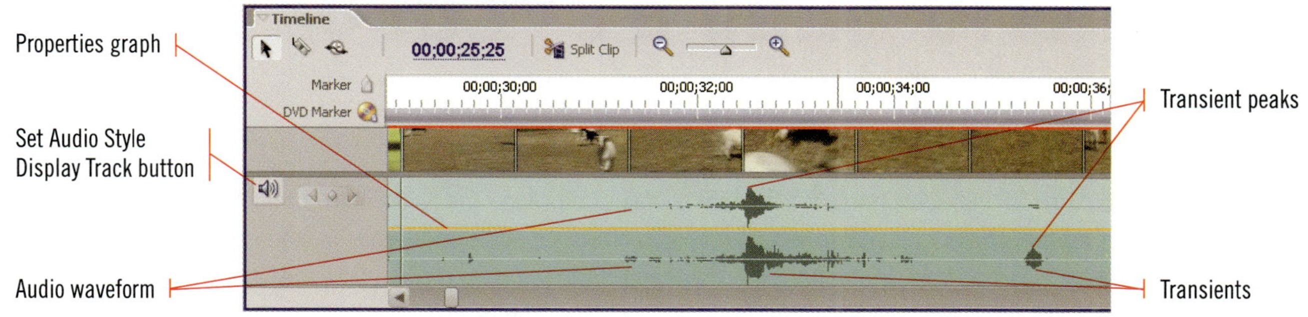


FIGURE E-8: Dragging the property graph to adjust volume

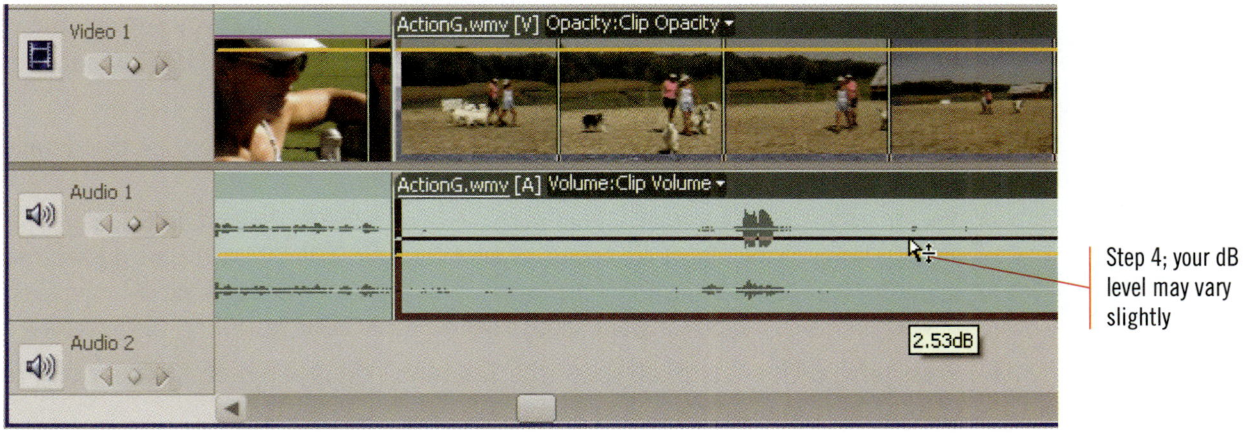


FIGURE E-9: Dragging a keyframe to adjust volume

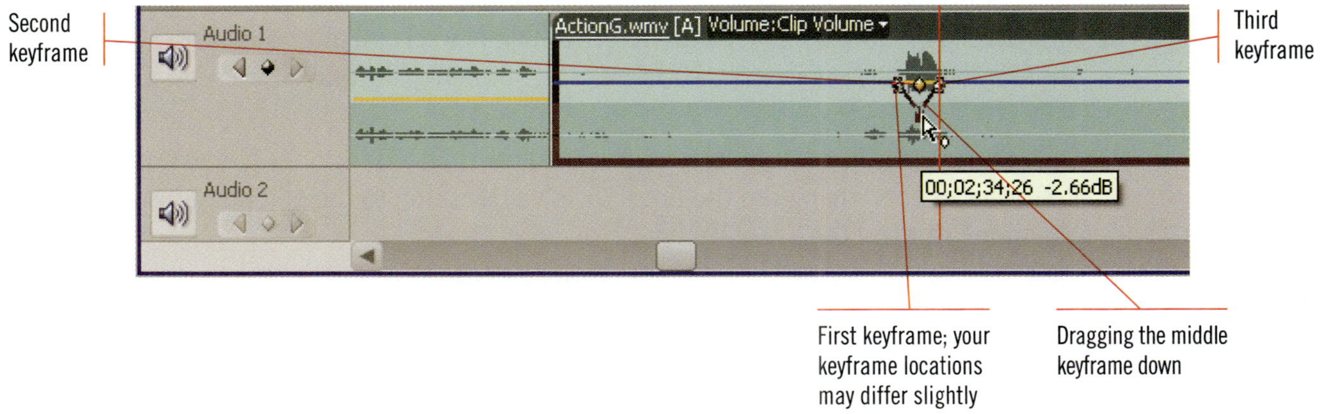


Premiere Elements 2.0

UNIT
E
Premiere Elements 2.0

# Performing a J-Cut or an L-Cut

You can trim individual tracks of a clip that contains both video and audio. Two common edits that incorporate linked but differently trimmed video and audio tracks are J-cuts and L-cuts. In a **J-cut,** the audio track starts before the video track; on the Timeline, the shape of the complete clip looks like the letter J, hence the name. In an **L-cut**, the audio track ends after the video track, resulting in a clip that is shaped like an L. In both types of edits, the audio track extends past the video track, but in a J-cut the extension is at the beginning of the clip, while in an L-cut the extension is at the end. Creating a J-cut or L-cut in conjunction with another clip on the Timeline (instead of at the beginning or end of a movie) can serve to hide unwanted audio or video, push the narrative action, or simply add visual interest. You want to adjust the edit point between the last two clips of the movie, Shannon1 and Client10. At the end of the Shannon1 clip, you want the audio to end just after Shannon says, "I want the ranch house," but you also want to show Shannon's face before moving to the next clip. You can achieve this by creating a J-cut.

## STEPS

1. **Move to the end of the movie, arrange the workspace so that you can see the edit point between the Shannon1 clip and the Client10 clip, then play the last few seconds of the Shannon1 clip and the first few seconds of the Client10 clip**
2. **Move to frame 00;03;16;00, then zoom in if necessary so you can see the detailed audio waveform**

   You can use the audio waveform to trim a clip more precisely. The current-time indicator is positioned just after the words, "I want the ranch house," as shown in Figure E-10. Notice the two thicker areas that follow it: the first is a laugh, and the next is the speaker saying, "Okay?" The shapes are pronounced on the bottom waveform, while the upper waveform shows a more constant audio signal.
3. **Press [Alt], click the audio track of the Shannon1 clip, then drag the out point to the current-time indicator**

   The audio track is trimmed to frame 00;03;16;00, and the video track remains intact. You can create an L- or J-cut by trimming frames from the audio track of the previous clip or by trimming video frames of the next clip.
4. **Click the Shannon1 clip, drag right until the audio track aligns to the in point of the Client10 clip, press [Ctrl], then when the pointer changes to ⇱, as shown in Figure E-11, release the mouse button**

   The clip aligns at the beginning of the Client10 clip, and the last few video frames of the Shannon1 clip overlay the first few video frames of the Client10 clip.
5. **Move to the beginning of the Shannon1 clip, right-click the blank area in the video or audio track, then click Delete and Close Gap**
6. **Play the movie from a few seconds before until a few second after the J-cut**

   The J-cut removes the unwanted audio while allowing you to keep the visual of Shannon's face at the end of the clip.
7. **Expand the Video Transitions category in the Effects and Transitions panel, expand the Dissolve category, then drag the Cross Dissolve transition to the edit point between the Shannon1 clip and the Client10 clip**
8. **Save your changes to the project, restore the Edit workspace, then play the transition**

   The dissolve transition softens the shift from one clip to the next, as shown in Figure E-12.

**TROUBLE**

Make sure you don't press [Ctrl] until you are ready to release the mouse button or you will rearrange the clip instead of overlaying it. If this happens, undo the edit and repeat Step 4.

**FIGURE E-10: Viewing audio waveform to position an edit**

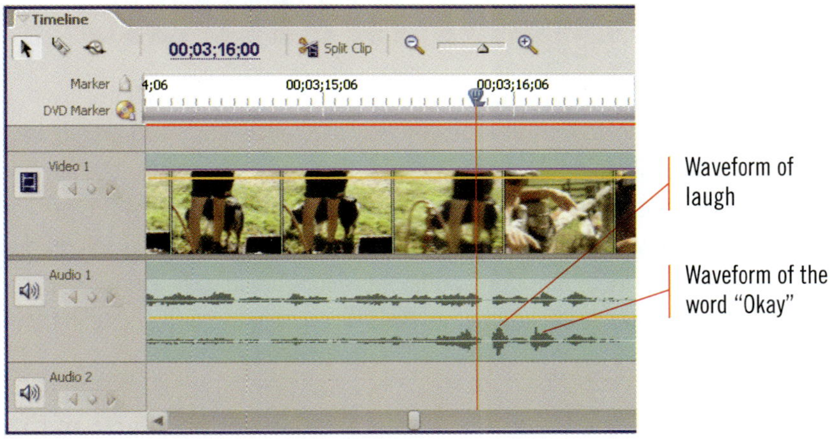


**FIGURE E-11: Performing a J-cut**

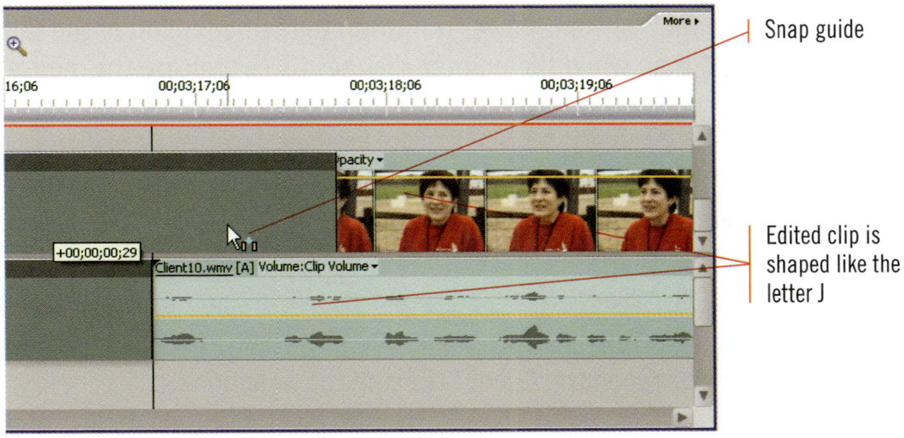


**FIGURE E-12: Completed J-cut**

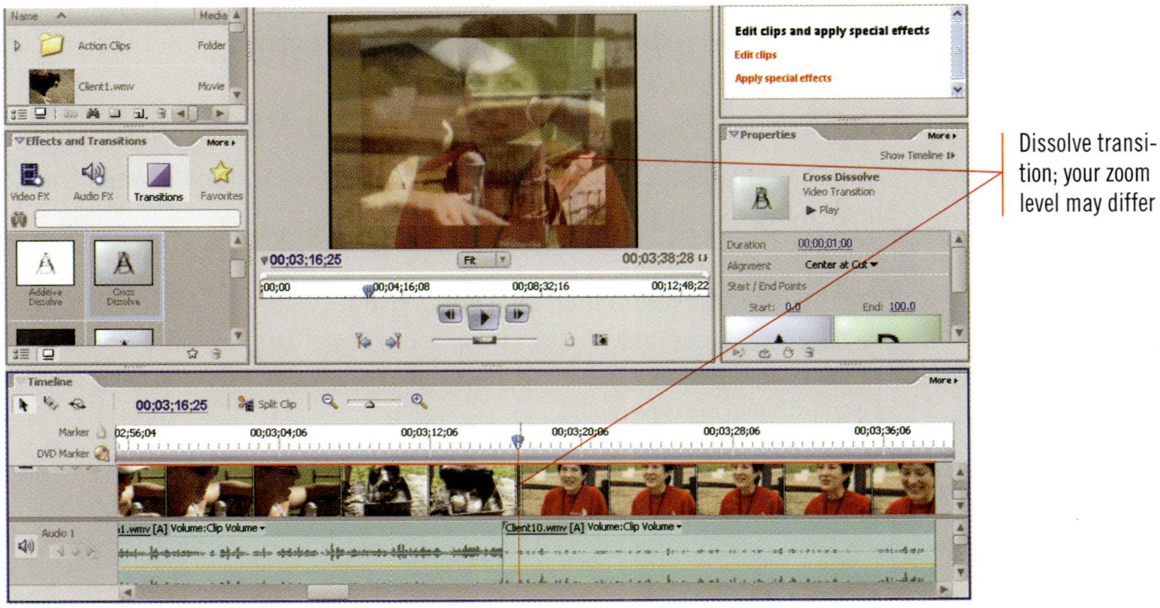

UNIT
E
Premiere Elements 2.0

# Applying an Audio Transition

You can apply audio transitions just as you do video transitions, by dragging them from the Effects and Transition panel to the Timeline; the only difference is that you drag them to the audio track instead of to the video track. Premiere Elements includes two audio transitions, both in the Crossfade category. A **crossfade** in audio is analogous to a dissolve in video; the content from the previous clip and the next clip intersect, with the previous clip fading out as the next one fades in. The default duration of an audio transition is one second. Like video transitions, audio transitions are initially aligned depending on the presence or absence of trimmed frames at the edit point. You want to add an audio transition to the J-cut you created.

## STEPS

1. **Collapse the Video Transitions category in the Effects and Transitions panel, expand the Audio Transitions category, then expand the Crossfade category**
   Although the default transition displays a dark blue border and the current selection displays a light blue border, you cannot preview an audio transition by clicking it. **Constant Power**, the default transition, creates a smooth, gradual crossfade from one sound clip to the next; **Constant Gain** gradually increases the gain of the next clip while reducing the gain of the previous clip.
2. **Drag the Constant Power transition to the beginning of the Client10 clip on the Audio 1 track, then when the pointer changes to , release the mouse button**
   The transition is added to the Client10 clip. It's left-aligned at the beginning of the clip because the out point of the Shannon1 clip contains trimmed frames, and the in point of the Client10 clip does not. The Properties panel displays the properties for the transition, as shown in Figure E-13.
3. **Change the Alignment property on the Properties panel to Center at Cut, then play the transition**
   The combination of the audio and video transitions creates a smooth progression to the Client10 clip.
4. **Drag the Constant Power transition from the Effects and Transitions panel to the edit point between the Client7 clip and the Shannon1 clip**
   The transition is center-aligned at the edit point because both the out point of the Client7 clip and the in point of the Shannon1 clip contain trimmed frames.
5. **Zoom out if necessary so you can see all the clips on the Timeline, then add a Constant Power transition to the edit point between the following clips starting at frame 00;00;58;24: Shannon1 and Client1, Client1 and Client9, and Client9 and Client8**
6. **Add a Constant Power transition between the ActionF clip and ActionE clip, change the Duration property to 3 seconds in the Properties panel, render the Timeline, then play the transitions you added**
7. **Add a Constant Power transition to the out point of the last clip**
8. **Drag the Constant Gain transition on top of the transition between the ActionF clip and the ActionE clip, as shown in Figure E-14**
   You can replace an audio transition by dragging a new transition on top of it.
9. **Play the new transition, then save your changes**
   The difference between the Constant Power and Constant Gain transitions might be hard to hear. In the Constant Gain transition, the audio in the second clip replaces the first clip more steadily, and the perception of blended audio is less perceptible.

**TROUBLE**

If you try to drag the transition to the video track, the pointer changes to ; you can only add an audio transition to the audio track.

**QUICK TIP**

You can quickly fade in or fade out both audio and video by right-clicking a clip, pointing to Fade, and then clicking a command in the shortcut menu.

FIGURE E-13: Audio transition added to Timeline

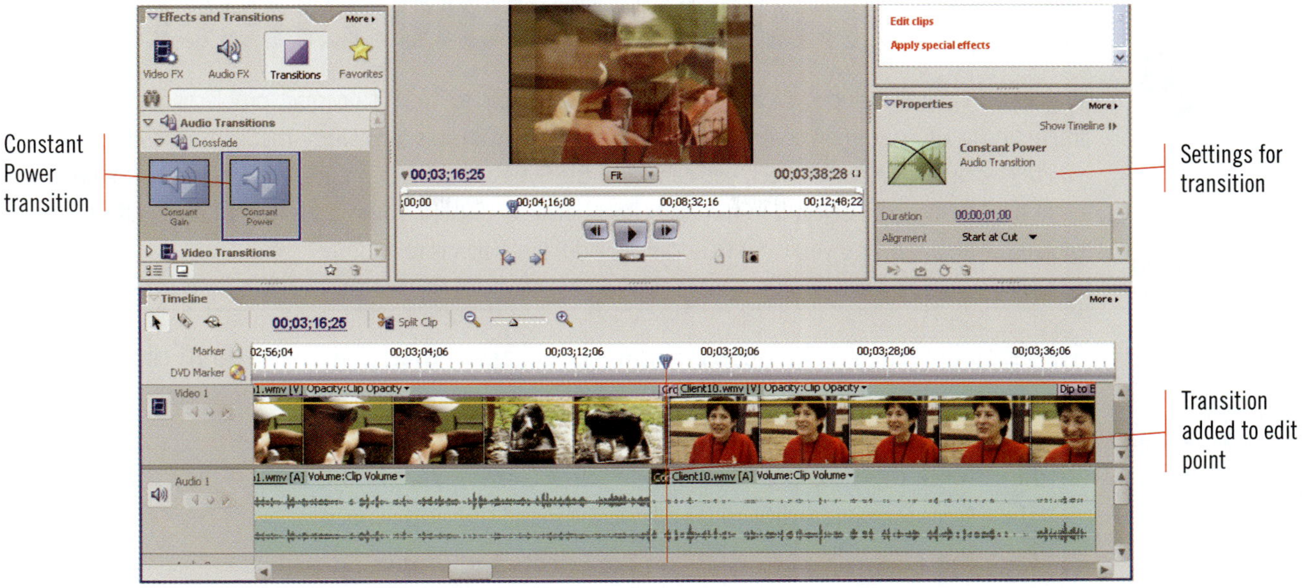


FIGURE E-14: Replacing a transition

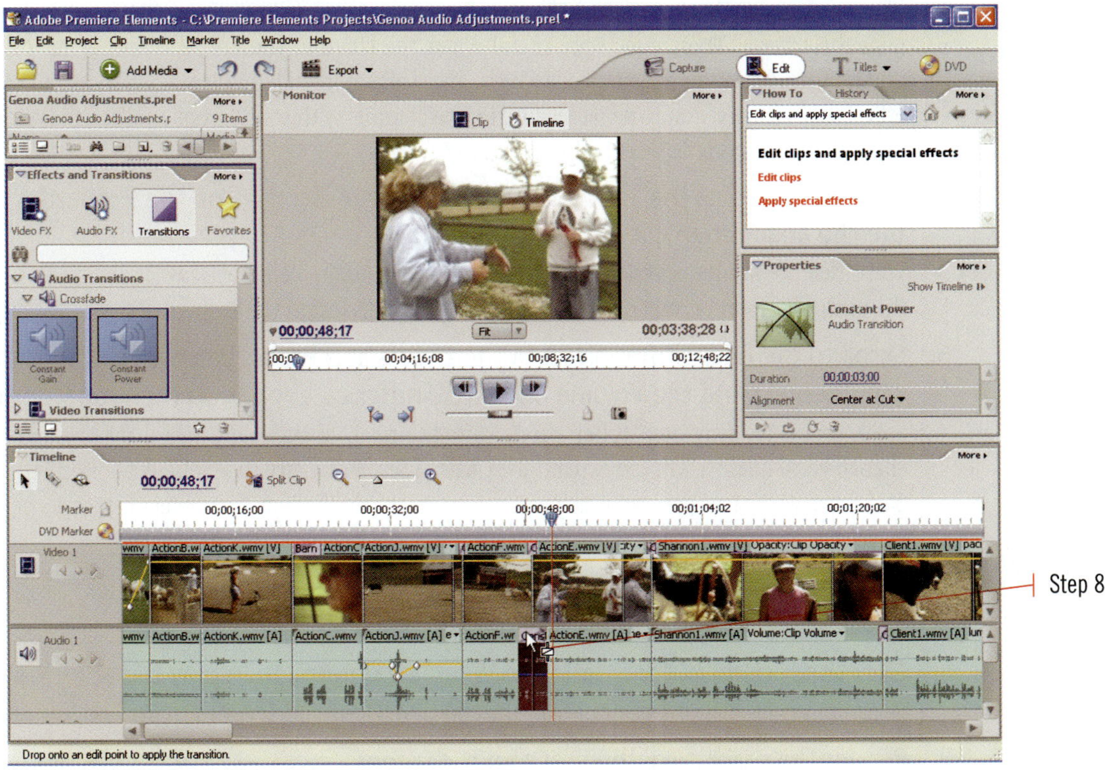

UNIT E

Premiere Elements 2.0

# Applying an Audio Effect

Premiere Elements includes 17 audio effects you can apply to a clip to correct problems, enhance quality, or intentionally add distortion. Every audio effect contains a **Bypass property** that turns the effect off or on. If you're keyframing an audio effect, you can select the Bypass check box on the Properties panel to turn the effect off at a keyframe, or deselect it to turn the effect back on. You want to use an audio effect to correct a problem with a clip, and you want to add some additional effects to another clip.

## STEPS

**QUICK TIP**

For best results when sound editing, wear headphones so you can correctly distinguish between right and left channels and hear subtle differences in properties.

1. **Verify that the Audio Meters window is still open, then play the ActionC clip**

   The dialogue in this clip sounds somewhat flat. As shown in the Audio Meters window and the audio waveform on the Timeline, most sound is coming from the right channel only.

2. **Right-click the clip, click Audio Gain, click Normalize, press OK, then play the clip**

   The volume increases slightly to 2.7 dB, but the sound still lacks resonance.

3. **Click the Audio FX button on the Effects and Properties panel**

   All available audio effects are listed within this category. They include effects to balance sound between channels, increase bass or treble frequencies, add reverberation, and more. Many effects allow you to adjust the intensity of decibel level, frequency, and other factors such as **gate**, which specifies the level at which a sound must occur before it's affected by the effect.

4. **Scroll down if necessary, then drag the Fill Right effect to the Audio 1 track of the ActionC clip**

   The effect is added to the clip and appears in the Properties panel, as shown in Figure E-15. The Fill Right effect replaces audio in the left channel with a copy of the audio in the right channel. The Fill Left channel does the reverse. These effects are useful when the channel you are replacing is not only weak, but also doesn't include any audio you need to keep. These effects include a Bypass check box, but no additional properties. Because they simply replace sound in one channel with sound from another, there is nothing to adjust other than activating or deactivating the effect.

**QUICK TIP**

The audio waveform does not reflect this change because it depicts the waveform of the original clip; to monitor audio effects in a selected clip, use the Properties panel.

5. **Play the clip, click the Toggle the effect on or off icon on the Properties panel, play the clip again, then click**

   The difference in sound, which you can observe in the Audio Meters window, is obvious; when the effect is on, the quality of sound is fuller, and no significant sound is lost in the absence of signal from the left channel.

6. **Scroll to the PitchShifter effect in the Effects and Properties panel, drag it to the ActionK clip, then expand the Volume and PitchShifter categories on the Properties panel**

   See Figure E-16. The PitchShifter effect shifts the pitch of the audio signal up or down, allowing you to change vocal quality. You can expand the Custom Setup category to manually adjust pitch by **semitones**, or half-steps, and view your adjustment settings in the Individual Parameters category; or, you can use the Presets menu to apply predesigned pitch settings.

7. **Click the Presets button, click Cartoon Mouse, play the clip, click, click Female becomes secret agent, then play the clip again**

8. **Click the Fade In button in the Volume category, then play the adjusted clip**

   The sound fades in at the beginning of the clip, and a keyframe is added to the Audio 1 track.

9. **Render the work area, then save your changes**

FIGURE E-15: Audio effect added to clip

Fill Right effect

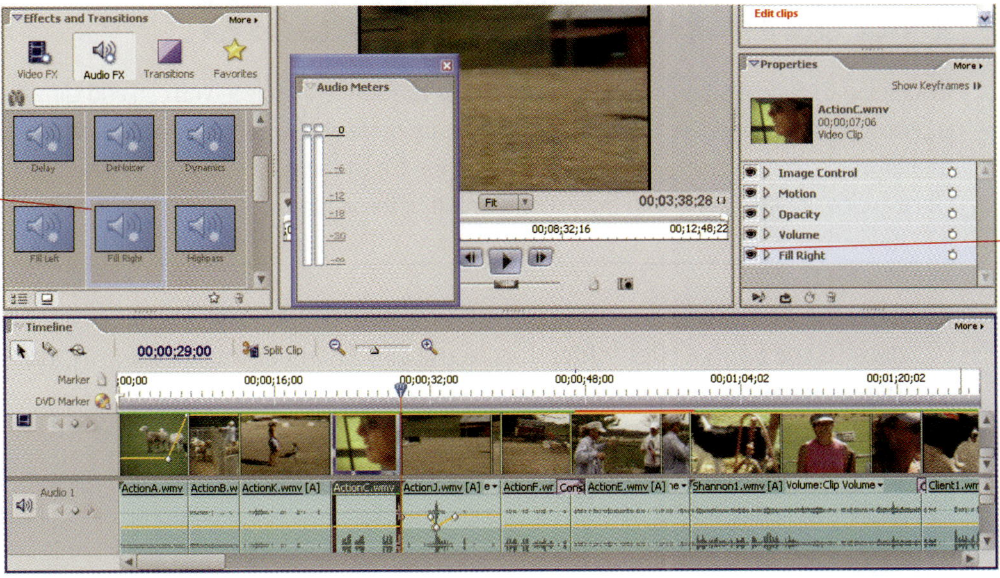


Toggle the effect on or off icon

FIGURE E-16: Adjusting audio effects

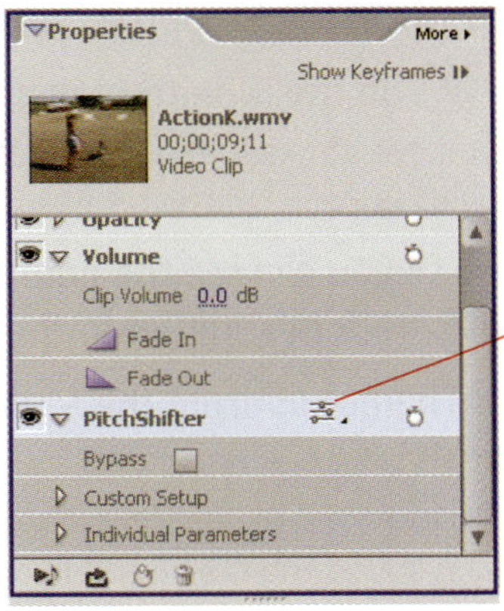


Presets buttons

## Production Matters

### Understanding sound and sound measurements

Sound comprises many components. We hear by perceiving the vibration of sound waves and the movement of particles of matter through the air. A **sound wave** consists of amplitude, wavelength, and frequency. **Amplitude** describes the power of the vibration, or the distance of the displacement of a particle in a cycle of vibration. **Wavelength** is the distance the wave travels in a cycle. **Frequency** is the rate at which the waves vibrate, and is measured in Hertz (Hz), or cycles per second. The human ear typically perceives vibrations within the range of 20 Hz to 20,000 Hz. We perceive increases in frequency as higher-pitched sounds and increases in amplitude as louder sounds. Decibels measure sound power or intensity, which corresponds to amplitude, but in a simpler, relative unit of measurement that's easier to remember and compare among different sources of sound. Actual results and preferences vary depending on each person's hearing abilities, but 0.0 decibels is considered the normal threshold of human hearing, and 130 dB is about the point at which sound is painful to the ear.

In Premiere Elements, most audio effects are measured in decibels. This keeps matters simple, rather than requiring you to make complex calculations regarding amplitude, wavelength, and frequency every time you want to make a change. However, some effects in Premiere Elements do include additional controls related to sound. For example, the Notch control reduces frequencies within a narrow range you specify (defined as the center); you can use this to remove problems such as the hum of a nearby refrigerator, air conditioner, or power line in a clip.

UNIT
E
Premiere Elements 2.0

# Adding a Sound Clip

In addition to audio that is contained in video clips you add to a project, you can add clips that are audio-only, such as music or sound effects. See Table E-1 to learn more about supported audio formats. You want to add music to the movie, so you need to add the file to the project and then add it to the Audio 2 track. Once added, it plays along with the existing sound of the video clips.

## STEPS

**QUICK TIP**
To see the audio waveform of a video clip that contains audio in the Monitor window, double-click the clip or drag it to the Monitor panel, then click the Toggle Take Audio and Video button on the Monitor panel.

**QUICK TIP**
Resize the track height and scroll as needed.

1. **Click the Add Media button on the toolbar, click From Files or Folders, navigate to the Source Files folder, locate the clip The Pharaos Theme.wav, then click Open**
   The clip is added to the project.
2. **Double-click the The Pharaos Theme clip on the Media panel**
   The clip opens in the Monitor panel, as shown in Figure E-17. Because this is an audio-only clip, the Monitor displays an audio waveform instead of images. This clip is a stereo recording of a song saved in WAV format.
3. **Right-click in the Monitor, then click Properties**
   Information about the clip is displayed in the Properties window. When you add an audio clip to a project, Premiere Elements converts it to Dolby digital stereo. If the source file was recorded in mono (one-channel) format, Premiere Elements copies the single channel so that it will play in stereo. This song was recorded in stereo, and the source file is a 16-bit stereo WAVE audio file.
4. **Click the Close button on the Properties window**
5. **Click the Play button on the Monitor panel, then listen to the clip for several seconds**
   The current-time indicator moves through the clip, just as it does a video clip. You can navigate the Monitor Timeline, set an in point and out point, and add markers.
6. **Zoom out as necessary so you can see the entire movie, then resize the Timeline panel so you can see the Audio 2 track in addition to the Audio 1 and Video 1 tracks**
7. **Drag the The Pharaos Theme clip from the Monitor panel to the Audio 2 track at the beginning of the Timeline**
   The clip is added to the beginning of the movie, as shown in Figure E-18. By default, a Premiere Elements project contains three audio tracks. You can add additional tracks by clicking the More button on the Timeline panel, then clicking Add Tracks, or by right-clicking in the track header area, then clicking Add Tracks.
8. **Save your changes to the project**

FIGURE E-17: Viewing an audio clip in the Monitor panel

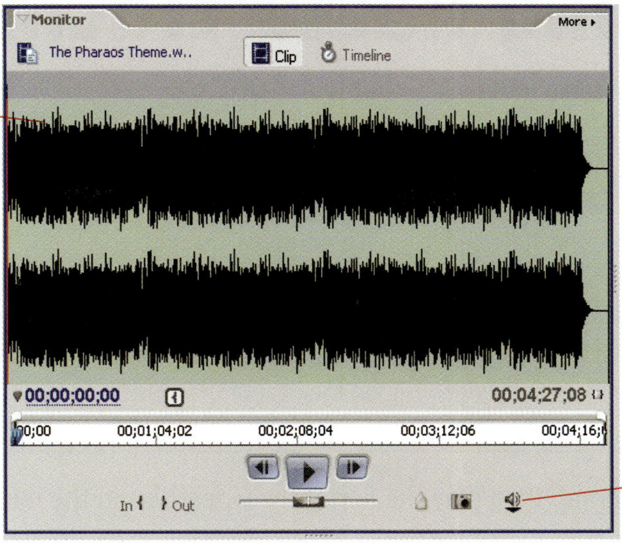


FIGURE E-18: Audio clip added to Audio 2 track

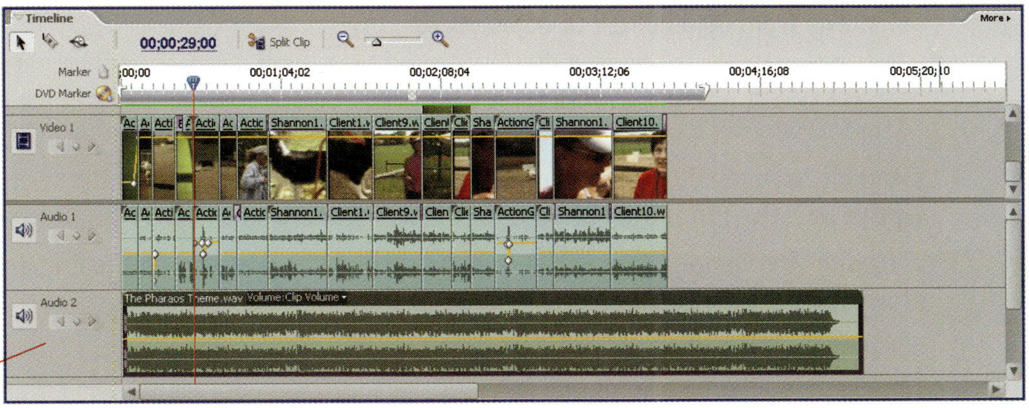


## Production Matters

### Adding music from a CD or the Internet

You can add songs from CDs or the Internet to your projects. To add a song from a CD, you first need to **rip** the song—that is, convert it from the CD to a different format, in this case, one compatible with Premiere Elements, such as WAV or MP3. To rip songs from a CD, you can use Windows Media Player (included in Microsoft Windows), Apple iTunes, or dedicated CD-ripping software such as SmartSoft Smart CD Ripper or Adobe Audition. In order to play properly in Premiere Elements, the file must be in a compatible format and be compressed using a format that Premiere Elements can decompress. Some CDs are formatted so their contents cannot be extracted, and some audio files downloaded from the Internet may have settings that render them unusable in Adobe Premiere Elements. If a song is copyright-protected, you should not use it in projects intended for public or commercial viewing without permission. If you are able to rip a song but find the quality is unacceptable, try ripping it again with a different file format or with a different compression setting.

UNIT E

Premiere Elements 2.0

# Mixing Audio Tracks

Using multiple audio tracks in a project is as easy as using multiple video tracks, but there are some important differences. When you have multiple video tracks, the clip on the highest track hides images on the tracks below. With multiple audio tracks, you can hear the sounds from all tracks. That means you can combine, or **mix**, sounds together. You can change the volume of different sounds to make certain sounds louder or softer, crossfade between different sound sources, edit to the beat of the music, and create richly layered soundtracks. With up to 99 audio tracks available in a Premiere Elements project, the possibilities are almost limitless. You want the music clip to play without dialogue on the Audio 1 track at the beginning of the movie, and then you want the dialogue to fade in gradually as the music fades out. You also want to cut to the second video clip on the beat of the music.

## STEPS

1. **Press [Home], then play the first three video clips in the movie**
   Right now, you can hear the music and dialogue evenly in the first three clips. You want the movie to start with the music fading in and playing without any dialogue audible.
2. **Click the ActionA clip, press and hold [Shift], click the ActionB clip, right-click the selection, click Delete Audio, then click in a blank area of the audio track to deselect the remaining video clips**
   The two audio clips are deleted.
3. **Zoom in so you can see the Audio 2 track in detail, then drag the current-time indicator slowly from 00;00;05;20 to 00;00;06;20**
   The transients on the waveform of the clip represent the beats of the music, as shown in Figure E-19. The transient peak at frame 00;00;06;05 is the exact point at which you want to cut to the next clip on the Video 1 track.
4. **Drag to frame 00;00;06;05, click the Set Unnumbered Marker button, drag out of the way, then trim the out point of the ActionA clip so it aligns with the marker**
5. **Click the The Pharaos Theme clip, expand the Volume property on the Properties panel, then click the Fade In button**
6. **Play the first two clips**
   The song fades in at the beginning of the movie, and the second video clip starts on the first strong beat of the music. Now, you want to fade the music out as the sound of the dialogue in the ActionK clip fades in. The ActionK clip already contains an audio fade in.
7. **Move to frame 00;00;11;05, click the Add/Remove Keyframe button on the Audio 2 track, move to frame 00;00;14;05, click, then drag the second keyframe to the bottom of the track until –oo dB appears in the pop-up window**
   The keyframe is adjusted as shown in Figure E-20. The symbol **–oo** represents negative infinity, which is inaudible in the soundtrack.
8. **Move to frame 00;03;32;00, click on the Audio 2 track, click, move to frame 00;03;38;15, click, then change the Clip Volume property in the Properties panel to 0**
   You faded the music out for most of the movie, and then faded it back in at the end of the movie, as shown in Figure E-21. Currently, the song extends past the end of the movie, which is useful if you want that part of the song to play under the movie credits, which you learn about in the next unit.
9. **Play the movie, save your changes to the project, then close it and exit Premiere Elements**

**QUICK TIP**

You can also select multiple clips by clicking a blank track area above or below the track and dragging a selection marquee around the desired clips.

**QUICK TIP**

You can click the on either the Timeline panel or on the Monitor panel.

**QUICK TIP**

As an alternative to dragging the properties graph, you can use the Properties panel to adjust levels for keyframes you set on the Timeline panel.

FIGURE E-19: Editing to the beat

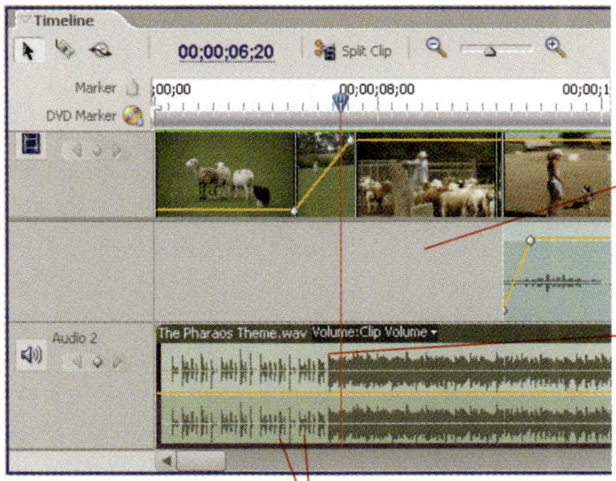


FIGURE E-20: Mixing audio

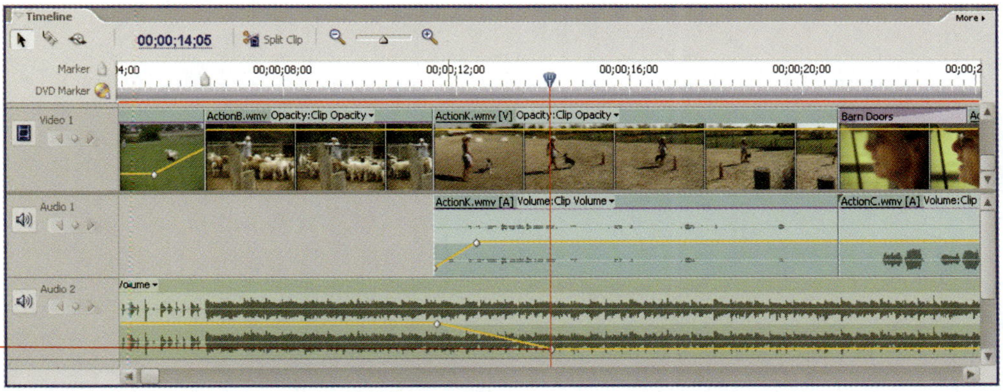


FIGURE E-21: Fading the music up

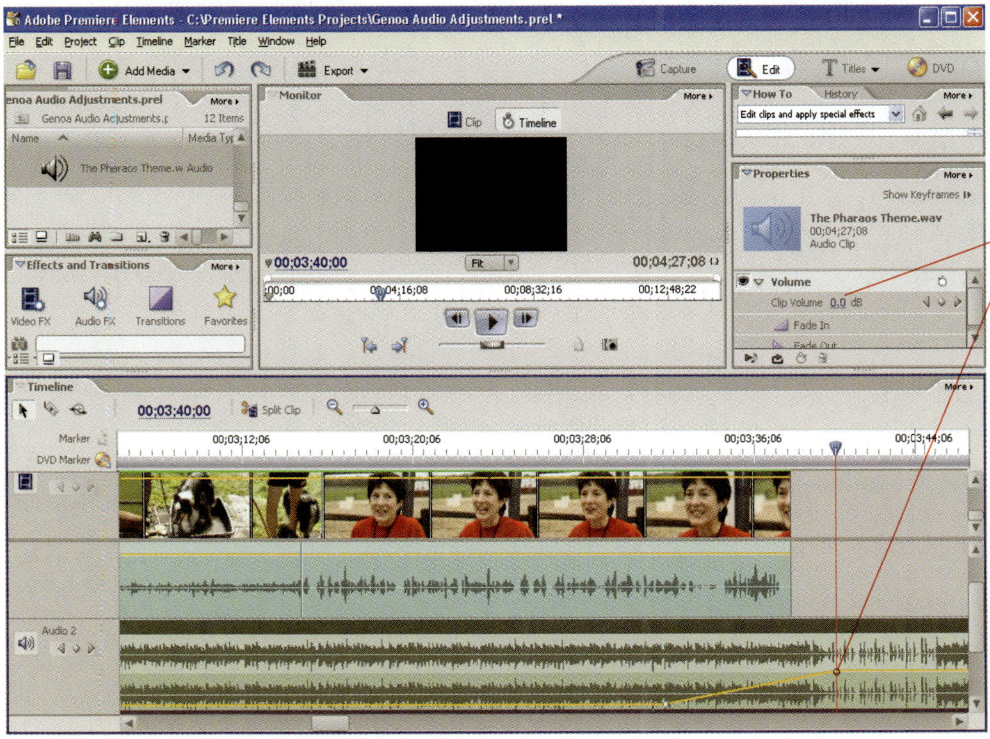

# Practice

## ▼ CONCEPTS REVIEW

**Label the elements of the Premiere Elements program window shown in Figure E-22.**

FIGURE E-22

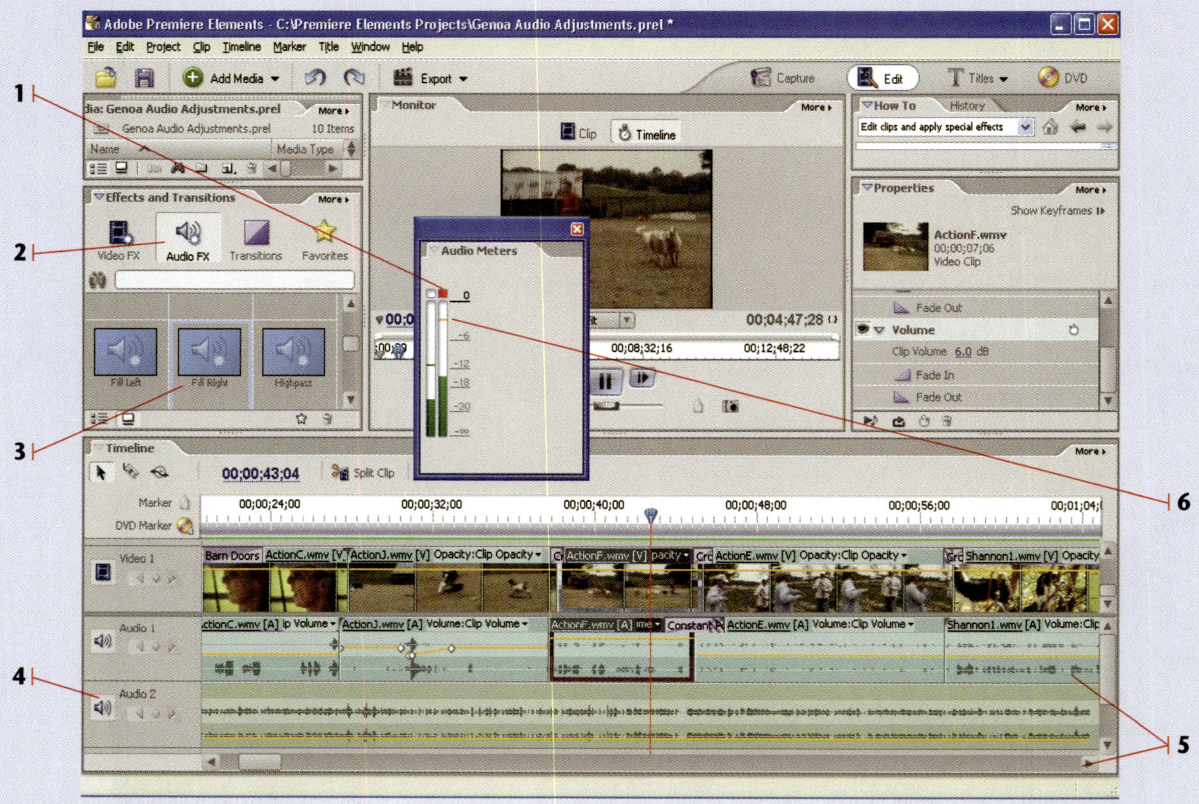


**Match each term with the statement that best describes it.**

7. **Normalize button**
8. **Set Audio Track Display Style button**
9. **Clipping**
10. **J-cut**
11. **Crossfade**
12. **Bypass**
13. **L-cut**
14. **Transient**

**a.** Hides or shows the audio waveform
**b.** Audio effect property that turns the effect on or off
**c.** Edit in which the out point of an audio track extends past the out point of a linked video clip
**d.** Dissolve-type audio transition
**e.** Adjusts the audio level of a clip to optimize overall volume
**f.** Graphical representation of a loud burst of sound
**g.** Occurs when audio levels are above the recommended output range
**h.** Edit in which the in point of an audio track extends before the in point of a linked video clip

**Select the best answer from the list of choices.**

**15. Amplitude is a measure of:**
- **a.** Frequency.
- **b.** Decibels.
- **c.** Treble tones.
- **d.** Loudness.

**16. Unintended hiss or distortion in an audio clip is known as:**
- **a.** Volume.
- **b.** Noise.
- **c.** Levels.
- **d.** Transience.

**17. The default duration of an audio transition is:**
- **a.** Half a second.
- **b.** One second.
- **c.** Two seconds.
- **d.** Three seconds.

**18. The Fill Right effect:**
- **a.** Adds sound from the right audio channel to the left audio channel.
- **b.** Adds sound from the left audio channel to the right audio channel.
- **c.** Replaces sound in the right audio channel with sound from the left audio channel.
- **d.** Replaces sound in the left audio channel with sound from the right audio channel.

**19. How many audio tracks can a Premiere Elements project contain?**
- **a.** Up to 24
- **b.** Up to 56
- **c.** Up to 99
- **d.** Up to 124

**20. To edit video clips to the beat of a musical sound track, cut each clip at the:**
- **a.** Keyframe on the audio track.
- **b.** Clipping point of the audio track.
- **c.** Beginning of a transient on the waveform.
- **d.** Transient peak on the waveform.

## ▼ SKILLS REVIEW

**1. Adjust gain in a clip.**
- **a.** Start Premiere Elements.
- **b.** Open the file PE E-2.prel from the drive and folder where your Data Files are located.
- **c.** Save the file as **Clown Audio Transitions** in the *YourName* folder where you are saving files for this book.
- **d.** Open the Audio Meters window.
- **e.** Play the Cam2_b clip, observing the Audio Meters window as it plays.
- **f.** Open the Clip Gain dialog box.
- **g.** Normalize the gain, then close the dialog box.
- **h.** Normalize the gain in all the clips, starting with Cam2_b and ending with Cam2_d (a total of seven clips).
- **i.** Play the Cam2_b clip, then save your changes to the project.

## ▼ SKILLS REVIEW (CONTINUED)

**2. Adjust clip volume.**

- **a.** Normalize the audio gain of the Cam2_a clip.
- **b.** Expand the Volume category for the Cam2_a clip on the Properties panel.
- **c.** Activate audio looping, then play only the audio of the current clip.
- **d.** Stop the playback of the audio.
- **e.** Change the Clip Volume property to 2.0.
- **f.** Move to the beginning of the clip, then on the Properties panel, display keyframes and toggle animation on for the Clip Volume property.
- **g.** Move to frame 00;00;10;00, add a keyframe, move to frame 00;00;10;15, then change the Clip Volume to –0.2.
- **h.** Move to frame 00;00;11:05, then change the Clip Volume to 2.0.
- **i.** Save your changes to the project, then play the clip.

**3. View an audio waveform.**

- **a.** Select the Cam1_b clip, then zoom in on the Timeline as large as possible and so that the you can see the entire clip.
- **b.** Change the Track Size to Large.
- **c.** Normalize the gain of the selected clip.
- **d.** Drag the properties graph of the audio track up until the pop-up window reads approximately 2 dB.
- **e.** Drag the current-time indicator slowly over the transient that begins at frame 00;00;22;04.
- **f.** Move to just before the transient at frame 00;00;22;03, add a keyframe on the Audio 1 track, click the transient peak at frame 00;00;22;06, add a keyframe, then add a third keyframe near the end of the transient, at frame 00;00;22;13.
- **g.** Drag the middle keyframe down to approximately –.68 dB.
- **h.** Save your changes to the project, then play the clip.

**4. Perform a J-cut or L-cut.**

- **a.** Play the Cam2_d and Cam1_e clips, observing the edit point between them.
- **b.** Extend the out point of the audio track of the Cam2_d clip by approximately 2 seconds. (*Hint*: Press [Alt] while dragging the out point.)
- **c.** Select the entire Cam2_d clip, drag it right to align the video out point with the beginning of the Cam1_e clip, then overlay the clip.
- **d.** Close the gap created by the move.
- **e.** Save your changes to the project, then watch the edited segment.

**5. Add an audio transition.**

- **a.** Add a Constant Power transition to the edit point between the Cam2_d audio clip and the Cam1_e audio clip, then change the duration of the transition to 2 seconds.
- **b.** Add a Constant Gain transition that aligns at the beginning to the Cam2_d clip.
- **c.** Add a Constant Power transition between the Cam2_b clip and the Cam1_c clip.
- **d.** Add a Constant Gain transition between the Cam1_c clip and the Cam2_c clip at frame 00;00;36;16, then change the alignment of the transition to Center at Cut.
- **e.** Replace the transition you just added with a Constant Power transition.
- **f.** Fade out the volume at the end of the Cam1_e clip using a button on the Properties panel.
- **g.** Save your changes to the project.

## ▼ SKILLS REVIEW (CONTINUED)

**6. Apply an audio effect.**

**a.** Add the PitchShifter effect to the Cam1_c clip.
**b.** Change the PitchShifter preset to Booo!
**c.** Add the PitchShifter effect to the Cam1_d clip, then change the preset to A quint up.
**d.** Add the Delay effect to the Cam2_c clip and the Cam1_d clip.
**e.** Add a DeNoiser filter to the Cam2_a clip.
**f.** Expand the Custom Setup category in the Properties panel, click the Reduction text box, type **–10**, then press [Enter].
**g.** Render the work area, then save your changes to the project.

**7. Adding a sound clip.**

**a.** Open the Add Media dialog box, then add the Theme Song.mp3 file to the project.
**b.** View the Theme Song clip in the Monitor panel.
**c.** View the Properties window for the clip, then close the Properties window.
**d.** Play the first few moments of the clip.
**e.** Add the clip to the Audio 2 track, aligning it at the beginning of the movie.
**f.** Save your changes to the project.

**8. Mix audio tracks.**

**a.** Delete the audio track of the Cam1_a clip.
**b.** Drag the first keyframe in the Cam2_a clip down to –oo dB.
**c.** Add a keyframe to the Audio 2 track at frame 00;00;09;00, and another keyframe at frame 00;00;11;00.
**d.** Drag the second keyframe on the Audio 2 track to –11.28 dB. Compare your Timeline to Figure E-23.

FIGURE E-23

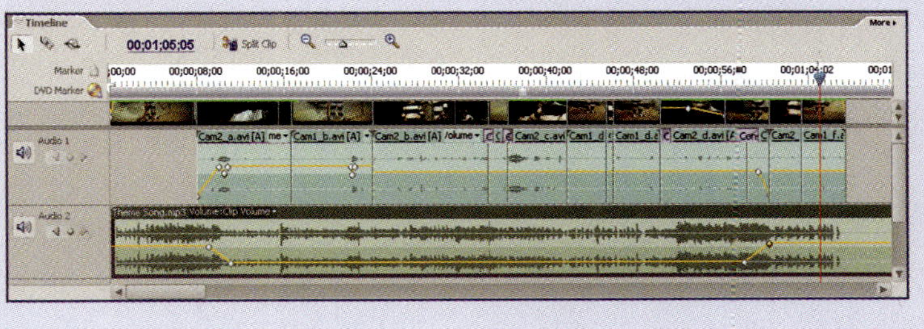

**e.** Add a keyframe to the Audio 2 track at frame 00;00;58;04, and a second keyframe at frame 00;01;00;12.
**f.** Drag the second keyframe up to .85 dB. Compare your screen to Figure E-23.
**g.** Save your changes, play the movie, then close it and exit Premiere Elements.

## ▼ INDEPENDENT CHALLENGE 1

The head of the film festival has provided you with a soundtrack to add to your trailer for the fest. She's asked that you mix it with the existing sound so that music plays under the entire trailer, except where other music is present. First, you'll need to trim the clip to an appropriate size for the movie. Currently, the clip is over two minutes long. You want to leave a little extra music at the end to play under the titles that will contain information about the film festival, so you want the clip to run approximately 1 minute and 20 seconds.

**a.** Start Premiere Elements.
**b.** Open the file PE E-3.prel from the drive and folder where your Data Files are located, then save it as **Film Fest With Soundtrack** in the *YourName* folder where you are saving files for this book.
**c.** Add the file Twelve Empty Cups.mp3 to the project, then open the new clip in the Monitor panel.
**d.** Trim the end point to 00;01;20;00, then add the trimmed clip to the Audio 2 track at the beginning of the Timeline.
**e.** Use the Fade In button on the Properties panel to fade the music clip in during the Dress for Success clip, then let the music play at 0.0 dB throughout the clip.
**f.** Add keyframes to fade the music to –6 dB during the first second of the Muffin Control clip.
**g.** Fade the music back in to 0.0 db during the first second of the Silent Breakfast clip, then fade it out to –oo dB during the last 15 frames of this clip.

## ▼ INDEPENDENT CHALLENGE 1 (CONTINUED)

**h.** Normalize the gain of the Tax Help audio clip.

**i.** Begin fading the Audio 2 back in to 0.0 dB at frame 00;00;51;20 so that it returns to 0.0 dB in two seconds, and fade the Audio 1 track out to –oo dB at these same two points. Compare your screen to Figure E-24.

FIGURE E-24

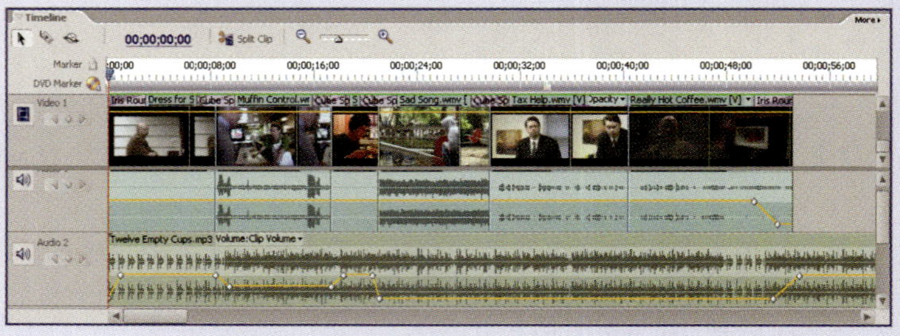

**Advanced Challenge Exercise**

ACE

- Perform a J-cut between the Tax Help clip and the Really Hot Coffee clip, so that the audio from the Really Hot Coffee clip plays for 00;00;01;15 over the video of the Tax Help clip. To create the cut, first delete audio-only frames from the out point of the Tax Help clip, then delete video-only frames from the in point of the Really Hot Coffee clip.
- Apply an audio effect of your choice to any clip in the movie.

**j.** Render the work area, save your changes to the project, watch the movie, then close the project and exit Premiere Elements.

## ▼ INDEPENDENT CHALLENGE 2

Review your documentary and decide what types of audio adjustments you want to make. Based on your vision and goals for this movie, use the skills you've learned in this unit to solve audio problems, add effects and transitions, and mix additional sounds such as music, recorded narration, or other sources.

**a.** Start Premiere Elements if necessary, open the file My Documentary Effects and Transitions.prel from the *YourName* folder where you are saving files for this book, then save it as **My Documentary With Audio Adjustments**. (*Note*: If you did not create and edit this movie, consult your instructor.)

**b.** Adjust the gain and volume in clips as needed.

**c.** Add transitions to smooth the progression of sound from one clip to the next.

**d.** Add at least one audio effect, either to solve a problem or to enhance a scene.

**e.** If you want, add a musical soundtrack, using one of the audio files in the Source Files folder, or another file if one is available on your computer.

**f.** Render the work area, then save your changes to the project.

**g.** Close the project and exit Premiere Elements.

## ▼ INDEPENDENT CHALLENGE 3

Jim, your boss at Fig Media, loves the video you are creating for the internship program. He asks you to make a few audio adjustments and add music to the piece.

**a.** Open the file Dream Job Effects and Transitions.prel from the *YourName* folder where you are saving files for this book, then save it as **Dream Job With Audio Adjustments**. (*Note*: If you did not create and edit this movie, consult your instructor.)
**b.** Add at least one J-cut or L-cut to any edit point in the movie.
**c.** Adjust the gain and volume of any clips that are too loud or too soft.
**d.** Add the Reverb audio effect with the Preset of your choice to each clip that contains dialogue.
**e.** Add at least three audio transitions.
**f.** Add the Singer Strange Theme.mp3 clip to the movie, adjust the volume to –8 dB, then fade the clip up at the beginning of the movie and out at the end.

**Advanced Challenge Exercise**

- Mix the two audio tracks so that the music dominates the soundtrack in some places, and dialogue dominates in others.
- Remove audio from the Audio 1 track in any clips where you think it is unnecessary.

**h.** Save your changes, render the work area, then preview the movie.
**i.** Save and close the project, then exit Premiere Elements.

## ▼ INDEPENDENT CHALLENGE 4

You are continuing to work on the Internet Education video for the upcoming conference on Cinema and Education. You want to add a soundtrack that will play softly under parts of the movie so that you can talk over parts of the video as it plays without adjusting the volume manually.

**a.** Connect to the Internet, then use your favorite search engine to search for sites that offer public domain song files, such as www.mp34u.com. For each Web site you visit, read the About page and/or Copyright pages on the site to learn whether you can legally download songs. Because you are using the file for educational purposes, downloading is often permissible, but the rules and guidelines vary by site.
**b.** Download a file to use as the soundtrack.
**c.** Open the file Internet Education Transitions.prel from the *YourName* folder where you are saving files for this book, then save it as **Internet Education With Soundtrack**. (*Note*: If you did not create and edit this movie, consult your instructor.)
**d.** Add the music clip to the Audio 2 track, adding two or more instances of the clip if it is too short to span the entire movie.
**e.** Mix the two audio tracks so that dialogue is audible in only the beginning and end of each clip, and then fades out completely as music fades in to approximately –6 dB.
**f.** Fade the music up to 0.0 dB at the end of the movie.
**g.** When you are finished, close the project and exit Premiere Elements.

## ▼ VISUAL WORKSHOP

Open the file PE E-4.prel from the drive and folder where your Data Files are located, then save it as **Butterfly Soundtrack** in the *YourName* folder where you are saving files for this book. Add and arrange the clips as shown so that your screen matches the one shown in Figure E-25. Use the keyframes in the figure as a guide; you do not need to duplicate the exact frame numbers. (*Hint*: The same video transition is used between each video clip.) When you are finished, save your changes to the project. Press [PrtScr], paste the image into your word-processing program, print a copy, then exit your word processor and Premiere Elements.

FIGURE E-25

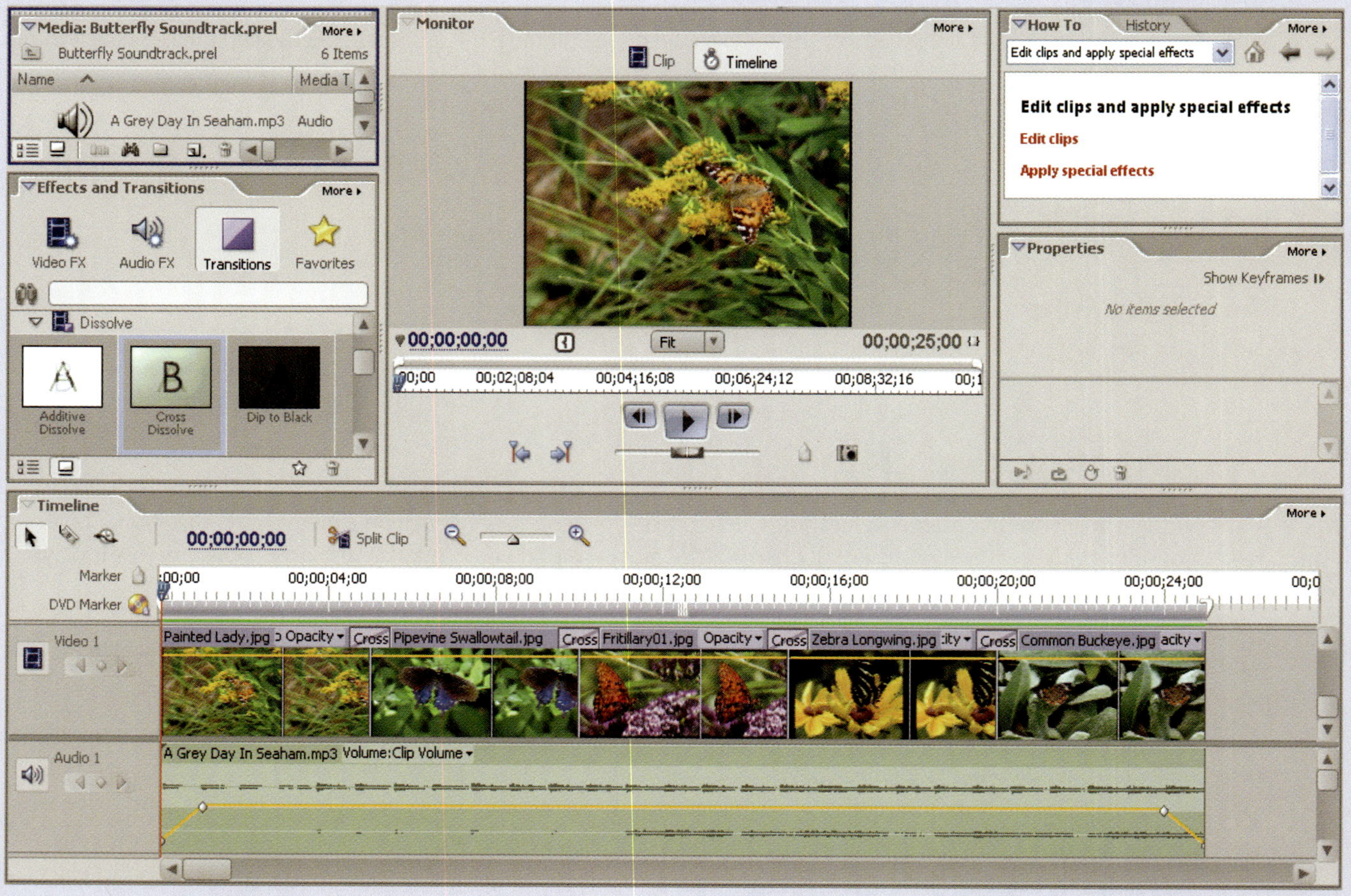

UNIT
F
Premiere Elements 2.0

# Adding Titles and Credits

## OBJECTIVES

- Create a title clip
- Edit a title clip
- Add a title to a movie
- Add an image to a title
- Work with crawling titles
- Create credits
- Work with rolling credits
- Work with shapes

Titles and credits are text within a movie that identifies its title, cast and crew, people, places, dates, or other important information. Premiere Elements includes a Titles workspace where you can create and edit titles and credits; you can then add them to the Timeline and work with them just like other clips in a movie. You're ready to add titles and credits to the Genoa Stock video. You've consulted with Shannon to finalize a title and subtitle for the movie, and she wants credits and contact information to appear at the end of the movie. You've also met with Luis to gather additional production information for the credits.

UNIT F
Premiere Elements 2.0

# Creating a Title Clip

A **title** usually appears at the beginning of a movie to introduce it. A **title sequence**, which consists of two or more titles, can be used to introduce other important information, including **credits**, or acknowledgments of the cast and crew. In Premiere Elements, you create a title in the Titles workspace, and it is automatically added to the project as a clip on the Media panel. You then add it to the Timeline to edit it just like other media clips. Shannon wants the title for her movie to include the film's main title and subtitle.

## STEPS

1. **Open the file PE F-1.prel from the drive and folder where your Data Files are located, then save it as Genoa Titles and Credits in the *YourName* folder where you are saving files for this book**

2. **Press and hold the Titles button on the task bar, then click Template**

   The Templates dialog box opens, listing nine categories of graphic and text templates suitable for common types of movies, such as narrative films (in the Entertainment category), vacation videos (in the Travel category), or business films (in the General category). Other Titles menu options include New Title, where you can create a title from scratch, and Scrolling Title or Crawling Title, where you can create a title that moves across the screen.

   > **QUICK TIP**
   > You can also start creating a new title by clicking the New Item button on the Media panel and then clicking Title.

3. **Click the Travel Expand icon, expand the Countryside theme, then click and preview each template in the Countryside theme**

   The Travel category includes 12 themes, and the Countryside theme contains four templates, as shown in Figure F-1. The countryside_title, countryside_frame, and countryside_upper3rd templates can be used for opening titles or as transitions during the movie; the countryside_credits template is intended for listing cast and crew credits. The gray checkerboard pattern indicates transparency (no background pixels) in this part of the template.

   > **QUICK TIP**
   > It's a good idea to use templates from the same theme throughout a movie, so that the movie has a consistent look.

4. **Click countryside_frame, then click OK**

   A new title clip, countryside_frame, is added to the Media panel and opens in the Titler panel of the Titles workspace, as shown in Figure F-2. This workspace contains several panels. In the **Titler panel**, you can edit and format text and graphic elements using tools on the **Tools panel**, font and alignment features on the **Main panel**, and font styles on the **Titler Styles panel**. You can also open an **Actions panel** by clicking the More button, then clicking Actions to access additional alignment options. The panels exclusive to the Titles workspace are collectively called the **Titler**. You can move or resize any Titler element, and you can float the Tools panel or the Actions panel anywhere in the workspace. Two margins offer guidance if you plan to show a video on a television. Televisions vary in how much of a video image they display, so the **title-safe margin** (the inner rectangle) indicates a reliable viewing area for text, and the **action-safe margin** (the outer rectangle) indicates a safe viewing area for action. **Placeholders** indicate suggested formatting and placement of text. The black background matte of the Timeline shows through the transparent part of the template.

   > **QUICK TIP**
   > To view safe margins in the Edit workspace, click the More button on the Monitor panel, then click Safe Margins. The margins appear in the Monitor panel where you can refer to them as you edit.

5. **Click the Countryside Title placeholder, select the text, then press [Delete]**

   The placeholder text is deleted, and the insertion point blinks in the blank text box.

6. **Type Genoa Stock & Training**

   The title is formatted like the placeholder. See Figure F-3. You can add text anywhere in a title frame by clicking; if you don't type any text, the new text box is deleted. The Subtitle placeholder is currently obscured by the main title.

7. **Save your changes to the project**

**FIGURE F-1: Templates dialog box**

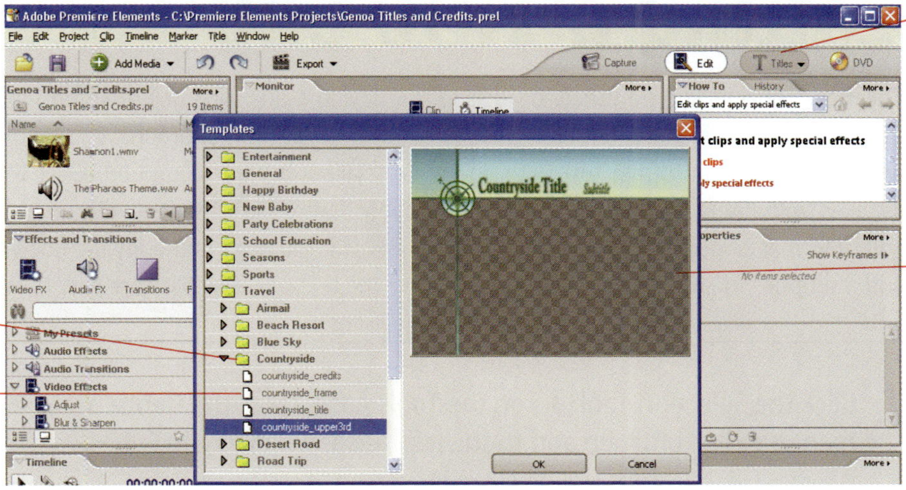


**FIGURE F-2: Titles workspace**

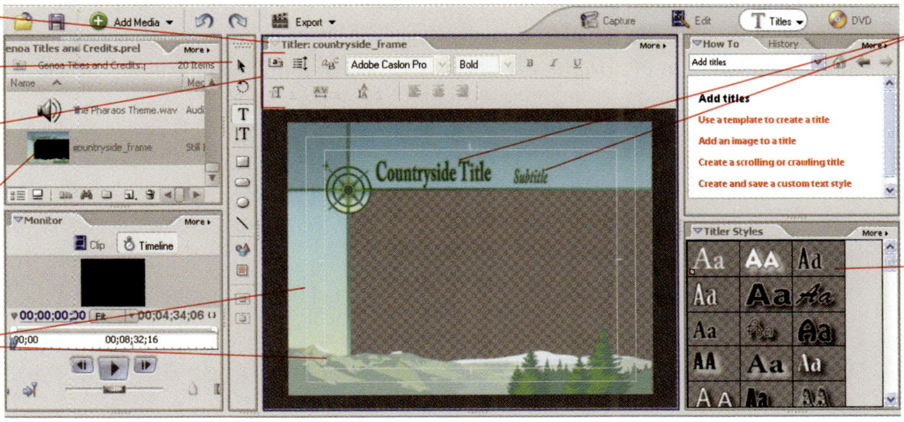


**FIGURE F-3: Title frame**

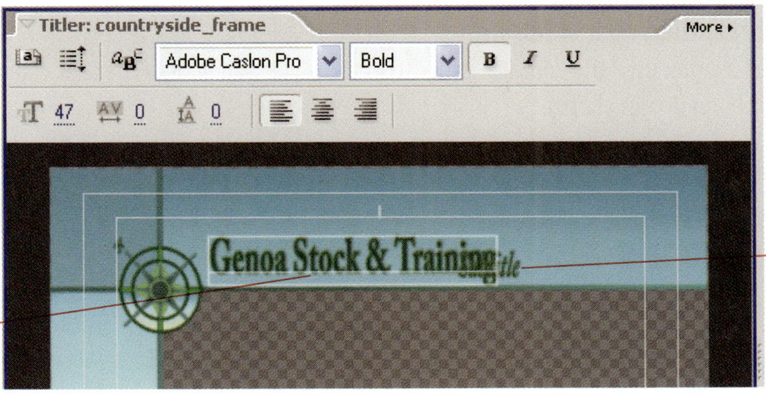


## Production Matters

### Understanding titles and credits

In the early days of filmmaking, titles were written or painted on title cards and then filmed for use in the movie. In silent films, these cards were also used to convey dialogue and summarize action. Today, you'll often hear the terms titles and credits used interchangeably. In general, a film starts with a title sequence, which includes the name of the film, the principal cast, and the most important production staff (such as director, cinematographer, and composer). Most films end with a long list of all cast and crew credits, plus any acknowledgements or other information about the film. However, some filmmakers choose to include detailed credits at the beginning of a film rather than saving these details for the end. In Premiere Elements, the term "title" can refer to either a title clip or a credit clip; technically, they are the same type of object. It's the filmmaker's intention that distinguishes a title or title sequence from a closing list of credits.

UNIT
F
Premiere Elements 2.0

# Editing a Title Clip

The Titler panel includes a variety of tools for modifying a title clip, including tools for editing text, adding graphics, and moving and formatting text and graphics. Any text or graphic you can modify is referred to as an **object**. You can format text with any font installed on your computer. Over two dozen fonts come installed with Premiere Elements, and you probably have others installed with other programs. In order to edit or format an object, you must first select it. You need to modify the title you created so you can add a subtitle. You also want to format and move the text boxes so they are easy to read.

## STEPS

**QUICK TIP**

The Type Tool on the Tools panel is selected by default.

**QUICK TIP**

If you don't have the Lithos Pro White 94 font installed on your computer, click a different swatch on the Titler Styles panel.

**QUICK TIP**

You can also activate the Text Tool by double-clicking in a text box.

**TROUBLE**

You may need to wait a few moments for the fonts beginning with "L" to appear.

1. **Click the Selection Tool on the Tools panel, click the Genoa Stock & Training text box, then drag it slightly up and to the left, as shown in Figure F-4**

   A border and sizing handles surround an object when it is selected.

2. **Click the Lithos Pro White 94 swatch on the Titler Styles panel**

   The selected text is formatted in the new style. The Styles panel includes **styles** for formatting objects with a preset combination of attributes. You can also format individual attributes by using the Font list, Style list, and formatting buttons on the Main panel.

3. **Drag the Font Size scrub pointer on the panel to 52**

   The Genoa text is enlarged. In addition to changing font, font style, and font size, you can use tools on the Main panel to browse for a font installed on your computer if it doesn't appear in the font list, and to create a new title clip that duplicates the changes you've made to the current title.

4. **Click the Subtitle placeholder, click the Type Tool on the Tools panel, select the text, then type An introduction**

5. **Click the Font list arrow Adobe Caslon Pro on the Main panel, press [L] to display fonts starting with L, then click Lithos Pro**

   Because you used the Font list rather than the Styles panel, only the font changes. The font color and other attributes do not change.

6. **Click the Color Properties button on the Tools panel**

   The Color Properties dialog box opens, where you can change thickness and color of the **stroke** or outline, the color of the **fill** or inside color, and the properties of the **shadow**, if one exists. You can also create a **gradient**, or blend of colors. See Table F-1 for an overview of all the ways you can use the Tools panel to create and modify text and shapes.

7. **Change the R: value to 94, the G: value to 130, and the B: value to 121, as shown in Figure F-5, then click OK**

   You can choose a color by clicking it on the palette, by entering red, green, and blue (RGB) values, or by clicking the Eyedropper button, and then clicking a color on the screen to sample it.

8. **Click on the Tools panel, drag the An Introduction text box slightly down and to the left so it doesn't intersect with the main title and is within the title-safe margin, then save your changes to the project**

   See Figure F-6. The two text boxes just barely touch, but the text within them does not overlap.

FIGURE F-4: Moving text

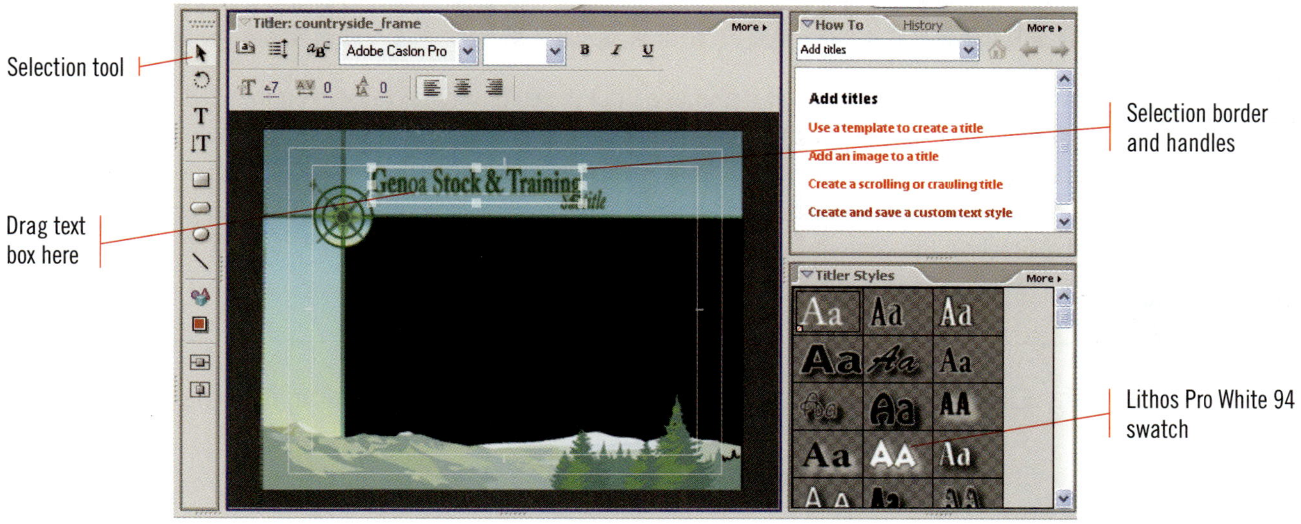


FIGURE F-5: Color Properties dialog box

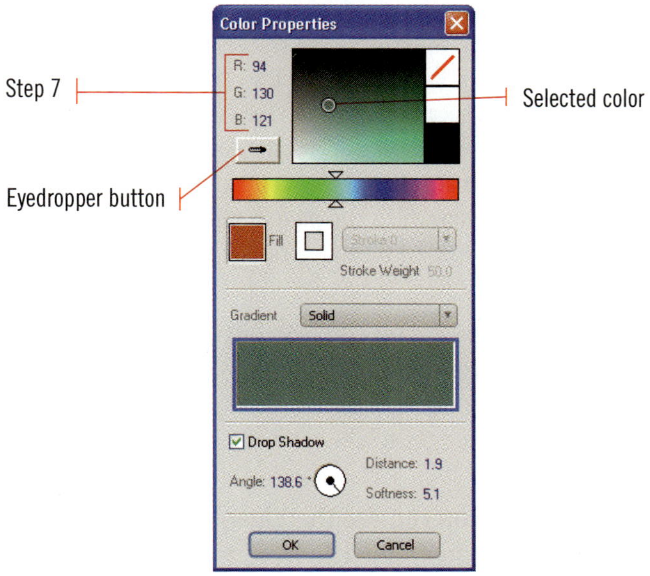


FIGURE F-6: Completed text

TABLE F-1: Tools panel tools

| button | name | button | name |
|---|---|---|---|
| | Selection Tool | | Ellipse Tool |
| | Rotation Tool | | Line Tool |
| | Type Tool | | Add Image |
| | Vertical Type Tool | | Color Properties |
| | Rectangle Tool | | Vertical Center |
| | Rounded Rectangle Tool | | Horizontal Center |

UNIT
F
Premiere Elements 2.0

# Adding a Title to a Movie

When you create a title clip, it becomes part of the current project (a clip on the Media panel), but it is not yet part of the movie. To add it to the movie, you drag it to the Timeline; you can then apply any effects and transitions you want, and you can trim or lengthen it as necessary. The default duration of a title clip is the same as a still image—five seconds. If you edit the contents of a title clip in the Titler panel after adding it to the Timeline, the contents of the clip are also updated in the Media panel. The title is complete, so you're ready to add it to the movie and then edit the clip on the Timeline.

## STEPS

1. **Click the countryside_frame clip in the Media panel, then drag it to the beginning of the Video 1 track on the Timeline**
   The other clips on the Timeline shift right to make room for the new clip.

2. **Press [Home] if necessary, then play the first two clips**
   The movie plays in the Monitor panel, which is docked under the Media panel in the Titles workspace and is much smaller than in the Edit workspace. The Titler panel does not preview the movie; rather it continues to display the title clip. However, when you pause the playback, the current frame appears in the Titler panel, as shown in Figure F-7. This is because the Show Video command under the More button in the Titler panel is active. The **Show Video command** displays the current video frame for reference purposes only, so that when you're editing and formatting titles that contain transparent areas, you can see how the title will interact with the video frames upon which you plan to superimpose the titles. This command is not a substitute for using the Monitor panel to view the movie on the Timeline.

3. **Click the Edit button on the task bar**
   While you can perform basic editing tasks using the Timeline and Monitor panel in the Titles workspace, once you create the title, it's easier to work in the Edit workspace, where you can take full advantage of all the available editing tools and view the results in a larger Monitor panel.

4. **Resize the Timeline so you can see the Video 1 and Video 2 tracks, zoom in if necessary, then drag the countryside_frame clip from the Video 1 track to the Video 2 track, aligning it with the beginning of the ActionA clip, as shown in Figure F-8**

5. **Close the gap created by the movie, render the work area, play the first clip, then save your changes**
   The title is superimposed over the ActionA clip, so the transparent area of the title clip shows the first five seconds of that clip.

6. **Drag the out point of the countyside_frame clip to 00;00;09;19, expand the Video Transitions category on the Effects and Transitions panel, expand the Slide category, then add a Slash Slide video transition to the end of the clip**

7. **Change the duration of the selected transition to 2 seconds, select the countyside_frame clip, then change the opacity properties so the clip fades in**

8. **Render the work area, play the first two clips, then save your changes**
   The title is integrated into the movie, and the transition occurs during the ActionB clip, as shown in Figure F-9.

**QUICK TIP**

You can also edit movies using a television monitor attached to your computer through your DV camcorder. Click Project on the menu bar, point to Project Settings, click General, click Playback Settings, and specify your equipment configuration.

**QUICK TIP**

You can use a title in a different project by exporting it; to do so, click File on the menu bar, point to Export, click Title, then name and save the file.

FIGURE F-7: Adding a title to the movie

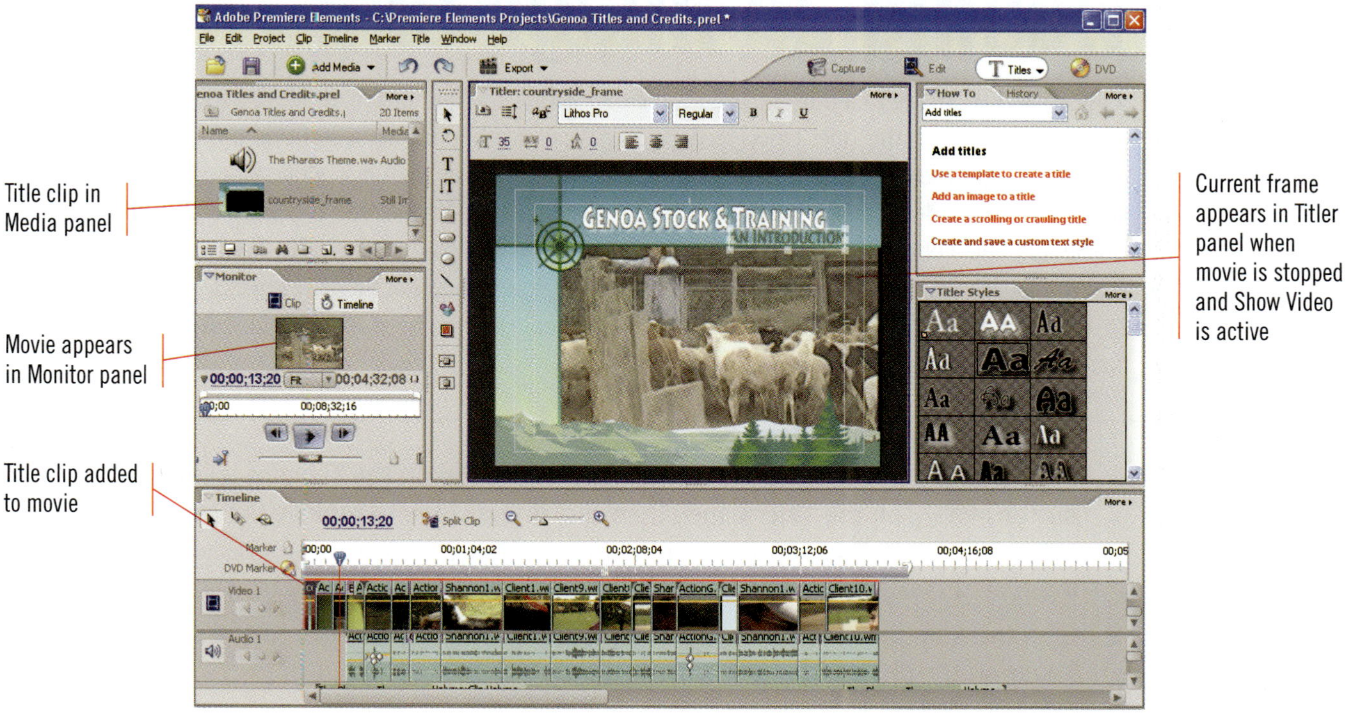


FIGURE F-8: Moving a title clip

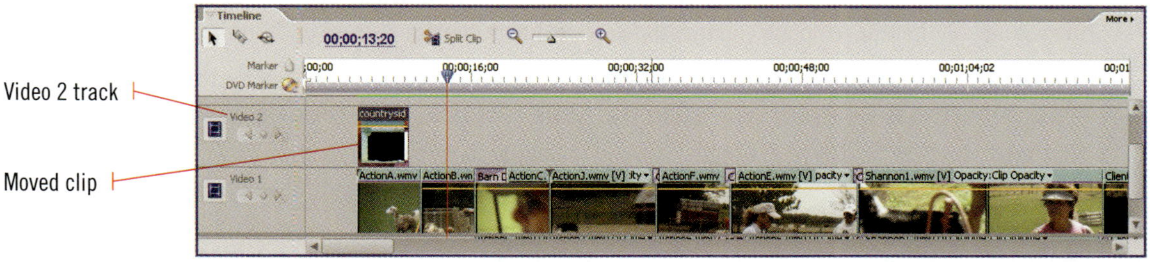


FIGURE F-9: Completed title in action

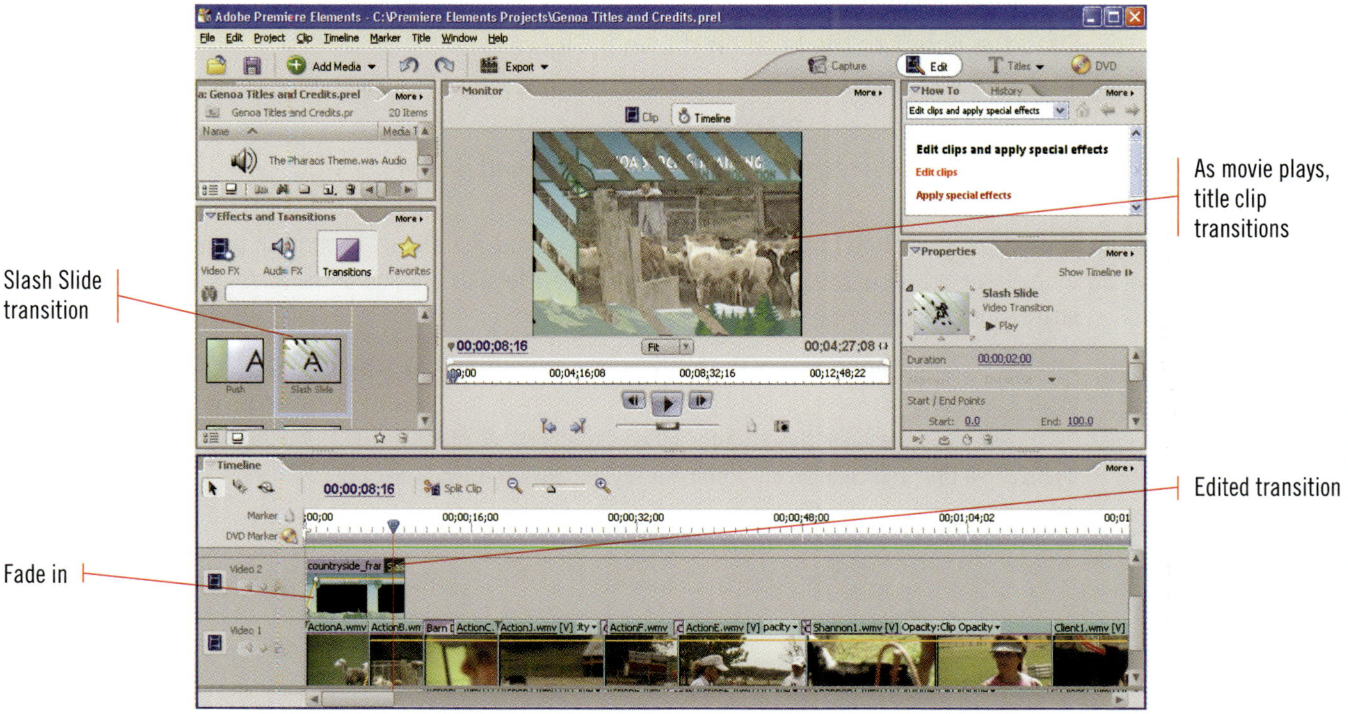

UNIT F

Premiere Elements 2.0

# Adding an Image to a Title

You can add an image to a title, and you can create simple images for use in titles by using the shape tools on the Tools panel in the Titles workspace. If you have Photoshop Elements installed on your computer, you can edit images there and use them in your titles. You can add an image to a title when you are creating it or after you've added it to the Timeline. Once you've added an image, you can work with it like any other object in a title. For example, you can use the Arrange commands to change the layer order of a image, so that it appears closer to the front or back of a **stack** or combination of multiple objects. You want to add an image of a herding dog to the title you created. First you need to open the title in the Titles workspace so you can modify it.

## STEPS

**QUICK TIP**
The background area in a title is black unless you superimpose it with another clip, change the background color, or reduce the opacity.

1. **Press [Home], double-click the countryside_frame clip on the Timeline, click the More button More ▸ on the Titler panel, then click Show Video to remove the check mark**
   The title opens in the Titles workspace, and the background has become transparent, as indicated by the checkerboard pattern. Viewing the video frame can be distracting when you're working on other aspects of a title.
2. **Click the Add Image button on the Tools panel, then navigate to the Source Files folder on the drive and folder where your Data Files are located**
   The Import Image as Logo dialog box displays still image files in the current folder.
3. **Click Django, then click Open**
   The image fills the screen and is selected, as shown in Figure F-10. The image is bordered by a white stroke; depending on the title template you use, added images may contain a stroke or drop shadow.

**QUICK TIP**
You can also open the Scale dialog box by clicking Title on the menu bar, pointing to Transform, and then clicking Scale.

4. **Right-click the image in the Titler, point to Transform, click Scale, verify that the Uniform option button is selected, type 20 in the Scale text box, then click OK**
   The image is scaled to 20% of its original size and maintains its original proportions. If you want to distort an image while resizing it, you can click the **Non-Uniform** option button in the Scale dialog box and enter different percentages in the Horizontal and Vertical text boxes.
5. **Click the Color Properties button on the Tools panel, change the Stroke Weight value to 0, then click OK**
   The stroke is removed.
6. **Drag the object to the location shown in Figure F-11**
   The dog image is in front of the Genoa Stock text. When you add an object, it is positioned at the top of the **stacking order**—in front of any other text or graphic objects.

**TROUBLE**
Be careful not to click Send to Back, or you will send the image to the back of the layer.

7. **Right-click the object, point to Arrange, click Send Backward, right-click the object again, point to Arrange, then click Send Backward**
   The dog image is behind the Genoa Stock text. You can use the Arrange commands to move an object closer to the front or back of the stacking order. See Table F-2 for a description of the Arrange commands and keyboard shortcuts.
8. **Switch to the Edit workspace, render the work area, play the title sequence, then save your changes**
   As shown in Figure F-12, the Monitor reflects the changes made to the title clip. Whenever you make a change to a title, the changes are automatically updated in the Edit workspace.

**FIGURE F-10:** Adding an image to a title

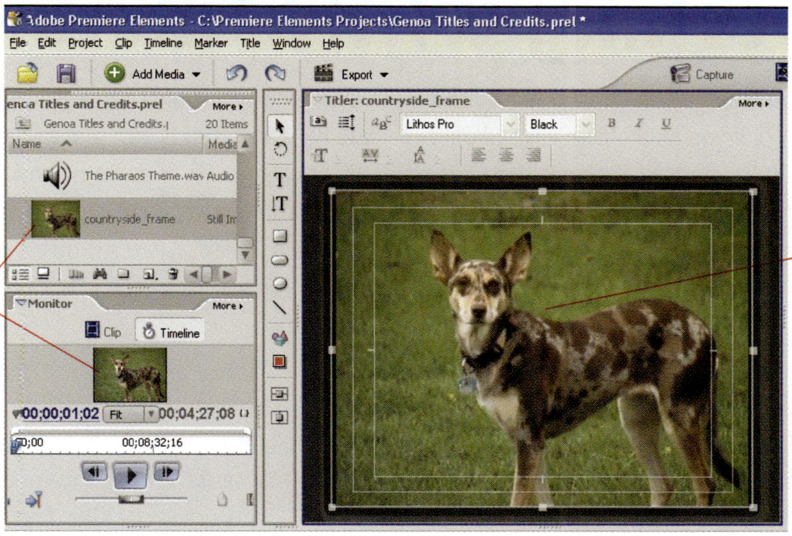


Changes to title are reflected in all panels

Added image

**FIGURE F-11:** Moving an image

Step 6

**FIGURE F-12:** Modified title in action

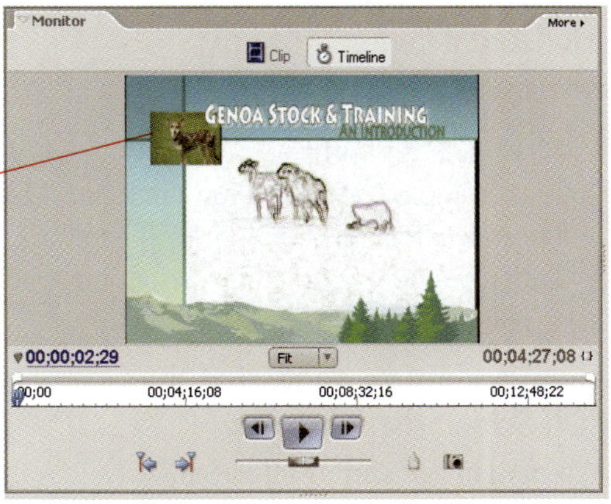


Image is behind title text

**TABLE F-2:** Arrange commands

| command | what it does | keyboard shortcut |
|---|---|---|
| **Bring to Front** | Moves the selected object to the front of the stack | [Ctrl][Shift] [ ] ] |
| **Bring Forward** | Moves the selected object one layer closer to the front | [Ctrl] [ ] ] |
| **Send to Back** | Moves the selected object to the back of the stack | [Ctrl][Shift] [ [ ] |
| **Send Backward** | Moves the selected object one layer closer to the back | [Ctrl] [ [ ] |

UNIT
F
Premiere Elements 2.0

# Working with Crawling Titles

Most title and credit templates are still images, and their appearance changes only if you apply transitions or effects or if you animate an effect. You can create titles and credits that move across the screen, or edit existing titles or credits to achieve these results. Text that moves up or down is a **rolling** title or credit, and text that moves left or right is a **crawling** title or credit. You use the Roll/Crawl options in the Titler to modify a title or credit made from a template or from scratch. You want to create a title that identifies Shannon to viewers and add it to the first Shannon1 clip.

## STEPS

1. **Click the New Item button on the Media panel, then click Title**

   The Templates dialog box opens. You could use one of the countryside templates to create the title so it matches the opening title in the movie. However, you want the title to include only text so that it conveys the information without distracting from the clip.

2. **Click Cancel, type Shannon intro in the New Title dialog box, then click OK**

   The Titler opens and displays the new Shannon intro title, a blank, transparent clip.

**TROUBLE**

If you used a different style in the Styles panel in Lesson 1, use that style in this lesson.

3. **Click the Lithos Pro White 94 style swatch on the Styles panel, click anywhere on the canvas, then type Shannon Wolfe**

   The text is formatted with the attributes of this style. The text box resizes automatically to fit the text you type, because you created the text box by clicking and typing text immediately. The work area adjusts if necessary to display as much text as possible. You can also create a text box by dragging to create the box before you start typing; in this case, the text **wraps**, or automatically moves to the next line, when it reaches the edge of the text box.

4. **Drag the Size scrub pointer over the Size value to change the font size to 35, press [Enter], type Owner, Genoa Stock, then click the Center button on the Main panel**

   The two lines of text are center-aligned. By default, text does not wrap when you reach the end of the title-safe margin. If you want the text to wrap automatically, you can right-click the text box and then click Word Wrap.

**QUICK TIP**

If you want to align three or more objects at once, use the options on the Actions panel; press and hold [Shift] while clicking the objects, click the More button on the Titler panel, then click Actions to open this panel.

5. **Select the Owner, Genoa Stock text, change the font size to 20, click the Selection Tool on the Tools panel, drag the text box so its bottom edge aligns with the title-safe margin, then click the Horizontal Center button**

   Compare your screen to Figure F-13.

6. **Click the More button More ▸ on the Titler panel, then click Roll/Crawl Options**

   The Roll/Crawl Options dialog box opens, as shown in Figure F-14. In this dialog box, you can set the current title or credit to roll or crawl, fine-tune how quickly the roll or crawl proceeds, and determine whether text remains stationary after reaching its destination or continues moving. See Table F-3 for a description of the options in this dialog box.

7. **Click the Crawl option button, verify that the Crawl Left option button is selected, then click the Start Off Screen check box**

   This sets the title to crawl in left, starting off-screen.

8. **Type 20 in the Ease Out text box, type 120 in the Postroll text box, then click OK**

   This sets the title to crawl in slowly and remain stationary for 120 frames after completing the crawl.

9. **Switch to the Edit workspace, drag the Shannon Intro title from the Media panel to the Video 2 track at frame 00;01;00;14, move to frame 00;01;11;14, drag the out point of the clip to the current-time indicator, as shown in F-15, render the work area, play the Shannon1 clip, then save your changes**

   The title crawls in as the camera pans to Shannon, then remains stationary for a few seconds.

**FIGURE F-13: Text box**

**FIGURE F-14: Roll/Crawl Options dialog box**

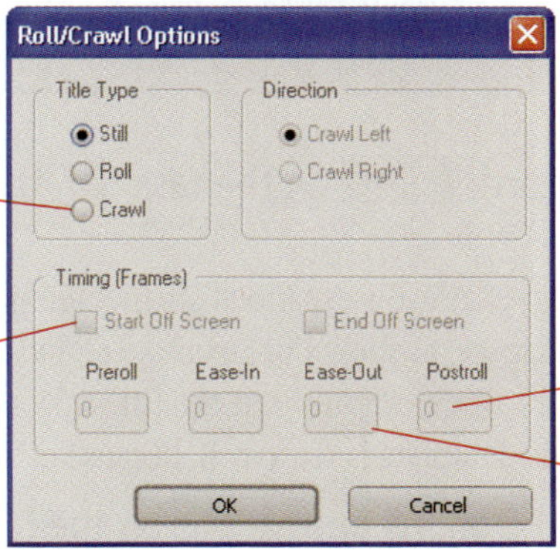


**FIGURE F-15: Adding a title to the Timeline**

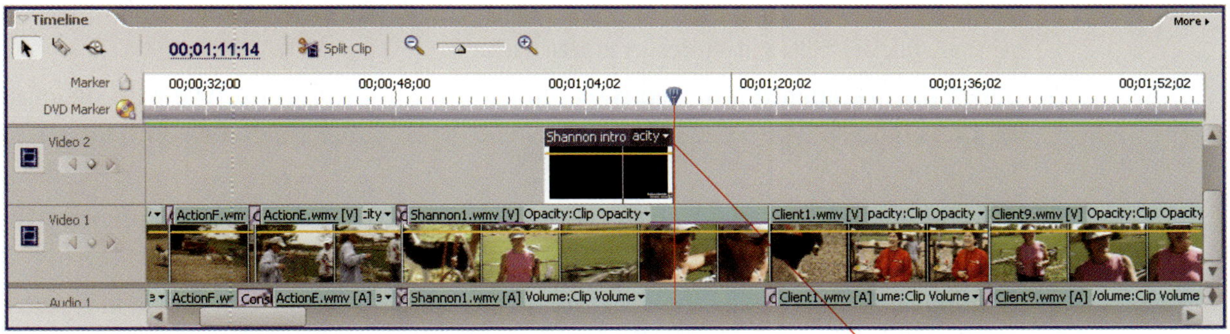


**TABLE F-3: Roll/Crawl options**

| option | description |
|---|---|
| **Still** | Title or credit does not move |
| **Roll** | Title or credit moves up or down |
| **Crawl** | Title or credit moves right or left |
| **Crawl Left/Crawl Right** | Title or credit moves left (from right edge) or right (from left edge) |
| **Start Off-Screen** | Title or credit begins off-screen, then moves in specified direction |
| **End Off-Screen** | After completing roll or crawl, title or credit continues moving off-screen |
| **Preroll** | Clip plays specified number of frames before rolling or crawling |
| **Ease-In** | Roll or crawl slowly speeds up during specified number of frames until the move completes |
| **Ease-Out** | Roll or crawl slows down during specified number of frames until the move completes |
| **Postroll** | Title or credit plays for specified number of frames after the move completes |

UNIT F

Premiere Elements 2.0

# Creating Credits

Among the more than 100 templates available for titles and credits, many are credit templates. Credits identify, or give credit to, the cast and crew of a movie; they may also provide additional information, such as the location where a movie was filmed, songs used, or a dedication. You can also use credits to thank people and organizations who assisted in the making of a movie or to provide contact information for learning more about the subject matter. Credits can come at the beginning of a movie or at the end; in many cases, some important credits are listed first as part of the title sequence, and more detailed credits come at the end. You want to add credits to the end of the movie to list the production staff and to provide contact information for viewers who want to learn more about Genoa Stock & Training.

## STEPS

**QUICK TIP**

Themes in the Templates dialog box remain expanded until you collapse them.

**QUICK TIP**

Some templates, such as blue sky_roll and woodland_roll, indicate a preset roll in their names, but others, such as countryside_credits, do not; it's always best to check the title once it's open in the Titler.

**QUICK TIP**

You can also press [Ctrl][Shift][C] to center selected text or images within a text box.

1. **Click the Titles button on the task bar, then double-click the countryside_credits template**

   The Countryside theme is already expanded in the Templates dialog box, and a countryside_credits title opens in the Titles workspace, as shown in Figure F-16. This template contains one large text box with several text placeholders. The text box extends past the title-safe margin and off the bottom of the screen. This is a good indication that this template is set to roll, because otherwise some text would be unreadable.

2. **Click the Roll/Crawl Options button on the Main panel, verify that the title is set to Roll, then click Cancel**

3. **Click the countryside_credits clip name in the Media panel, then type Production credits**

   The name of the clip changes to "Production credits" in the Media panel and in the Titler panel. You can rename a title or credit so that it's easier to keep track of.

4. **Select the first countryside credits placeholder text under Credits, type Shot on location at, press [Enter], type Genoa Stock & Training, press [Enter], then type in Genoa, Wisconsin**

5. **Select the next countryside_credits text placeholder, type Edited by, press [Enter], then type *Your Name***

6. **Continue deleting the placeholder text and replacing it with the text shown in Figure F-17; scroll down as necessary to see the bottom of the text box, then delete any remaining placeholder text**

   When working with rolling titles, the text box can be as long as necessary to include all the information. If the text box weren't longer than the frame, there wouldn't be a need to roll the credits.

7. **With the Type Tool and the text box selected, press [Ctrl][A] to select all the text, click the Font list arrow, press [L], click Lithos Pro, then click the Center button on the Main panel**

8. **Double-click the countryside_frame clip in the Media panel, click the Selection Tool on the Tools panel, click the dog image, click Edit on the menu bar, click Copy, double-click the Production credits clip in the Media panel, click Edit on the menu bar, then click Paste**

   You've created credits that are formatted consistently with the opening title, as shown in Figure F-18.

9. **Add the Production credits clip to the end of the movie on the Video 1 track, play the credits in the Monitor panel of the Titles workspace, then save your changes**

   The titles and graphic start on screen and then roll up the screen quickly.

**FIGURE F-16:** Countryside_credits title

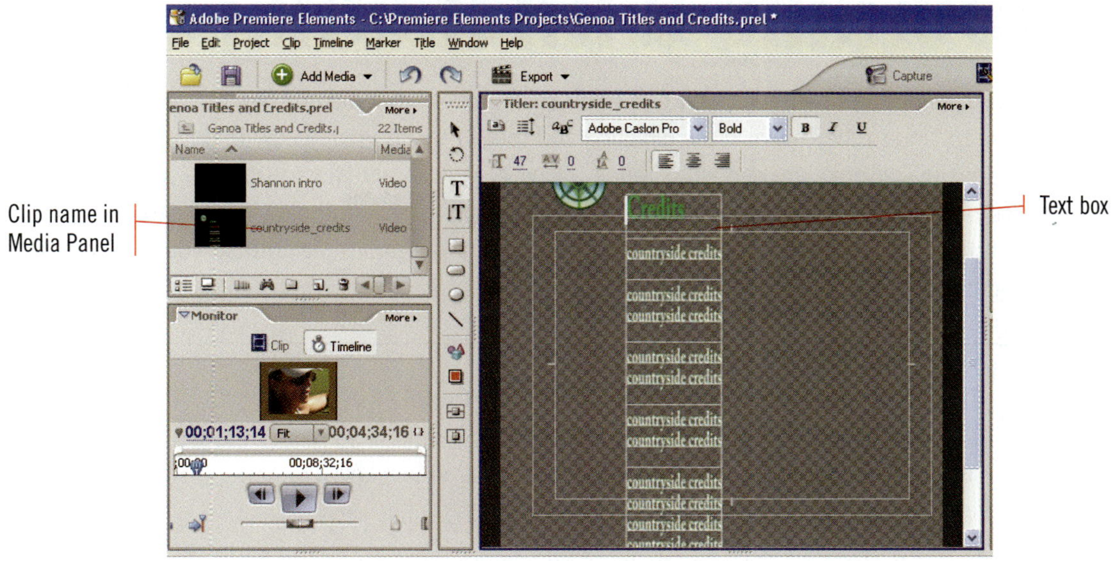


**FIGURE F-17:** Typing credits text

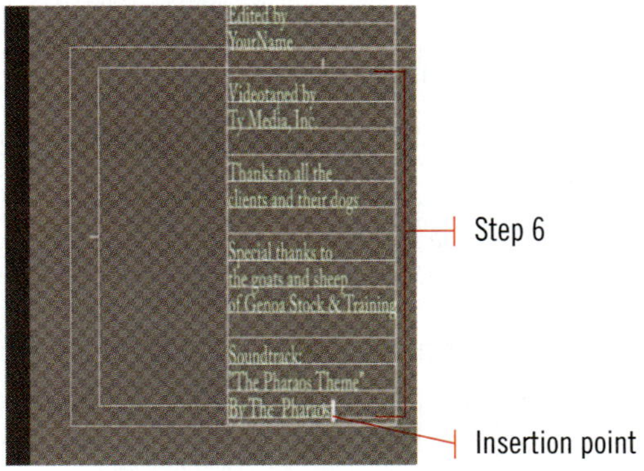


**FIGURE F-18:** Pasted image and formatted text

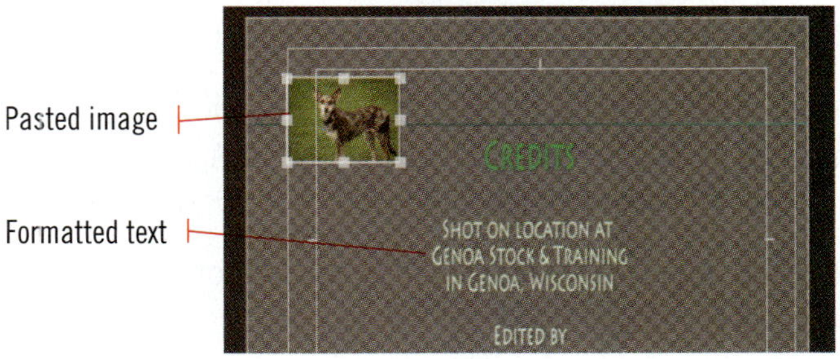


**TABLE F-4:** Main panel buttons

| button | name | button | name |
| --- | --- | --- | --- |
| | New Title Based on Current Title | | Underline |
| | Roll/Crawl Options | 100 | Size |
| | Browse | 0 | Kerning (spacing between letters) |
| Adobe Caslon Pro | Font | 0 | Leading (spacing between lines) |
| Bold | Font Style | | Left |
| | Bold | | Center |
| | Italic | | Right |

UNIT
F
Premiere Elements 2.0

# Working with Rolling Credits

Like crawling titles or credits, you can adjust rolling titles or credits so they start and end where you want them to, and so they move in the direction and speed that fits your needs. To do so, you use the Roll/Crawl Options dialog box. You can also change rolling or crawling credits to still credits. You want the credits to start on screen, begin rolling at a specified point, roll more slowly, and end on screen. To accomplish this, you make some adjustments in the Roll/Crawl Options dialog box. You also want to add a still credits clip that contains contact information for Genoa Stock.

## STEPS

**QUICK TIP**

In most cases, you want only text to crawl or roll; however, if you insert an image in a text box, the image moves, too.

**QUICK TIP**

When fine-tuning roll and crawl options, you often need to make repeated changes in the Roll/Crawl options dialog box and modify the duration of the clip until you achieve exactly the pacing that works for the clip and the movie.

**QUICK TIP**

If you want to copy the formatting in a single text or image object, rather than copying the entire clip, select the object, click the More button in the Styles panel, then click Save Style; you can then save the formatting as a swatch on the Styles panel.

1. **Click Title on the menu bar, then click Roll/Crawl Options**
   The settings in the Roll/Crawl dialog box include a Preroll of 10 frames, Ease-In of 10 frames, Ease-Out of 30 frames, and the clip ending off-screen. The Postroll text box is dimmed; it is available only if the title remains on screen after the roll completes.
2. **In the Roll/Crawl Options dialog box, double-click the Preroll text box, then type 70**
   This sets the credits to remain stationary for 70 frames before beginning to move.
3. **Click the End Off Screen check box to remove the check mark**
   The Postroll text box becomes active.
4. **Double-click the Postroll text box, type 90, compare your screen to Figure F-19, then press [Enter]**
   This sets the credits to remain stationary for 90 frames after the roll completes, and the dialog box closes. The text isn't visible in the clip thumbnail because the credits are now set to start off-screen.
5. **On the Timeline, move to frame 00;04;00;08, then drag the out point of the clip to the current-time indicator**
   The duration of the clip is now long enough to fit the settings you specified in the Roll/Crawl Options dialog box and allow the viewer ample time to read the information.
6. **Click the New Title Based on Current Title button on the Main panel**
   The New Title dialog box opens, as shown in Figure F-20.
7. **Type For more info in the Name text box, then click OK**
   A duplicate of the Production Credits clip opens in the Titler panel, named "For more info." Creating a duplicate is a quick way to copy the formatting and elements in one title or credit, for use in creating another.
8. **Click the Roll/Crawl Options button, click the Still option button in the Roll/Crawl Options dialog box, then click OK**
   The objects on this clip will not roll; they will remain stationary.
9. **Select the text Credits in the text box, type Contact us, delete the remaining text in the text box, type the text shown in Figure F-21, then save your changes**

FIGURE F-19: Adjusted settings in Roll/Crawl Options dialog box

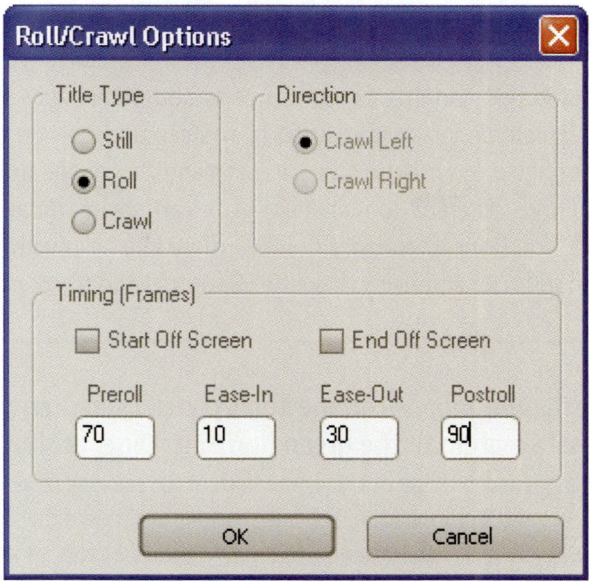


FIGURE F-20: New Title dialog box

New Title Based on Current Title button

New Title dialog box

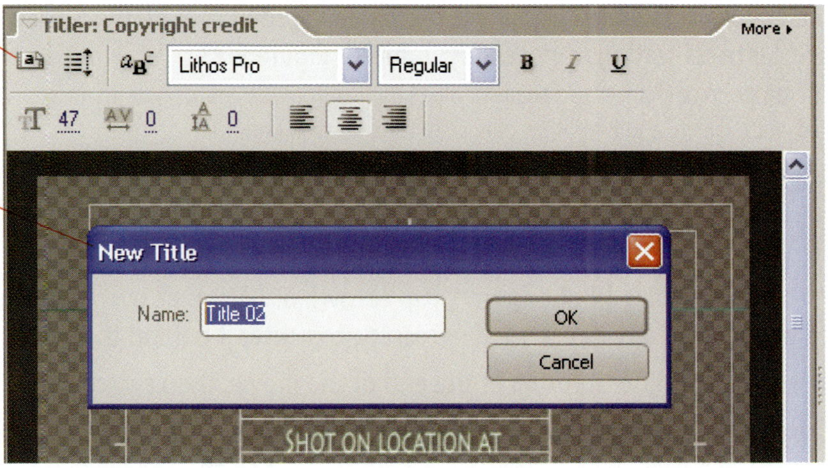


FIGURE F-21: Text for still credits clip

Step 9

# Working with Shapes

In addition to adding text and images, you can also add original designs to a title or credit, whether it's created from a template design or from scratch. You can use tools on the Tools panel to add and format lines and shapes, and you can use the Arrange commands to change the stacking order of multiple shapes. By experimenting with different combinations, you can create visual effects that range from subtle to stunning. You want to enhance the "For more info" clip with a shape that samples a color from the countryside_credits clip and helps draw the viewer's eye to the contact information.

## STEPS

**QUICK TIP**

If you create a title from scratch, the default color properties are white fill, white stroke, and no drop shadow.

**TROUBLE**

Your color values do not need to match the dialog box exactly; however, if you did not sample a shade of blue, try sampling the color again.

**QUICK TIP**

To insert an image directly into a line of text, click Title on the menu bar, point to Image, then click Insert Image into Text.

1. **Click the Rectangle Tool on the Tools panel, then drag from the upper-left corner of the title-safe margin to the green horizontal line, as shown in Figure F-22**

   A rectangle shape is added to the canvas at the front of the stacking order and is selected. The shape has a white fill, a green stroke, and a drop shadow. The initial color properties of the shape are based on the template used to create the title. See Table F-5 to learn how to use keyboard shortcuts and selection handles to draw shapes with greater control.

2. **Verify that you can see the countryside_frame clip in the Media panel, right-click the rectangle in the Title panel, then click Color Properties in the shortcut menu**

3. **Click the Stroke button, click the Eyedropper button, click the upper-left corner of the countryside_frame clip in the Media panel; then change the Stroke Weight, Distance, and Softness settings if necessary to match Figure F-23**

   The stroke color changes to a shade of blue sampled from the countryside_frame clip, and the color values (R for Red, G for Green, and B for Blue) change to the color you sampled.

4. **Click OK, drag the rectangle on top of the text CONTACT US, right-click the shape, point to Arrange, then click Send to Back**

   The shape moves to the back of the stacking order, and frames the "CONTACT US" text.

5. **Press [Left Arrow], [Right Arrow], [Up Arrow], or [Down arrow] to move the selected shape by one pixel in any direction, if necessary, to center it behind the text**

6. **Insert the For more info clip at the end of the movie, then switch to the Edit workspace**

7. **Expand the Dissolve category on the Effects and Transitions panel, add a Cross Dissolve transition between the Production credits clip and the For more info clip, then change the Opacity properties of the For more info clip so it fades out**

8. **Trim the out point of the The Pharaos Theme clip on the Audio 2 track so it aligns with the end of the For more info clip, change the Clip Volume properties so the clip fades out, render the work area, play the closing credits sequence, then save your changes**

   As shown in Figure F-24, the new shape helps to draw attention to the contact information clip, and the transition you added to the clips creates a smooth ending to the movie.

9. **Close the project, then exit Premiere Elements**

FIGURE F-22: Drawing a rectangle

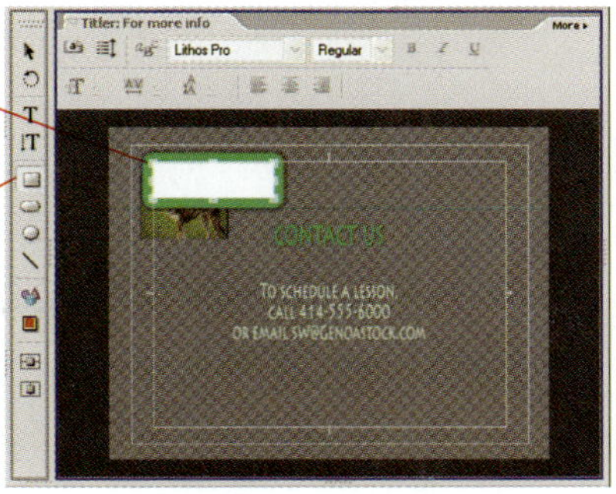


FIGURE F-23: Changing the stroke color

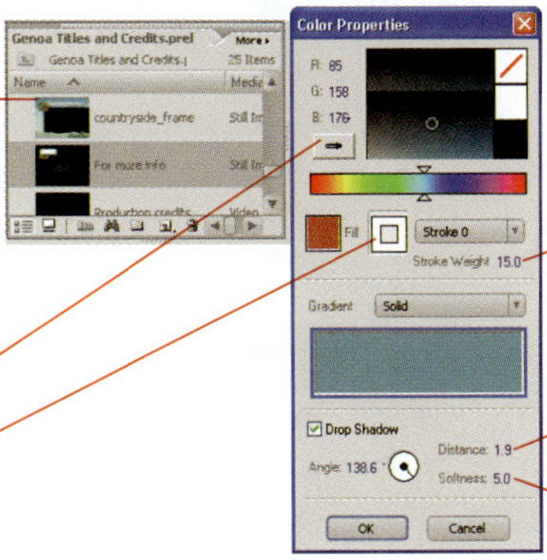


FIGURE F-24: Credits sequence in action

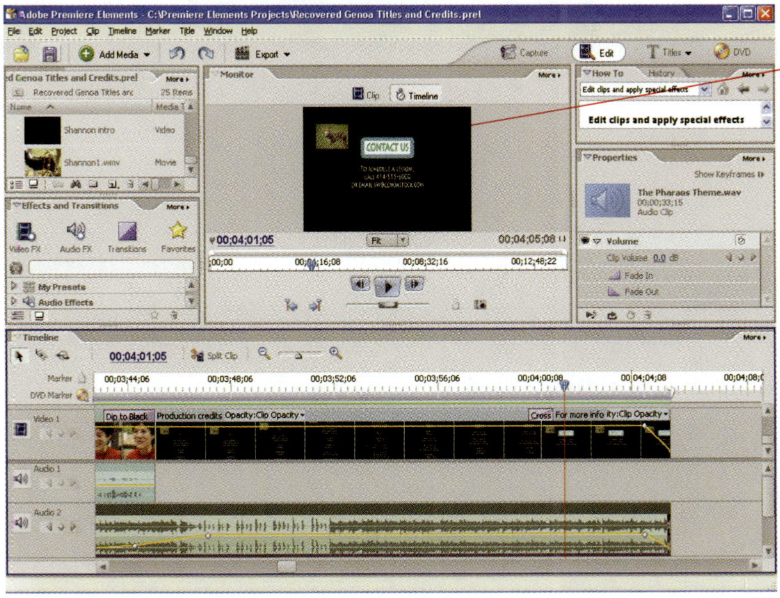


TABLE F-5: Additional techniques for creating a shape

| if you want to | do this to create the shape |
|---|---|
| Maintain the shape's aspect ratio | Press [Shift] while dragging |
| Anchor the center of the shape to a desired point | Press [Alt] while dragging |
| Maintain the aspect ratio and anchor the center | Press [Alt][Shift] while dragging |
| Flip the shape horizontally or vertically | Drag horizontally or vertically across the shape |
| Flip the shape diagonally | Drag diagonally across the corner selection points |

# Practice

## ▼ CONCEPTS REVIEW

**Label the elements of the Premiere Elements program window shown in Figure F-25.**

FIGURE F-25

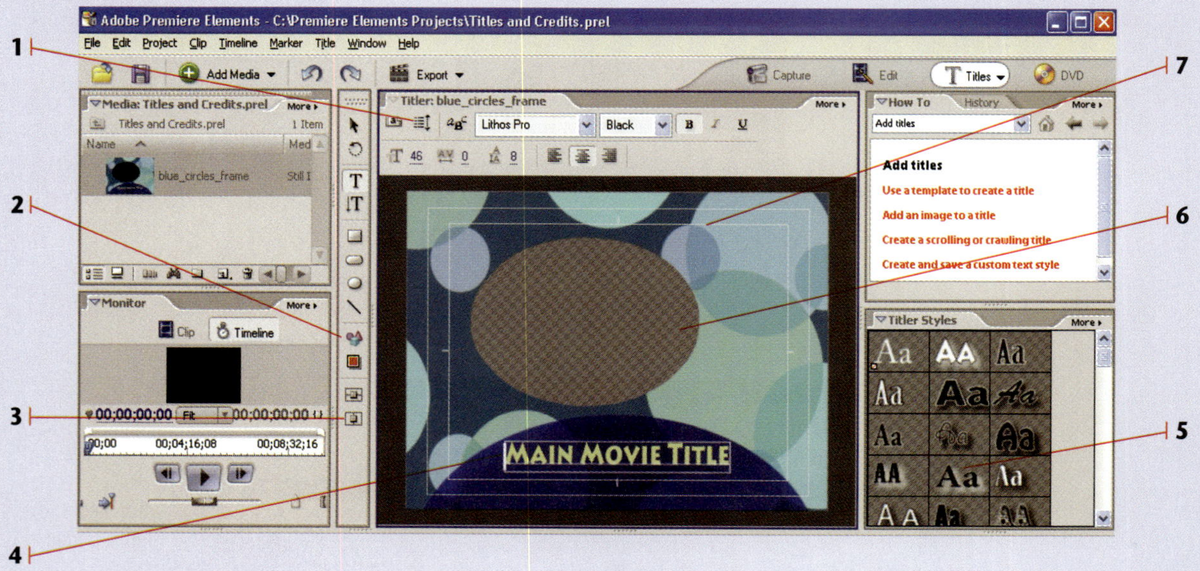


**Match each term with the statement that best describes it.**

| | |
|---|---|
| **8. Titler Styles panel** | **a.** This setting is unavailable if the End Off Screen option is active. |
| **9. Rolling** | **b.** This setting controls how long text remains stationary before moving. |
| **10. Title-safe margin** | **c.** Contains preconfigured combinations of formatting attributes |
| **11. Templates dialog box** | **d.** Text that moves vertically across the screen |
| **12. Preroll** | **e.** Contains preinstalled title and credit designs |
| **13. Crawling** | **f.** Text that moves horizontally across the screen |
| **14. Postroll** | **g.** Border within which text should be readable on all televisions |

**Select the best answer from the list of choices.**

**15. A title sequence usually appears:**
- **a.** At the end of a movie.
- **b.** Halfway through a movie.
- **c.** At the beginning of a movie.
- **d.** After the closing credits.

**16. A gray checkerboard pattern on a title indicates that:**
- **a.** Part of the title is damaged.
- **b.** Part of the title is transparent.
- **c.** The title includes an audio component.
- **d.** The title must be rendered.

**17. To add a transition to a title clip, you must:**
- **a.** Add the clip to the Timeline.
- **b.** Change the clip's Roll/Crawl options.
- **c.** Create the title from scratch.
- **d.** Create the title using a template.

**18. Which tool do you use to create a square shape on a title?**
- **a.** 
- **b.** 
- **c.** 
- **d.** 

**19. If you play a clip in the Titles workspace:**
- **a.** The movie plays in the Titler panel only.
- **b.** The movie plays in the Monitor panel only.
- **c.** The movie plays in both the Titler panel and the Monitor panel.
- **d.** The movie does not play.

**20. If you want to move an object you just created so it appears behind all other objects in the title, use the:**
- **a.** Bring to Front command.
- **b.** Bring Forward command.
- **c.** Send to Back command.
- **d.** Send Backward command.

## ▼ SKILLS REVIEW

**1. Create a title clip.**
- **a.** Start Premiere Elements.
- **b.** Open the file PE F-2.prel from the drive and folder where your Data Files are located, then save it as **Clown Titles and Credits** in the *YourName* folder where you are saving files for this book.
- **c.** Click the Titles button on the task bar.
- **d.** Expand the Entertainment category, expand the Stage theme, then double-click the stage_title template.
- **e.** Delete the text in the Stage Curtain Title placeholder text, type **Kapoot**, press [Enter], then type **Clown Theatre**.
- **f.** Click below the text box, then type **Shows for all ages**.
- **g.** Save your changes to the project.

## ▼ SKILLS REVIEW (CONTINUED)

**2. Edit a title clip.**

**a.** Select the top text box, then click the Charlemagne Std Gradient 67 style swatch in the Titler Styles panel. (*Hint*: The style swatch is toward the bottom of the Styles panel and is shown in light green.) (*Note*: If you don't have the Charlemagne font installed on your computer, you won't see this Style swatch; in that case, click a different swatch.)

**b.** Click the Text Tool, if necessary, select the first line of text in the text box, then change the font size to **48**.

**c.** Select the second line of text, then change the Font size value to **58**.

**d.** Drag the text box up slightly in the frame so that the second line of text drops about halfway beneath the inner curtains.

**e.** Select the bottom text box, then change the font size to **38**.

**f.** Open the Color Properties dialog box, verify that Linear Gradient is selected, change the R, G, and B values to **255**, then close the dialog box.

**g.** Center both text boxes horizontally, click another part of the canvas to deselect the objects, then compare your screen to Figure F-26.

**h.** Save your changes.

**3. Add a title to a movie.**

**a.** Drag the stage_title clip from the Media panel to the Video 1 track on the Timelime, aligning it at 00;00;00;00.

**b.** Play the title clip.

**c.** Switch to the Edit workspace.

**d.** Add a Dip to Black Dissolve transition between the title clip and the Cam1_a clip.

**e.** Change the alignment of the transition to Center at Cut.

**f.** Render the work area, play the first two clips, then save your changes.

FIGURE F-26

**4. Add an image to a title.**

**a.** Open the Templates dialog box.

**b.** Create a new title based on the stage_frame title.

**c.** Click the Add Image button on the Tools panel, then add the Kapoot4 image.

**d.** Open the Scale dialog box, verify that the Uniform option button is selected, then change the Scale to **125%**.

**e.** Center the image horizontally and vertically, then use the Arrange menu to send it to the back of the stacking order.

**f.** Select the title placeholder, then type **The Clowns Present...** (Type three periods after the word "Present.")

**g.** Save your changes to the project.

**5. Work with crawling titles.**

**a.** Open the Roll/Crawl Options dialog box.

**b.** Change the Title Type to Crawl.

**c.** Select the Start Off Screen check box.

**d.** Change the Postroll value to **60**.

**e.** Close the dialog box, then insert the clip on the Video 1 track at the beginning of the Timeline. Verify that the other video and sound clips shift right to make room.

**f.** Add a Cross Dissolve transition between the stage_frame clip and the stage_title clip, then center-align the transition if necessary.

**g.** Render the work area, play the opening sequence, then save your changes.

## ▼ SKILLS REVIEW (CONTINUED)

**6. Create credits.**

**a.** Open the Templates dialog box, then create a new title based on the stage_credits template.

**b.** Rename the clip name **Closing credits**.

**c.** Replace the Stage Rolling Credits placeholder text with the following lines of text, leaving a blank line between each block of text:

**Videotaped at**
**The Oak Theatre**
**by Ty Media, Inc.**

**Edited by**
***YourName***

**Music**
**composed & performed by**
**Mark Kmit**

**Kapoot offers**
**Performances for all ages**
**Residencies**
**Master classes**
**Team building**

**For more information**
**contact pr@kapoot.com**

**d.** Format the text in bold and change the font size to **25**.

**e.** Change the font of the Credits heading to Charlemagne Std, then change the Kerning value to **–2**.

**f.** Drag the black and red graphic object so it is below the last line of text.

**g.** Add the clip to the end of the movie, render the work area, watch the credits in the Monitor panel, then save your changes.

**7. Work with rolling credits.**

**a.** Open the Roll/Crawl Options dialog box, then deselect the End Off Screen check box.

**b.** Change the Ease In value to **0**.

**c.** Change the Ease Out value to **60**.

**d.** Change the Postroll value to **90**, then click OK.

**e.** Drag the out point of the clip so it aligns with the end of the sound clip on the Audio 2 track.

**f.** Save your changes.

## ▼ SKILLS REVIEW (CONTINUED)

8. **Work with shapes.**
   - **a.** Click the Ellipse Tool on the Tools panel.
   - **b.** Draw an ellipse that extends over the two lines of text that read "Edited by" and your name. The shape should be wider than it is tall, and the top and bottom of the shape should not overlap the lines of text above and below it.
   - **c.** With the shape selected, open the Color Properties dialog box.
   - **d.** Change the Fill color to a shade of red sampled from the upper-left corner of the "D" in the word "CREDITS" on the title frame. (*Hint*: Drag the dialog box out of the way if you can't see this part of the frame.)
   - **e.** Select the Drop shadow check box, then change the distance value to **10.5** and the Softness value to **30**.
   - **f.** Close the dialog box, move the shape to the back of the stacking order, then compare your screen to Figure F-27.
   - **g.** Render the work area, then switch to the Edit workspace.
   - **h.** Play the credits clip, save your changes, close the project, then exit Premiere Elements.

FIGURE F-27

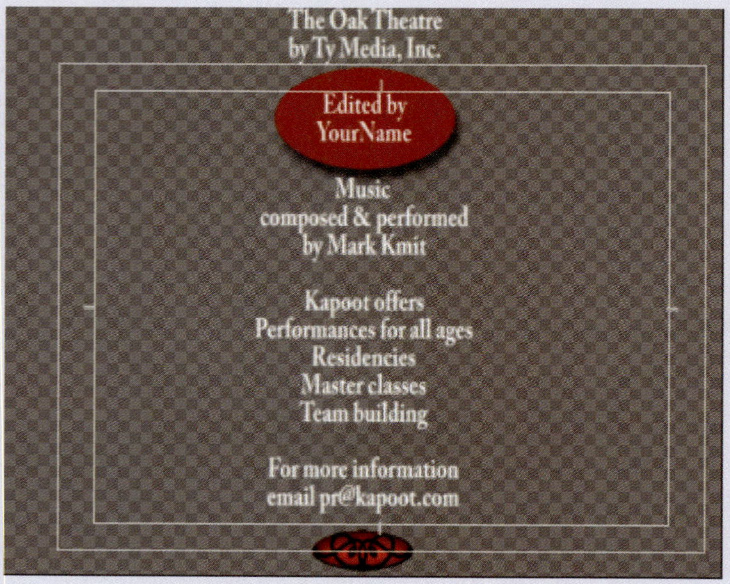


## ▼ INDEPENDENT CHALLENGE 1

Your film festival trailer is almost complete. The head of the film fest does not want an opening title for the trailer; instead, she wants titles included with each clip, identifying the name of the film and the director.

- **a.** Start Premiere Elements.
- **b.** Open the file PE F-3.prel from the drive and folder where your Data Files are located, then save it as **Film Fest Titles** in the *YourName* folder where you are saving files for this book.
- **c.** Open the Titles menu on the task bar, click Crawling Title, then name the title **Dress for Success title**.
- **d.** Starting anywhere on the work area, type **"Dress for Success"** (include the quotation marks), press [Enter], then type **dir. Clark Wigby**.
- **e.** Change the font size of the text on the first line to **40**, and the size of the text on the second line to **30**.
- **f.** Select all the text, then change the font color to white. (*Hint*: Use the Color Properties dialog box.)
- **g.** Position the text box so its lower-left corner is aligned with the lower-left corner of the title-safe margin.
- **h.** Use the Rectangle Tool to draw a rectangle that starts just slightly above the text box and extends from the left edge to the right and bottom edges of the action-safe margin. Change the fill color to black, if necessary.
- **i.** Move the rectangle to the back of the stacking order.

## ▼ INDEPENDENT CHALLENGE 1 (CONTINUED)

j. Open the Roll/Crawl Options dialog box, change the settings so the crawl starts off-screen and ends off-screen, and has an Ease-Out of 60. Compare your screen to Figure F-28.

FIGURE F-28

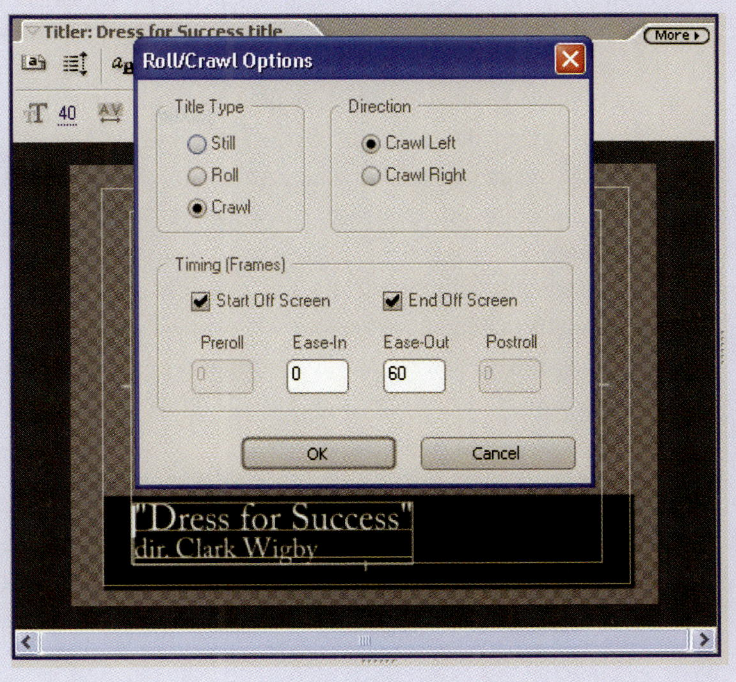


k. Add the clip to the Video 2 track on the Timeline, aligning it with the beginning of the Dress for Success clip on the Video 1 track. Drag the out point of the title clip so it is the same duration as the clip on the Video 1 track.

l. Create a new title from the current title, then save the new title as **Muffin Control title**. Change the text in the text box so it reads **"Muffin Control"** on the first line, and **dir. Bryan Jordan** on the second line. Add the new title clip to the Video 2 track on the Timeline, aligning it with the beginning of the Muffin Control clip on the Video 2 track and changing its duration to match it.

m. Continue this process to create and name a new title for each of the remaining four clips in the movie, and add it to the movie, adjusting the clip duration as necessary. Use the clip name as the movie title, and make up a name for the director.

**Advanced Challenge Exercise**

ACE

- Create a still title of your own design at the end of the movie. Include the following information: The date and time of the film festival is **Friday, June 15**, at **8:00 p.m.**, the location is **Regis Theatre**, and admission is **$5.00**.
- Add the image Still from Dress for Success.bmp, located in the Source Files folder, to the title. Place and format it so it's attractive and the title is still readable, then add the clip to the Timeline.

n. Render the work area, save your changes, watch the movie, then close the project and exit Premiere Elements.

## ▼ INDEPENDENT CHALLENGE 2

Create titles and credits for your documentary. The titles can be short and simple, long and detailed, or somewhere between. Use the skills you've learned in this unit to create titles and credits that reflect your filmmaking style and that convey all the information appropriate for this movie. Make sure you credit yourself as the filmmaker and editor of the movie.

- **a.** Start Premiere Elements, open the file My Documentary With Audio Adjustments.prel from the *YourName* folder where you are saving files for this book, then save it as **My Documentary Titles and Credits**. (*Note*: If you did not create and edit this movie, consult your instructor.)
- **b.** Add an opening title sequence. The sequence can consist of one or more titles, but should at least include the name of the movie.
- **c.** If appropriate, add titles that identify people or places during the movie.
- **d.** Add credits that identify everyone who worked on the movie. Be sure to thank anyone who helped make the movie possible, and credit anyone who contributed music or other elements.
- **e.** When you're finished, save and close the project and exit Premiere Elements.

## ▼ INDEPENDENT CHALLENGE 3

Jim, your boss at Fig Media, has asked you to add titles and credits to the video you're making for the internship program. He wants you to include an opening title, as well as a few additional pieces of information throughout the movie.

- **a.** Start Premiere Elements, open the file Dream Job With Audio Adjustments.prel from the *YourName* folder where you are saving files for this book, then save it as **Dream Job Titles**. (*Note*: If you did not create and edit this movie, consult your instructor.)
- **b.** Locate a title template you like in the Templates dialog box.
- **c.** Add an opening title that briefly welcomes the viewer to Fig. The message can be casual, inspirational, or over-the-top excited. Change the font formatting or add text boxes as necessary to convey the information in a way that suits the style of the movie you have edited.
- **d.** Insert the clip at the beginning of the Timeline and add a transition from it to the next clip.
- **e.** Use another template from the same theme to add credits to the end of the movie. Include your name as the Editor, and credit the music used in the movie. The name of the song is "Singer Strange Theme," and the composer is Derek R. Audette. Include a closing message if you want.
- **f.** Add the clip to the end of the movie, or superimpose it over the last clip using the Video 2 track. If you want, add a transition of your choice.

**Advanced Challenge Exercise**

ACE

- Add an additional title to the end of the movie based on the same theme you used for the previous credits. Delete any text boxes, then use the Vertical Type Tool to type **The End**. If you want, format the text in a style that makes it easier to read.
- Add the clip to the end of the movie.

- **g.** Render the work area, save your changes, then watch the clips you added.
- **h.** Save and close the project, then exit Premiere Elements.

## ▼ INDEPENDENT CHALLENGE 4

You are almost finished with the Internet Education video for the upcoming conference on Cinema and Education. You need to add an opening title sequence and titles that identify each film excerpt during the movie. The title of the movie is "Cinema & You." You want to add an image to the opening title that reflects the theme of the conference.

- **a.** Connect to the Internet, then use your favorite search engine to search for sites that offer public domain or open access images, such as www.flickr.com. For each Web site you visit, read the About page and/or Copyright pages on the site to learn whether you can legally download images. Because you are using these images for educational purposes, downloading is often permissible, but the rules and guidelines vary by site.
- **b.** Download the image, then edit it in an image editing program such as Photoshop Elements, if necessary.
- **c.** Open the file Internet Education With Soundtrack.prel from the *YourName* folder where you are saving files for this book, then save it as **Internet Titles and Credits**.
- **d.** Create an opening title sequence that includes the movie title (**Cinema & You**) and the text **Presented by**, followed by ***Your Name***. Include the image file you downloaded and format it any way you like.
- **e.** Add a title to each clip in the film, identifying the title. Format the title clips any way you like, and add a roll or crawl if appropriate.
- **f.** Add the title clips to the Timeline, edit them to adjust length, and add and adjust transitions as appropriate.
- **g.** When you are finished, render the work area, view the movie, save your changes, then close the project and exit Premiere Elements.

## ▼ VISUAL WORKSHOP

Open the file PE F-4.prel from the drive and folder where your Data Files are located, then save it as **Butterfly Title** in the *YourName* folder where you are saving files for this book. Using Figure F-29 as a guide, create a new title based on a template and add it to the Timeline where necessary to create the effect shown. (*Hint*: The template is available in the Templates dialog box, and you do not need to change any formatting or color properties.) When you are finished, save your changes to the project. Press [PrtScr], paste the image into your word-processing program, print a copy, then exit your word processor and Premiere Elements.

FIGURE F-29

# Outputting a Movie

## OBJECTIVES

- Understand output options
- Prepare a movie for DVD
- Export an auto-play DVD
- Create DVD menus
- Export a DVD with menus
- Export a movie to DV or VHS tape
- Export a video file
- Export an image file

A project file is not a stand-alone movie. While you can preview a project in Premiere Elements by watching the contents of the Timeline on the Monitor panel, you can't distribute it simply by e-mailing the file to a friend. Even if your viewers have Premiere Elements installed, they still need the source files used in the project to view it. Besides, the whole point of digital editing is to share your work using a common delivery method. Premiere Elements offers many options for distribution, from DVD to videotape to transmission over the Internet. You need to distribute the Genoa Stock video in a variety of formats. Shannon, the owner of Genoa Stock & Training, wants to post it on the company Web site and distribute it on DVD to prospective clients. She also wants a still from the movie to use in a brochure. Luis, a producer at Ty Media, wants a DV tape of the movie for archival purposes. You prepare to create the necessary files.

UNIT G
Premiere Elements 2.0

# Understanding Output Options

**Outputting** converts a movie on the Timeline into a stand-alone video. Depending on the intended playback method, outputting writes directly to the medium or generates a separate file or set of files. Each output format includes options that affect file size, output quality, and other factors in playback. In many cases you can use the default setting, but depending on disk space and other considerations, you may need to make some adjustments. You can output a movie in as many playback formats as you like; the project file remains unchanged. See Table G-1 for a description of the video file formats you can export in Premiere Elements. You need to output the Genoa Stock video in several formats, so you review your choices.

DETAILS

**The major output methods available in Premiere Elements include:**

**QUICK TIP**
Standard, single-sided DVDs hold 4.7 gigabytes (GB) of data, but Premiere Elements also supports double-sided DVDs, which hold 8.5 gigabytes and are becoming more widely available.

- **Burning to DVD**

  You can output directly to a DVD if your computer includes a DVD burner and you have a compatible DVD. You can create a disc compatible with the NTSC or PAL standard, no matter which standard you used to create the project. You can also burn to a folder instead of to a disc, provided you have enough space on that drive. This is a useful option if you don't have a compatible DVD available, or if you plan to use a dedicated DVD authoring program for advanced features such as subtitles, multiple aspect ratios on one disk, or burning an audio DVD. Burning to DVD creates an **MPEG-2** file, a high-quality format that contains video, audio, and menu navigation data. The extension **.vob** stands for **Video Object**.

  Premiere Elements can burn to most commercially available types of DVDs, including DVD-R, DVD+R, and DVD-RW or DVD+RW. "R" stands for recordable but not re-writable, and "RW" stands for both. The + and – symbols refer to different DVD standards.

**QUICK TIP**
You can export part or all of the contents of the Timeline or export just the audio or video.

- **Exporting to a file**

  You can save a video file to a hard disk or CD, post it to the Internet, or e-mail it. The file can then be played on a computer, mobile phone, or personal digital assistant (PDA) running compatible software, such as Windows Media Player or Apple QuickTime Player.

  The format and settings you choose affect the size of the file and the quality of the movie. For example, exporting to an MPEG or AVI movie format results in clear, sharp images and vivid colors, but produces a large file, whereas exporting to a Windows Media Video or QuickTime Movie format yields less detail and fewer colors, but can result in a much smaller file size. Figure G-1 shows a three-minute movie exported in Microsoft DV AVI (.avi) format at the default 720 x 480 frame size. Figure G-2 shows the same movie exported to MOV (.mov) format at a frame size of 160 x 120, the default MOV setting for movies intended for transmission over a broadband Internet connection. The AVI file is 667MB, and the MOV file is 12MB.

**QUICK TIP**
You can convert a project to motion picture film, such as 16mm or 35mm, using a commercial service provider with video-to-film transfer equipment.

- **Recording to video tape**

  You can output a movie to VHS or DV videotape using a FireWire or i.Link connection and a compatible camcorder or recording deck.

- **Exporting a still image or still image sequence**

  You can turn any frame on the Timeline into a still image file, which you can then insert in a document or open in an image-editing program. Figure G-3 shows a frame exported as a still image file and opened for editing in Adobe Photoshop Elements. You can also export a sequence of still images to use in an animation program that cannot open video files.

FIGURE G-1: Movie saved in Microsoft AVI format

FIGURE G-2: Movie saved in QuickTime MOV format

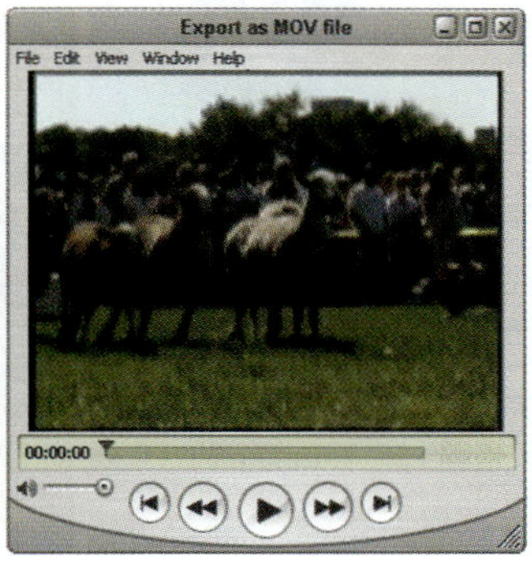


FIGURE G-3: Frame saved as still image and opened in Adobe Photoshop Elements

TABLE G-1: File formats available for export

| file type | file formats |
|---|---|
| Audio-Video | MPEG-1, MPEG-2, Microsoft AVI and DV AVI Movie, QuickTime, Filmstrip, or Windows Media |
| Audio-only | Microsoft AVI, DV AVI, or Windows WAVE |
| Still image | Adobe Title Designer, GIF, JPEG, Truevision Targa, TIFF, or Windows Bitmap |
| Sequence | GIF, Animated GIF, JPEG, Truevision Targa, TIFF, or Windows Bitmap sequence |

UNIT
G
Premiere Elements 2.0

# Preparing a Movie for DVD

Before burning a movie to DVD, you can make a few additions to create a more professional-looking product that is easy for viewers to navigate. You can add a few seconds of blank video to the beginning of the Timeline so there is a slight pause before the movie starts. To generate blank video, you can use the **Black Video** command to add a still black clip, or the **Color Matte** to add a still clip in the color you choose. You can also add **DVD markers**, which viewers can use to jump to specific points using the Next and Previous buttons on their DVD players or remotes. DVD markers are especially useful in a DVD with menus, but can also be used in auto-play DVDs. You want to prepare the Genoa Stock & Training video for exporting to DVD.

## STEPS

**QUICK TIP**

If you create a clip using the Color Matte command, after you specify the color, you are prompted to name it in the Choose Name dialog box; the clip is then added to the Media panel.

**QUICK TIP**

If you create an auto-play DVD, the Stop Marker and Thumbnail offset features do not apply.

1. **Start Premiere Elements, open the file PE G-1.prel from the drive and folder where your Data Files are located, then save it Genoa Stock & Training in the *YourName* folder where you are saving files for this book**

   This project contains the final edit of *Genoa Stock & Training: An Introduction*, starting at the beginning of the Timeline. It also contains a slideshow of still images, starting just after the movie credits sequence.

2. **Click the New Item button on the Media panel, then click Black Video**

   A still video-only clip with a black background and a duration of five seconds is added to the Media panel. The also contains the Color Matte command, which opens a Color Picker dialog box where you can create a still video clip of any color.

3. **Drag the Black Video clip from the Media panel to the beginning of the Video 1 track on the Timeline**

4. **Drag another instance of the Black Video clip from the Media panel to frame 00;04;54;20, the first frame of the slideshow**

   Two copies of the clip are inserted in the movie, as shown in Figure G-4. A blank video clip is almost unnoticeable to viewers, but it gives them a chance to focus on the screen before the opening title sequence or scene begins. Adding blank clips between movies on the Timeline provides a similar break between pieces.

5. **Move to frame 00;04;34;22, then click the Set DVD Marker icon on the Timeline**

   The DVD Marker dialog box opens, as shown in Figure G-5. The title bar of the dialog box displays the frame number where the marker will be added. In this dialog box, you can create three types of markers for use on a DVD; see Table G-2 for a description of each. You can change the frame number for the **Thumbnail offset**, the image that illustrates this marker in a DVD menu—for example, you might want to show a later frame in the credits sequence. This doesn't change the location of the marker, just the image that illustrates it on a menu.

6. **Verify that the Marker Type is Scene Marker, click the Name text box, type Movie Credits, then click OK**

   A scene marker is added to the Timeline for the credits sequence, which allows viewers to jump directly to this point on the DVD. The "Movie Credits" name you entered in the Name text box will be useful later; links to Scene markers are listed in the Scene menu of a DVD menu.

7. **Move to frame 00;04;54;20, click on the Timeline, click the Marker Type list arrow, click Main Menu Marker, click the Name text box, then type Photo Slideshow**

   A main menu marker is added for the second movie. Links to main menu markers appear on the main page of a DVD menu.

8. **Click OK, then save your changes to the project**

   The DVD markers are added just beneath the time ruler, as shown in Figure G-6.

**FIGURE G-4: Black Video clip added to two locations on the Timeline**

**FIGURE G-5: DVD Marker dialog box**

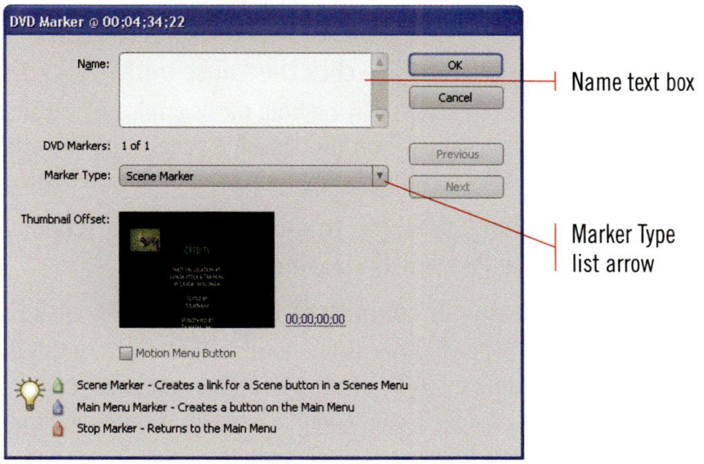


**FIGURE G-6: DVD markers on the Timeline**

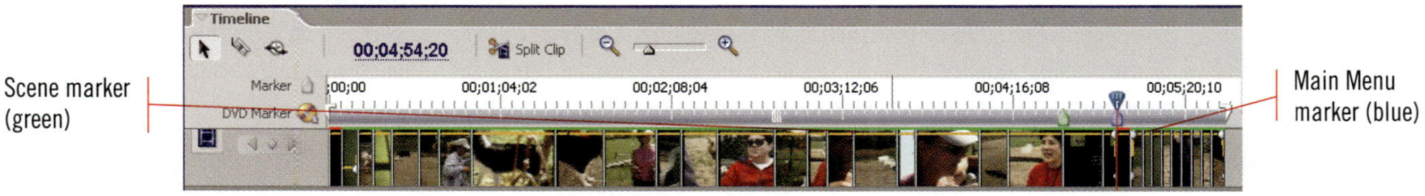


**TABLE G-2: DVD markers**

| marker | looks like | description |
|---|---|---|
| Scene |  | Use to designate a scene within a movie if you want the viewer to be able to skip to different scenes while watching the movie or from the DVD menu |
| Main Menu |  | Use to designate an additional movie or movies on a DVD following the first one (you don't need to set a Main Menu marker for the first movie on a DVD) |
| Stop |  | Use in a DVD with menus if you want the movie to return to the DVD menu when it reaches the end of a movie (if you create a DVD with no menus, there's no menu to return to, so the marker is ignored) |

UNIT G

Premiere Elements 2.0

# Exporting an Auto-Play DVD

In Premiere Elements, you can create auto-play DVDs and DVDs with menus. In an **auto-play DVD**, the movie begins playing immediately when you insert it in a DVD player, and any additional movies on the DVD play in succession after the first one. Adding **menus** to a DVD displays a set of choices when the DVD is inserted in a DVD player, such as scenes and bonus material. An auto-play DVD is the simplest type of DVD to create because you don't have to create menus for it. Although the absence of menus somewhat limits a viewer's navigational choices, if the movie includes Main Menu or Scene Markers, viewers can jump to those points using the Next and Previous buttons on their DVD players. You are ready to create an auto-play DVD for Shannon so she can review your work. (*Note*: Steps 5–7 require a DVD burner attached to your computer. If you do not have a DVD burner, stop at Step 4.)

## STEPS

**QUICK TIP**

When purchasing blank DVDs, choose a format compatible with both the burner and the player(s) on which you plan to play the DVD; check your user's guide for more information.

1. **Click the DVD button on the task bar, verify that the Auto-play DVD with no Menus option button is selected, then click OK**

   The DVD workspace opens, as shown in Figure G-7. In this workspace, a DVD Layout panel appears above the Timeline, and a smaller Monitor panel replaces the Effects and Transitions panel.

2. **Click Preview DVD on the DVD Layout panel**

   The Preview DVD window opens. Device controls under the preview area allow you to navigate as if you were watching the finished DVD on a DVD player. When the window first opens, only the Play button is active.

3. **Click the Play button, click the Pause button, then click the Next Scene button**

   A preview of the DVD starts playing from the beginning of the Timeline (even though the current-time indicator is at a different frame on the Timeline panel), and the other device controls available for this DVD become active. After pausing, the DVD jumps to the credits sequence, as shown in Figure G-8.

4. **Press [Spacebar], press [N] to move to the next scene, watch the Photo Slideshow movie, then close the Preview DVD window**

**TROUBLE**

If you forget to insert a DVD before you open the Burn DVD dialog box, insert it and then click Rescan.

5. **Insert a DVD in your computer's DVD drive, then click Burn DVD on the DVD Layout panel**

   The Burn DVD dialog box opens, as shown in Figure G-9. In this dialog box, you specify final settings before you start recording to DVD. In the Disc Name text box, you can enter a name for the disc to replace the default numeric name. If your computer system includes multiple DVD burners, you can click the Burner Location list arrow to choose a different burner drive. You can change the quantity in the Copies list box to burn more than one copy in this session. It can take several hours to compress a movie into the MPEG-2 format of a DVD; if you specify multiple copies, the most time-consuming part of the process happens just once, and burning additional DVDs is much faster. If you leave the Fit Contents to available Space check box selected, Premiere Elements compresses the movie only as much as possible to fit it on the DVD at the highest possible quality. You can deselect the check box and drag the slider to manually adjust the **bitrate**, or amount of data space consumed by a second of video.

**QUICK TIP**

When burning to a DVD, it is recommended that you not use your computer to perform other tasks; even on a high-end system, this can slow progress dramatically or cause data transfer errors or even a system crash.

6. **Click Burn**

   The Burn DVD Progress dialog box opens and updates the progress of the burning process. The **Current Task Progress bar** shows the progress of the current task, such as **Encoding Media** (compressing the data) or **Burning Media** (writing to disc). The **Overall Progress bar** provides a visual measure of how much longer the process will take. Burning takes several minutes even on a fast system. When burning is complete, the dialog box displays the message "Export completed," and a Close button appears.

7. **Click Close, if necessary**

FIGURE G-7: DVD workspace

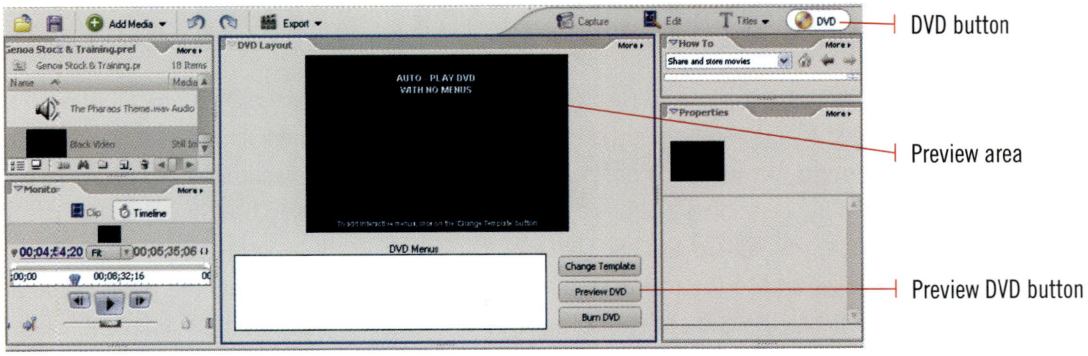


FIGURE G-8: Preview DVD window

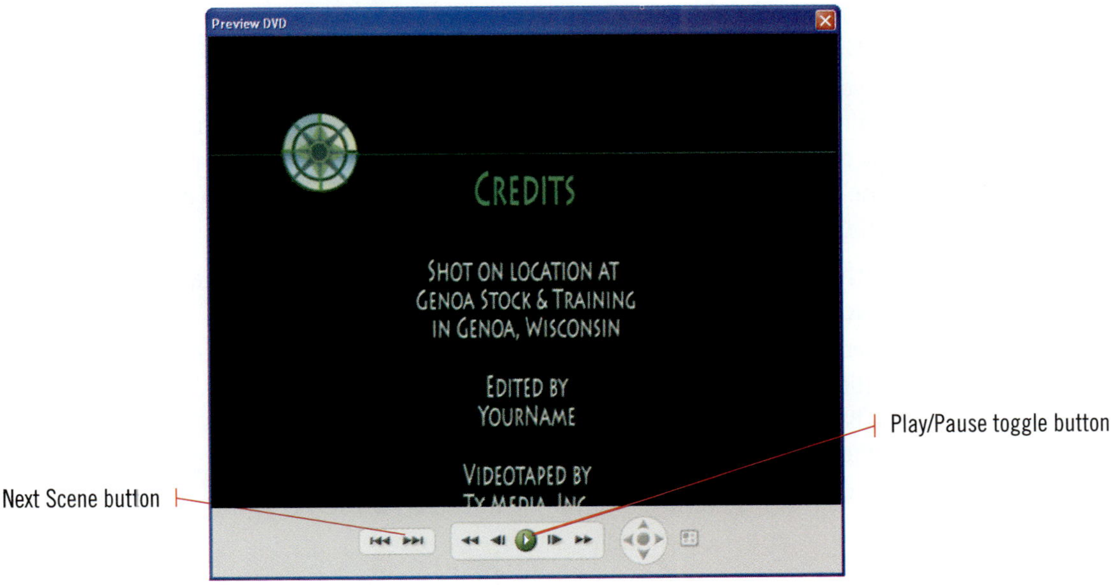


FIGURE G-9: Burn DVD dialog box

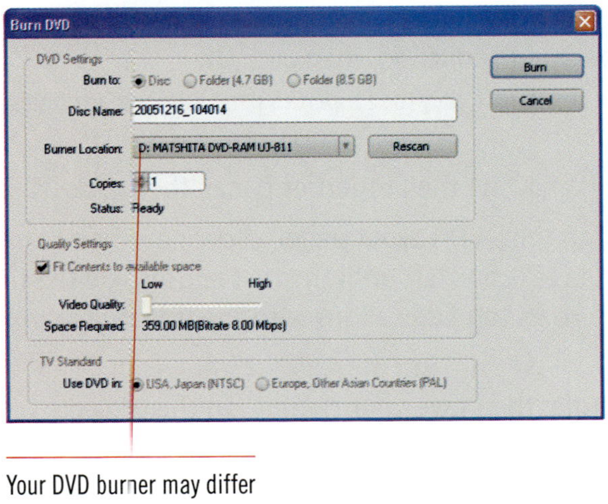


FIGURE G-10: Burn DVD Progress dialog box

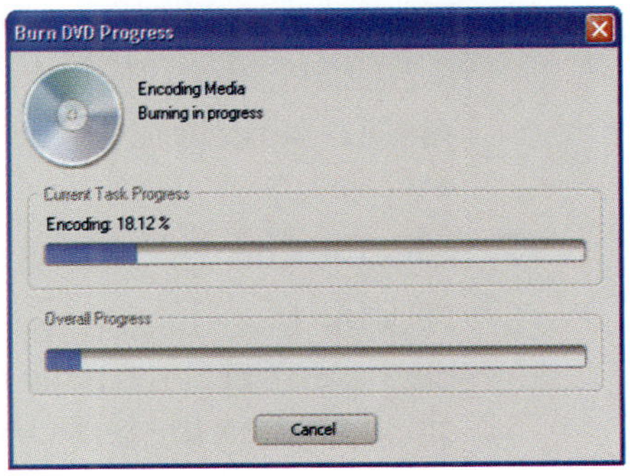


Premiere Elements 2.0

UNIT
G
Premiere Elements 2.0

# Creating DVD Menus

Adding **menus** to a DVD provides a table of contents for the DVD when it plays. Instead of the movie starting immediately, a menu system opens onscreen. Each menu links to a marker on the DVD. The viewer clicks a **menu** to move to a different scene or movie, or to a submenu of **chapters** or links to scenes. To add menus, you choose a template in the DVD Templates dialog box, and then edit the menus in the DVD workspace. For the final DVD for Genoa Stock, you want a menu system that includes links to the two movies and to the movie credits in a design that complements the project. You also want to add a Stop marker to the end of the first movie so the DVD will return to the main menu when it reaches this point.

## STEPS

1. **Click Change Template on the DVD Layout panel**
   The DVD Templates dialog box opens, as shown in Figure G-11. Premiere Elements includes themes for DVD templates to match all the themes in the Title templates dialog box.

**QUICK TIP**
Premiere Elements adds or removes buttons if you have more or fewer markers on the Timeline than necessary; it generates extra menus if you add more markers than are in the selected template.

2. **Click the Theme list arrow, click Travel, then scroll down to the CountrySide Main Menu and CountrySide Scenes Menu template**
   Each theme includes a template for the Main menu and one for the Scenes menu. A **main menu** appears when you insert the DVD in a player; a **scenes menu** appears when you click the Scene Selection menu on the main menu. Premiere Elements uses one Main Menu button for the first movie on the DVD, and another to link to the Scenes menu. The Countryside template includes three Main Menu buttons, which is perfect because you have one additional movie to list on the main menu. It also includes six Scenes Menu buttons, even though you need only one to link to the movie credits.
3. **Click the Countryside theme, click OK, then resize the DVD Layout panel if necessary, so your screen matches Figure G-12**
   The menus for this DVD are generated, and the Main Menu 1 menu appears in the DVD Layout panel. The Properties panel displays information about the selected object and lets you change its attributes; by default, Menu Background is selected. You can change the background by dragging an image, video, or audio clip from the Media panel to a **media drop zone** on the Properties panel.
4. **Click the Scenes Menu 1 thumbnail in the DVD Menus section, view the menu, then click the Main Menu 1 thumbnail**
   The menu names are numbered so that if additional menus need to be generated to accommodate additional links, each menu will have a unique name.

**QUICK TIP**
To add a still image or video clip to the menu background, drag it to the Video Media drop zone; if the clip is not in the Media panel, click Browse, navigate to the file in the Select Background Media dialog box, then click Open.

5. **Drag the The Pharaos Theme clip from the Media panel to the Audio media drop zone on the Properties panel, then click the Apply Default Transition before loop check box**
   A looping audio clip is added to the menu background. Audio clips have a maximum duration of just under 30 seconds, and the loop can include the default audio transition.
6. **Double-click the Countryside Title text, in the Change Text dialog box type Genoa Stock & Training:, press [Enter], type An Introduction, then click OK**
   The DVD Layout panel displays the edited text, and the Properties panel displays attributes for the selected text object.
7. **Click the Change Text Font list arrow on the Properties panel, then click Lithos Pro**
8. **Click the More button More ▸ on the DVD Layout panel, click Show Safe Margins, drag the right selection handle of the text box left until the text ends inside the title-safe margin, then drag the text box up so its top edge aligns with the title-safe margin, as shown in Figure G-13**
9. **Click outside the title-safe margin, then save your changes to the project**

FIGURE G-11: DVD Templates dialog box

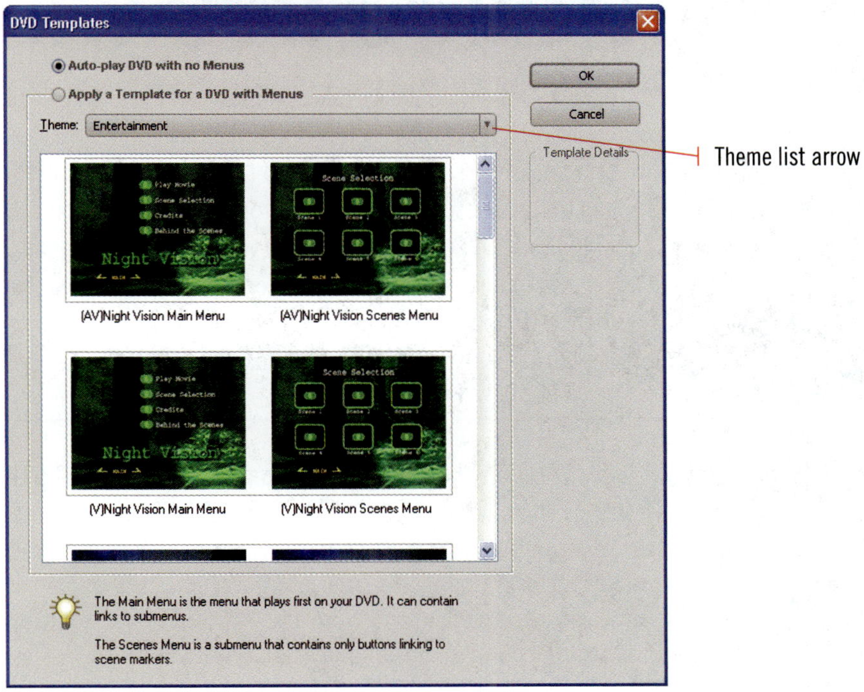


FIGURE G-12: DVD menus in DVD workspace

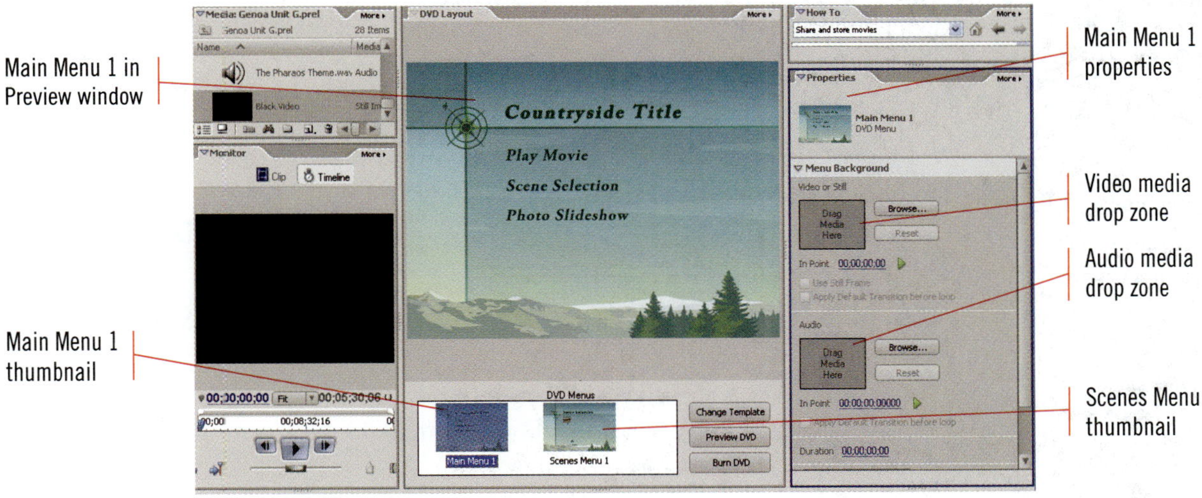


FIGURE G-13: Formatted, resized, and repositioned text

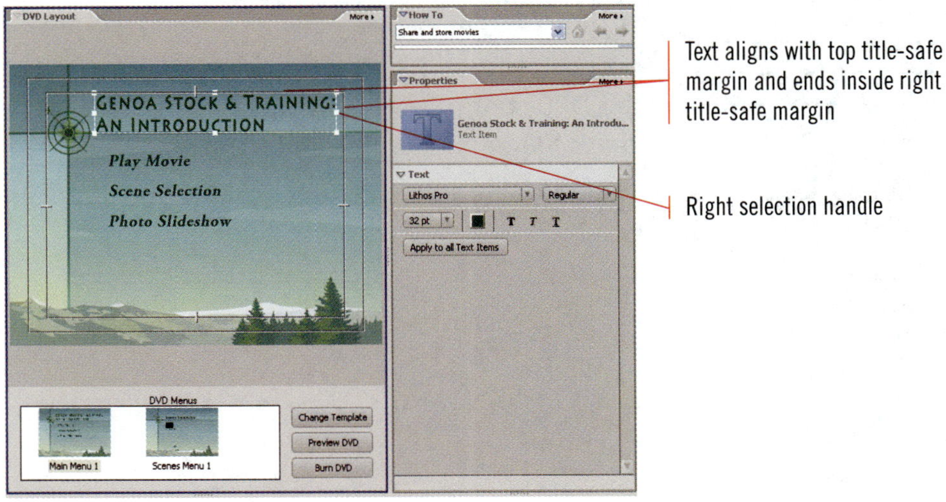


Premiere Elements 2.0

UNIT
G
Premiere Elements 2.0

# Exporting a DVD with Menus

Adding menus to a DVD can enhance its value and appearance, but menus also increase its complexity. The actual process of burning a DVD with menus is just like burning an auto-play DVD, but it usually takes more time to preview and finalize the DVD. You need to take time to check the functionality of all the menus, and you may often need to refine it so the navigation works just the way you like before you burn to disc. You may also want to add additional DVD markers to a DVD with menus to give the user more navigation options. You can add DVD markers in either the Edit workspace or the DVD Layout workspace. (*Note*: Steps 8 and 9 require a DVD burner attached to your computer. If you do not have a DVD burner, stop after Step 7.) You are ready to preview the Genoa Stock DVD and make any final changes before burning to disc.

## STEPS

1. **Click Preview DVD on the DVD Layout panel, then listen to the audio clip**

   The Preview DVD window opens, as shown in Figure G-14. The main menu appears first, and the audio clip plays in the background. By default, audio clips are set to loop in the menu background, so the clip repeats once it reaches the background clip limit of 30 frames. The Remote buttons and Main menu buttons are active because you can use them to navigate the DVD just as you would if you were playing the finished DVD in a DVD player. A decorative cursor indicates the current link.

2. **Click Scene Selection in the Preview DVD window**

   The Scenes menu opens, as shown in Figure G-15. It displays a single scene, Movie Credits, and the audio clip does not play because you added the clip only to the Main Menu background. The button displays a thumbnail image of the clip.

3. **Click Movie Credits**

   The DVD jumps to the credits sequence in the Genoa Stock movie and plays. When the credits clip ends, the DVD plays the black video clip you inserted and then plays the photo slideshow.

4. **Click the Close button on the Preview DVD window, resize the Timeline panel if necessary to see the Video 1 track, move to frame 00;04;54;19, then click the Set DVD Marker icon on the Timeline**

5. **In the DVD Marker dialog box, click the Marker Type list arrow, click Stop Marker, then click OK**

   A Stop Marker icon is added, though you may need to zoom in closely to see it beneath the Main Menu Marker icon at frame 00;04;54;20. Now the DVD will return to the main menu after the end of the Genoa Stock movie instead of continuing with the next movie.

6. **Click Preview DVD, click Play Movie, then verify that the movie plays properly and returns to the main menu after it ends**

7. **Click the Down button twice until the cursor points to Photo Slideshow, click the Enter button, verify that the slideshow plays properly, then close the Preview DVD window**

8. **Click Burn DVD on the DVD Layout panel, then change your settings as necessary so they match those shown in Figure G-16**

9. **If you want to create a DVD, click Burn; otherwise, click Cancel**

   You return to the DVD workspace.

**QUICK TIP**
To change this image, change the Thumbnail Offset frame in the DVD Marker dialog box when you create a marker.

**QUICK TIP**
You can press [S] to play a movie in the Preview window; or you can press [F] to fast forward through it.

**QUICK TIP**
Whenever you burn a DVD, it's a good idea to test it on as many different DVD players as possible before distributing it.

FIGURE G-14: Preview DVD window

FIGURE G-15: Scene Selection menu

FIGURE G-16: Completed Burn DVD dialog box

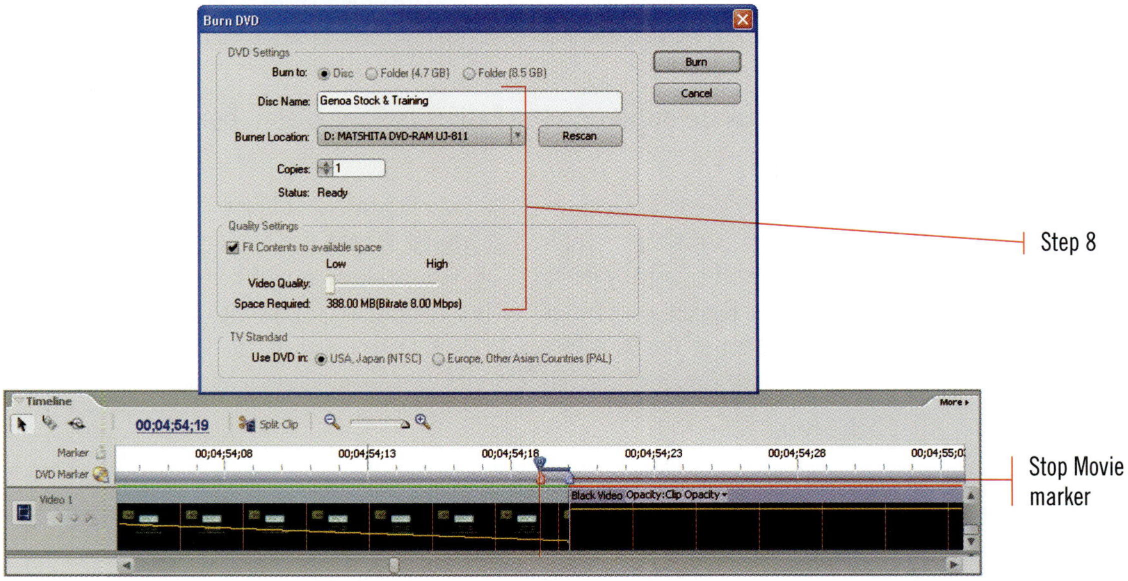

UNIT
G
Premiere Elements 2.0

# Exporting a Movie to DV or VHS Tape

Exporting a project to videotape records it on tape so it can be played on a VCR or DV camcorder. Recording occurs in real time, so the process takes as long as the duration of your movie. You can control several aspects of the recording in the Export to Tape dialog box. (*Note*: This lesson requires a videotape and a DV camcorder. If you don't have a videotape and a DV camcorder, skip to the next lesson.) You need to create a videotape of the Genoa Stock video for archiving at Ty Media. You don't need to record the slideshow.

## STEPS

1. **Verify that your system is equipped for recording to a video camera**
   To record back to the DV camcorder you used to videotape the source footage, connect it using either a FireWire cable or a USB 2.0 cable, depending on the port.
2. **Connect the camcorder to your computer using an IEEE 1394 or USB 2 cable, turn on the camcorder, then set it to playback mode**
3. **Use the controls on the camera to move to the location on the tape where you want to start recording**
   Make sure the tape is not write-protected or it will not record; most tapes have a plastic tab you move to set write-protection on or off. It's a good idea to record a few seconds of blackness (recording with the lens cap on) before the point at which you want to begin recording.
4. **In Premiere Elements, open the project you want to export and adjust the work area if necessary**
   The Genoa Stock & Training movie is already open, and the work area includes just the movie.
5. **Render the work area, click the Export Project button Export on the task bar, then click To Tape**
   The Export to Tape dialog box opens, as shown in Figure G-17. In this dialog box, you can control the recording process and monitor its status. The Activate Recording Device check box, which is selected by default, allows Premiere Elements to control the camcorder or tape deck so that it records at the proper location on the tape and stops recording when the movie is finished. Selecting the **Assemble at timecode** option lets you designate the location on the tape where recording should begin, rather than moving to the location using the controls on the deck or camera. Selecting the **Preroll** check box rewinds the tape by a specified number of frames, to give it a chance to get up to speed before recording starts. See Table G-3 for an overview of the options in this dialog box.
6. **If desired, change options in the Export to Tape dialog box**
7. **Click Record**
   Premiere Elements begins recording. The status of the recording process, such as a total of any dropped frames, appears as the tape records. A **dropped frame** is a frame that doesn't get transferred from one medium to the other, usually due to a data transmission error. When recording is complete, the status area summarizes the process, as shown in Figure G-18. If the tape on which you are recording does not have timecode recorded on it, the Start Timecode location is 0 frames. The End Timecode displays the last frame recorded, and the Current Timecode indicates the current location of the tape.
8. **Click Stop**

**QUICK TIP**

You can record to an analog camcorder or VHS tape deck by connecting it to your computer through either an analog-to-digital converter or a DV camcorder that has an analog-out port.

**QUICK TIP**

The Assemble at timecode option is available only if a tape has timecode recorded on it. Timecode is recorded automatically when you record on a videotape; you can add timecode but maintain an otherwise blank tape by recording with the lens cap on.

**FIGURE G-17: Export to Tape dialog box**

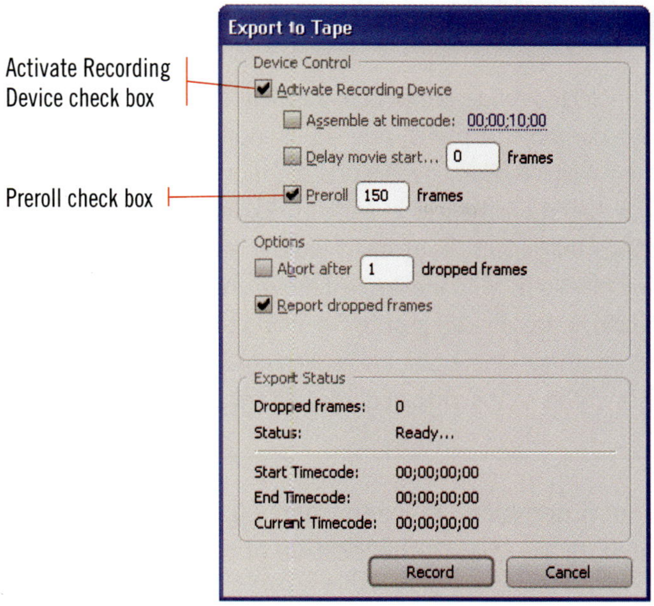


**FIGURE G-18: Status of completed recording**

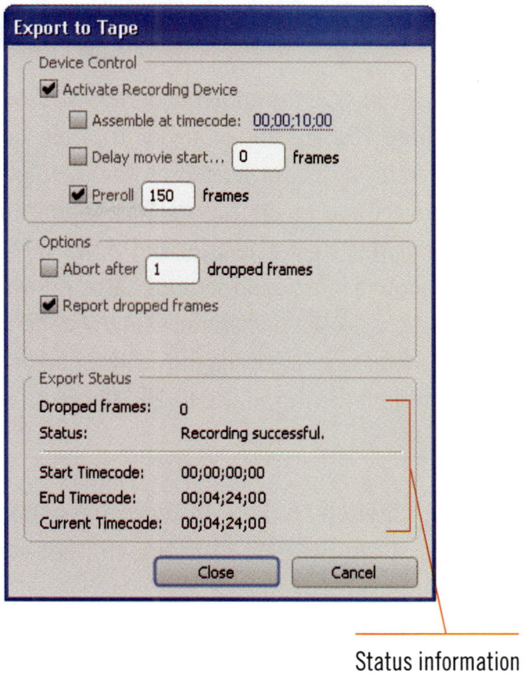


**TABLE G-3: Export to Tape dialog box options**

| option | what it does |
|---|---|
| **Activate Recording Device** | Allows Premiere Elements to control the device controls on the camcorder or tape deck for automatic cueing and recording |
| **Assemble at timecode** | Designates a location on the tape to begin recording; available only if Activate Recording Device is active and tape has timecode recorded on it |
| **Delay movie start** | Specifies a number of quarter-frames to delay the start of the movie once recording starts, which compensates the delay a camera or deck may have before recording |
| **Preroll** | Rewinds the tape by a specified number of frames, so the camera has time to reach a consistent speed before it begins recording the movie; a preroll of 150 frames is recommended |
| **Abort after** | Lets you specify a maximum number of allowable dropped frames in a recording; if more than the allowed number of frames are dropped, recording stops |
| **Report dropped frames** | Displays the total number of dropped frames, if any, at the end of the recording process |

## Clues to Use

### Archiving a project

If you want to send a project to another computer so you or another editor can work on it, but you don't want to copy and move all the source media separately from the file, you can archive the project. **Archiving** saves a copy of the project along with the media on the Media Panel so that it contains everything needed to open and edit the project. To archive a project, click Project on the menu bar, then click Project Archiver. In the Project Archiver dialog box, you can choose to **Archive Project**, which includes only the clips used on the Timeline (plus 30 seconds on either side of each in and out point, if available), or to **Copy Project**, which includes full copies of all the clips on the Media Panel whether you used them or not. The Disk Space area estimates the amount of disk space needed to archive the project. Depending on the size of the project and source clips, archiving can consume a lot of disk space. It copies not only the project and source files, but also the preview files necessary to render the project, so it can't always estimate the final size of the archived project ahead of time. For this reason, you may want to save the file to an external hard drive, network drive, or burn the file onto a CD.

UNIT G

Premiere Elements 2.0

# Exporting to a Video File

You can save the contents of the Timeline, or a selected range within it, in a variety of formats to create a **video file**, a stand-alone file that can be played in a media player, opened in another editing program, stored on disk, or posted on the Internet. When Premiere Elements exports the movie, it compresses the project and media clip data to optimize quality based on the export settings. **Export settings** include compression, frame size, and other specifications that affect the ultimate quality and size of a file. You choose a format and settings based on what you plan to do with the finished movie and on any file size limitations. Shannon wants a stand-alone movie file she can post to her Web site; she wants only the *Genoa Stock & Training* movie included, not the photo slideshow. Shannon's Web hosting service suggested she limit the movie size to 20 MB or less, so that visitors to the site can quickly download the movie.

## STEPS

1. **Switch to the Edit workspace, zoom out if necessary, move to frame 00;04;54;20, then drag the end-of-movie marker on the work area bar to the location of the current-time indicator**

   If you don't want to export the entire contents of the Timeline, adjust the work area so it includes only the part you want to export.

2. **Click the Export Project button Export on the task bar, then click Windows Media**

   The Export Windows Media dialog box opens, as shown in Figure G-19. Windows Media Video format (.wmv) is a popular video format for the Internet because it heavily compresses data and can be played in Windows Media Player, a popular media player that can **stream media**, or begin playing before the entire file has downloaded. This dialog box contains presets for popular Windows Media Video output methods, such as sending over a cable modem or DSL, or to a mobile phone. The Preset Description suggests the intended use and lists the file type and major export settings; see Table G-4 for an explanation of these settings. The Your Movie area lists the length of the contents of the Timeline and the estimated file size at the current settings. A file size of 65.84 MB is far above the 20MB limit Shannon requested.

3. **Click LAN (1024K), observe the Frame Size and File Size estimates, then click 128 Dual ISDN**

   This setting yields a movie that is well under 20MB, yet maintains the frame size of 320x240 and a frame rate of 30. The audio format is **mono** (one-channel) instead of stereo (two-channel), but that's acceptable for posting to the Web. To choose from all available export formats, you can click File on the menu bar, point to Export, click Movie, then click Settings. In the Export Movie Settings dialog box that opens, you can choose any file type or preset, and you can change individual export settings as well as preferences, such as whether you want to add the export file to the current project.

4. **Click Advanced, then click the Video tab if necessary**

   The Export Settings dialog box displays detailed export settings for the current Windows Media preset. For example, this preset includes settings to export both the audio and video tracks, and it uses the Windows Media Video 9 **codec**, or compression method.

5. **Click Cancel, then click OK**

   The Save File dialog box opens, where you can specify a filename and a range for export.

6. **Navigate to the *YourName* folder where you are saving files for this book, type Genoa Stock for Web in the File name text box, click the Export Range list arrow, click Work Area, compare your screen to Figure G-20, then click Save**

   Premiere Elements creates the video file.

7. **Save your changes to the project**

**QUICK TIP**

The Export Windows dialog box doesn't calculate for the adjusted work area until you actually export a file, so take that into consideration if you plan to export only part of a movie; in this case, a brief slideshow containing still images does not add much to the overall file size.

**QUICK TIP**

Changing individual settings can result in an incompatible combination of settings; use the settings for the preset unless you have specific guidelines or reasons for changing a value.

**QUICK TIP**

When you export a video file, it's a good idea to open it in as many compatible media players as possible before distributing it, to test it.

FIGURE G-19: Export Windows Media dialog box

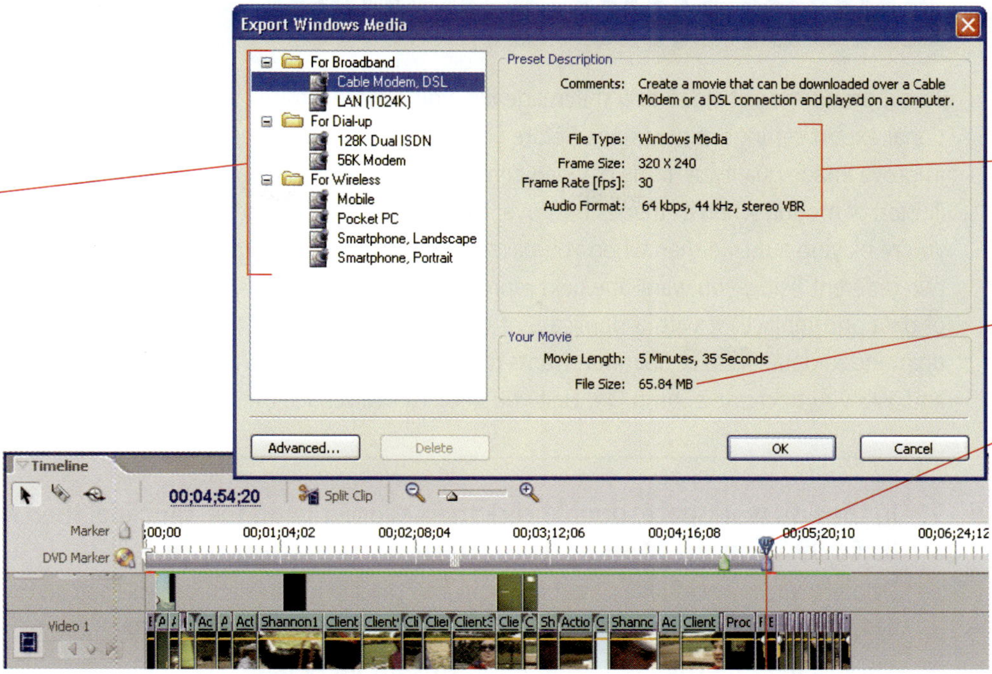


FIGURE G-20: Save File dialog box

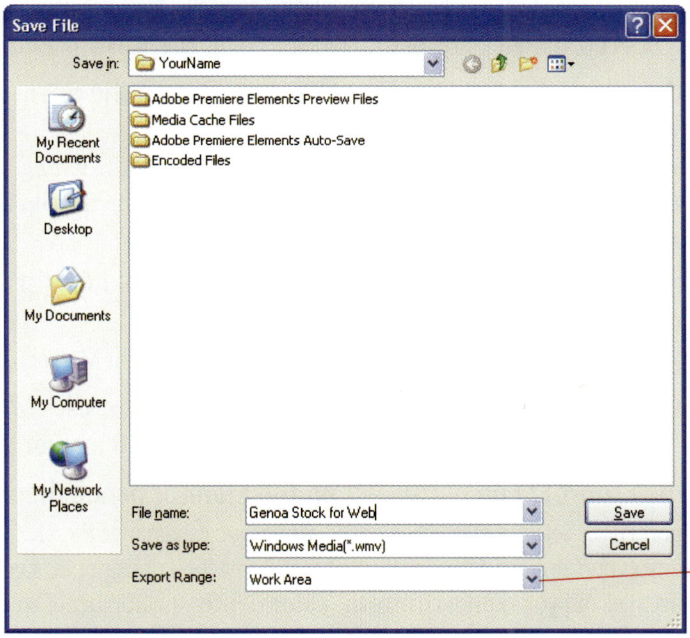


TABLE G-4: Important Export Settings

| setting | description |
|---|---|
| **Frame size** | Size of the screen that opens to play the movie (measured in the number of pixels wide by the number of pixels high |
| **Frame rate** | Speed at which frames play in playback (30 frames per second is the standard for video, though some formats play more slowly to accommodate a more compressed file size) |
| **Audio format** | Compression and stereo settings based on the selected audio codec |
| **Compressor** | Type of COmpressor/DECompressor algorithm (codec) used in export; Premiere Elements and other digital media programs use codecs to compress files for transferring and to decompress them for editing and playing; Windows Media Video 9 is the standard codec for Windows Media Player |
| **Quality** | Slider setting you can adjust to decrease the overall picture quality to achieve a lower file size; not available with all formats and codecs |

# Exporting an Image File

To export a frame of video as a still image file, you choose a frame and then specify a file format and additional export settings, if necessary. Before you export, you can deinterlace the frame you want to export to improve image quality. A frame of video consists of two fields of data **interlaced**, or combined to create the illusion of motion when all frames pass over the playback head. That's why the picture can look clearer when you're playing a movie than when you pause it. But with a still image, you don't want a frame that contains two different fields; you want one field reproduced as clearly as possible. **Deinterlacing** removes one field of data and replaces it with a duplicate of the remaining field, so the frame doesn't contain **artifacts**, or unintended data. Shannon wants to use a frame from the ActionF clip as a still image in a brochure and asks you to create a .bmp file. First you need to deinterlace the frame.

## STEPS

**QUICK TIP**
To export just the audio in a movie, make sure the Timeline is active, click File on the menu bar, click Export, then click Audio.

1. **In the Edit workspace, double-click the ActionF clip on the Timeline, then move to frame 00;00;09;12 on the Monitor time display**
   Deinterlacing is a two-step process: first you open the clip in the Monitor panel and add a Clip marker to the desired frame; then you **hold** or freeze the frame as a still with the settings you want.
2. **Click Marker on the menu bar, point to Set Clip Marker, click Other Numbered, type 0 if necessary in the Set Numbered Marker text box, then click OK**
   A Clip marker labeled "0" is added to the clip, as shown in Figure G-21. To deinterlace a frame, it must be the in point of a clip, the out point, or the Marker 0 point. The marker must be added in the Monitor panel.
3. **Click the selected clip on the Timeline, click Clip on the menu bar, point to Video Options, then click Frame Hold**
   The Frame Hold Options dialog box opens, where you can specify settings for the frame you want to export. To open this dialog box, the Timeline Panel must be active, and the clip containing the frame you want to export must be selected.

**QUICK TIP**
If a clip has effects applied to it that you don't want to appear in the still image, you can click the Hold Filters check box to select it.

4. **Click the Hold On check box to select it, click the Hold On list arrow, click Marker 0, click the Deinterlace check box to select it, then click OK**
   These settings tell Premiere Elements to freeze the frame that's at Marker 0, and to deinterlace it.
5. **Click anywhere to the left of the marker in the Timeline, click Marker on the menu bar, point to Go To Clip marker, click Numbered, verify that the 0 marker is highlighted, then click OK**

**QUICK TIP**
You can export a title clip by selecting it in the Media panel, clicking File on the menu bar, pointing to Export, then clicking Title. The file is saved in Adobe Title Designer (.prtl) format.

6. **Click the Export Frame button on the Monitor panel, then click Settings**
   The Export Frame Settings dialog box opens, where you can change the file format and export preferences. Note that many export options are unavailable for still images. For example, a codec is not used when exporting a still image file, and you cannot change the **color depth**, the number of colors used to produce the image.
7. **Click the File Type list arrow, click Windows Bitmap if necessary, click OK, scroll down in the Summary list, then compare your screen to Figure G-22**
   In the Export Frame dialog box, the File name text box displays a filename for the image based on the project filename, and a file format based on the last format and settings selected in this dialog box. Under Video Settings, the Fields setting displays "No Fields (Progressive Scan)" because you deinterlaced this frame. **Progressive scan** is another term for deinterlaced video.
8. **Click Save**
   Premiere Elements creates the file, then adds it to the Media panel, so you can use it in the project if you want.
9. **Save your changes to the project, then close it and exit Premiere Elements**

FIGURE G-21: Clip marker added to frame

FIGURE G-22: Completed Export Frame dialog box

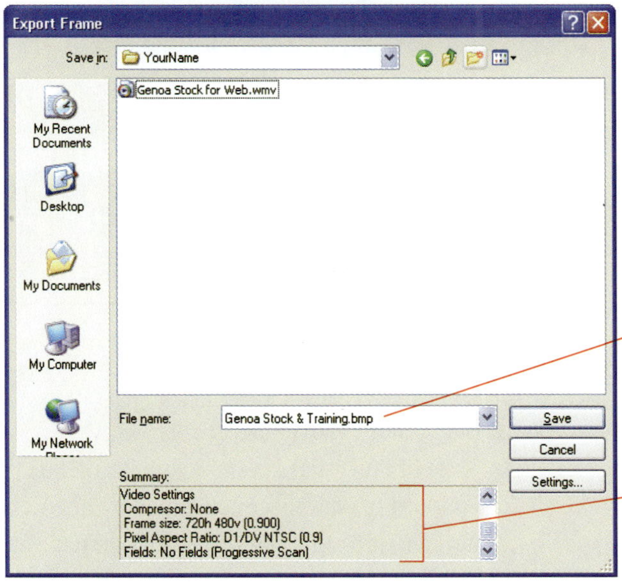


## Production Matters

### Adding bars and tone

Before exporting a movie to videotape, you may want to add a bars and tone clip to the beginning. **Bars and Tone** is a clip that is included with Premiere Elements. It consists of a standard television test pattern of color bars and a constant 1 kHz audio tone. Video professionals use it to calibrate or match the video and audio levels on one source when outputting to another source. While it's not necessary to include this clip for a movie you simply plan to play on your VCR, it can be useful if you plan to have several copies duplicated at a production house. To add this clip, click the New Item button on the Media panel, click Bars and Tone, drag the Bars and Tone clip from the Media panel to the beginning of the Timeline, then extend the duration of the clip to 30 seconds, the standard length of a bars and tone segment.

# Practice

## ▼ CONCEPTS REVIEW

**Label the elements of the Premiere Elements program window shown in Figure G-23.**

FIGURE G-23

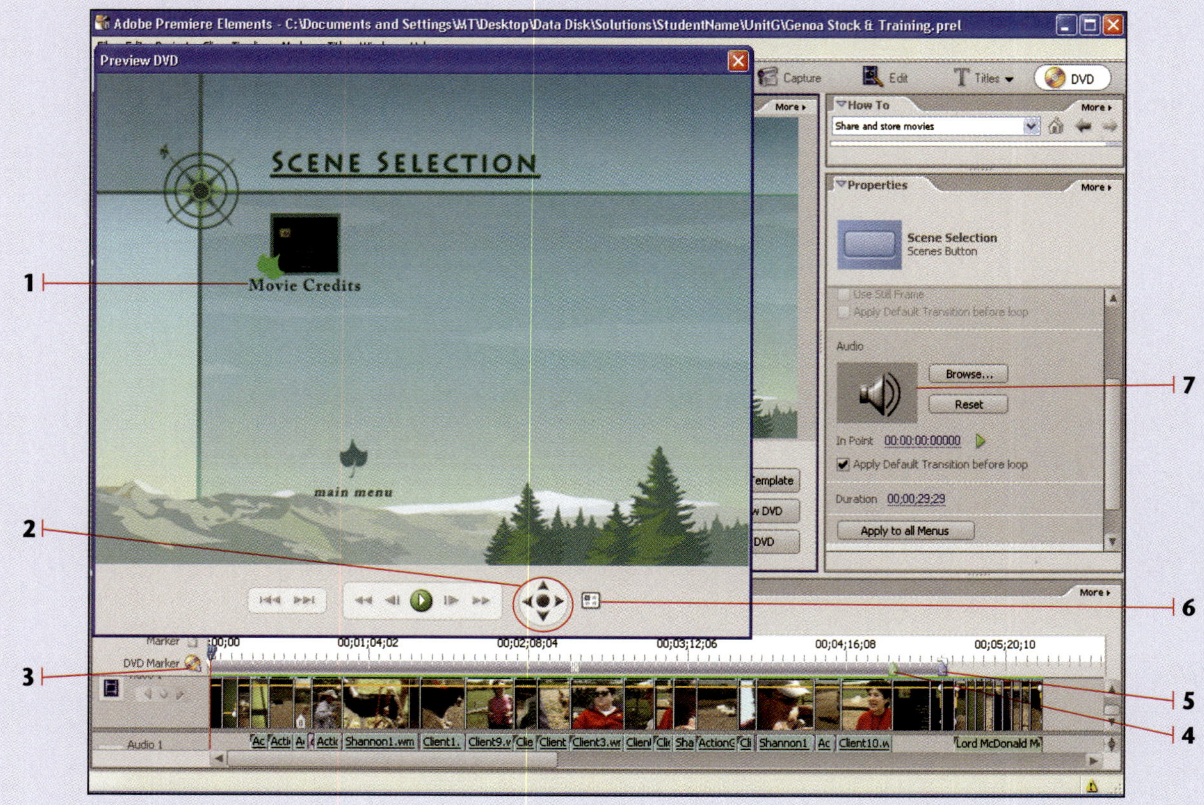


**Match each term with the statement that best describes it.**

8. **DVD marker**
9. **Video file**
10. **Preview window**
11. **Color Matte**
12. **Auto-play**
13. **Main Menu marker**
14. **Bitrate**

**a.** Stand-alone movie file
**b.** Type of DVD that does not contain menus
**c.** Amount of data space consumed by one second of video
**d.** You add it to a movie so viewers can navigate to specific points on a DVD
**e.** You add it to a movie so viewers can navigate to the first menu on a DVD
**f.** Lets you view a DVD and menus before burning to disc
**g.** Video clip you can use to separate movies on the Timeline

**Select the best answer from the list of choices.**

**15. To export a movie file, you choose a file type and:**
- **a.** File add-ons.
- **b.** Disc color.
- **c.** Audio clips.
- **d.** Export settings.

**16. Prior to exporting a frame as a still image file, you should:**
- **a.** Crop it.
- **b.** Deinterlace it.
- **c.** Interlace it.
- **d.** Resize it.

**17. A dropped frame is:**
- **a.** A frame trimmed from a clip.
- **b.** A deleted frame.
- **c.** A frame that isn't transferred from one medium to another, due to an error.
- **d.** A frame that isn't transferred from one medium to another, due to preferences.

**18. If you add Stop markers to the end of each movie on a multi-movie DVD with menus:**
- **a.** The DVD ejects when a movie ends.
- **b.** The DVD returns to the main menu when each movie ends.
- **c.** The movie plays again from the beginning when it ends.
- **d.** The DVD pauses when each movie ends.

**19. Which tool do you use to export a frame as a still image?**
- **a.** 
- **b.** 
- **c.** 
- **d.** 

**20. You can change the default text in a DVD menu in the:**
- **a.** Monitor panel.
- **b.** Properties panel.
- **c.** DVD Layout panel.
- **d.** DVD Menus area.

## ▼ SKILLS REVIEW

**1. Prepare a movie for DVD.**
- **a.** Start Premiere Elements.
- **b.** Open the file PE G-2.prel from the drive and folder where your Data Files are located, then save it as **Kapoot Clown Theatre** in the *YourName* folder where you are saving files for this book.
- **c.** Create a Black Video clip using a button on the Media panel.
- **d.** Add the new video clip to the Video 1 track at the beginning of the Timeline.
- **e.** Add another instance of the clip to the photo slideshow, which begins at frame 00;01;34;25.
- **f.** Move to frame 00;01;22;16, then open the DVD Marker dialog box.
- **g.** Add a Scene Marker named **Credits and Info**, then close the dialog box.
- **h.** Add a Main Menu marker named **Performance Photos** to frame 00;01;34;26.
- **i.** Save your changes to the project.

## ▼ SKILLS REVIEW (CONTINUED)

**2. Export an auto-play DVD.**

- **a.** Click the DVD button on the task bar.
- **b.** Choose the Auto play DVD with no Menus option button, then close the dialog box.
- **c.** Open the Preview DVD window.
- **d.** Play the DVD for a few moments, pause the playback, then jump to the next scene.
- **e.** If you have a compatible DVD and want to create a DVD of this project, insert it in your computer's DVD drive, then open the Burn DVD dialog box.
- **f.** If you are burning a DVD of this project, burn the DVD; otherwise, click Cancel in the dialog box.

**3. Create DVD menus.**

- **a.** Open the DVD Templates dialog box.
- **b.** Locate the Stage theme in the Entertainment category, then generate menus based on this theme.
- **c.** In the DVD Layout panel, switch to the Scenes Menu 1 menu.
- **d.** Double-click the Credits & Info thumbnail.
- **e.** In the DVD Marker dialog box, drag the Thumbnail Offset to frame 00;00;05;25, then click OK.
- **f.** Switch to the Main Menu 1 menu, double-click the Theatre Curtain Title text, type **Kapoot Clown Theatre** in the Change Text dialog box, then click OK.
- **g.** Change the Acts text to **ETC**.
- **h.** Change the font of the menu buttons on both menus to Charlemagne Std and the font size to 18pt. (*Hint:* If this font is not available on your computer, choose a different font.)
- **i.** Drag the menu text boxes on the Main Menu 1 menu into a centered column, as shown in Figure G-24, then save your changes to the project.

FIGURE G-24

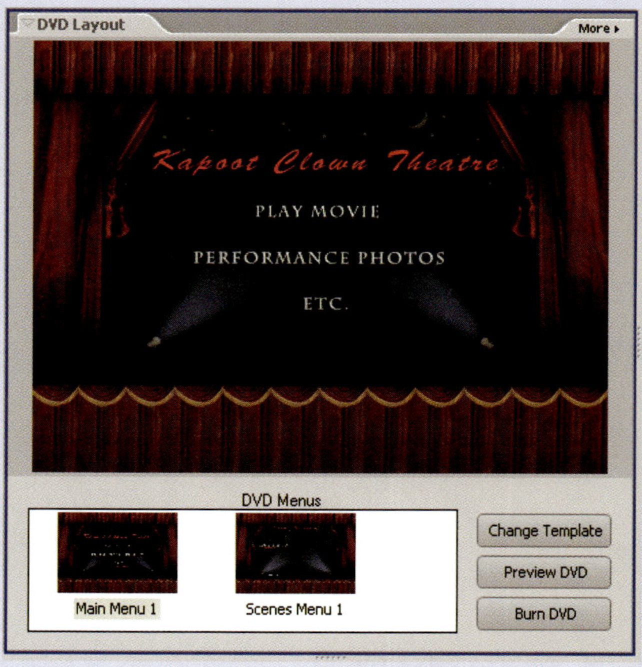


**4. Export a DVD with menus.**

- **a.** Open the Preview window.
- **b.** Click the ETC. link.
- **c.** Click the CREDITS & INFO link.
- **d.** After the credits play, return to the main menu, then close the Preview window.
- **e.** Resize the Timeline if necessary to see the Video 1 track, move to frame 00;01;34;25, then open the DVD Marker dialog box.
- **f.** Create a Stop marker, then close the dialog box.
- **g.** Preview the DVD, then make sure it stops after the movie ends.
- **h.** In the main menu, move to the Performance Photos link using a button on the Preview window, click the link, verify that the slideshow plays, then close the Preview DVD window.
- **i.** Open the Burn DVD dialog box, burn a DVD if you want, then close the dialog box.

**5. Export a movie to DV or VHS tape.**

- **a.** Review the steps to verify that your system is equipped for recording to a video camera.
- **b.** Review the steps for connecting the camcorder to your computer.
- **c.** Review the steps for moving to the tape location where you want to start recording.
- **d.** Review the steps for opening and completing the Export to Tape dialog box in Premiere Elements.
- **e.** Review the steps for completing the recording process.

## ▼ SKILLS REVIEW (CONTINUED)

**6. Export a video file.**

- **a.** On the Timeline panel, adjust the work area so it does not include the slideshow.
- **b.** Click the Export Project button on the task bar, then click QuickTime.
- **c.** In the Export QuickTime dialog box, review the Frame Size estimates for the following presets: LAN (1024K), 112 Dual ISDN, Mobile, and Smartphone Landscape. (*Hint*: When exporting to QuickTime, file size estimates are not available.)
- **d.** Click the Cable Modem, DSL preset, then open the Export Settings dialog box.
- **e.** Review the settings in the Video tab, click Cancel, then click OK in the Export QuickTime dialog box.
- **f.** In the Save File dialog box, change the Export Range to Work Area, then save the file as **Kapoot Clown Theatre** for Web in the *YourName* folder where you are saving files for this book.

**7. Export an image file.**

- **a.** Switch to the Edit workspace, open the Cam2_d.avi clip in the Monitor panel, then move to frame 00;01;07;23 on the Monitor time display.
- **b.** Click Marker on the menu bar, point to Set Clip Marker, then click Other Numbered.
- **c.** Type **0** in the Set Numbered Marker text box, then click OK.
- **d.** Activate the Timeline panel, leaving the clip selected, then open the Frame Hold Options dialog box using a command on the Clip menu.
- **e.** Select the Hold On check box and the Deinterlace check box, change the Hold On field to **0**, then click OK.
- **f.** Move to the 0 marker on the Timeline, then click the Export Frame button on the Monitor panel.
- **g.** In the Export Frame dialog box, open the Export Frame Settings dialog box, change the File Type to JPEG, then close the Export Frame Settings dialog box.
- **h.** Save the file as **Kapoot Clown Theatre** in the *YourName* folder where you are saving files for this book.
- **i.** Save your changes to the project, then close it and exit Premiere Elements.

## ▼ INDEPENDENT CHALLENGE 1

You are ready to output your film festival trailer so it can be posted to the Web. The head of the film festival wants the file in two formats, Windows MediaVideo and QuickTime. She asks you to create two video files, one for each format.

- **a.** Start Premiere Elements if necessary.
- **b.** Open the file PE G-3.prel from the drive and folder where your Data Files are located, then save it as **Film Fest Trailer** in the *YourName* folder where you are saving files for this book.
- **c.** Save one copy of the entire movie as a WMV file using the 128K Dual ISDN preset and the filename **Film Fest Trailer for Windows Media Player**.
- **d.** Save another copy of the movie as an MOV file using the Cable Modem, DSL preset and the filename **Film Fest Trailer for QuickTime Player**.

**Advanced Challenge Exercise**

ACE

- Open the Project Archiver dialog box. (*Hint*: Use a command on the Project menu.)
- Determine the estimated file size to archive this project including only the clips used on the Timeline. Do not archive the project, but instead cancel out of the dialog box.
- Open a word-processing document and record the information, adding your name to the top of the page, save the document as **Film Fest Trailer ACE**, print one copy, save and close the document, then exit your word processor.

- **e.** Save your changes to the project, then close it and exit Premiere Elements.

## ▼ INDEPENDENT CHALLENGE 2

It's time to output your documentary so you can share it with friends, colleagues, and perhaps submit it to a film festival or two. The output options you choose depend on your goals for distributing the movie and the output options available on your computer system.

- **a.** Start Premiere Elements if necessary, open the file My Documentary Titles and Credits.prel from the drive and folder where you are saving files for this book, then save it as **My Documentary Final**. (*Note*: If you did not create and edit this movie, consult your instructor.)
- **b.** Add DVD markers to the project. Include Scene markers for major scenes within the movie and for the credits sequence.
- **c.** Create menus for the DVD using a theme of your choice, then modify the text and formatting as appropriate.
- **d.** Preview the DVD and test the menu navigation.
- **e.** If you have a DVD burner and a blank DVD, burn the movie to DVD. If you are unable to burn a DVD, save the movie as a video file in a format appropriate for your distribution goals and data storage limitations, with the filename **My Documentary Final**.
- **f.** When you're finished, close the project and exit Premiere Elements.

## ▼ INDEPENDENT CHALLENGE 3

Jim, your boss at Fig Media, has requested a copy of your Dream Job video so he can use it in his presentation to new interns. Jim plans to play the movie using a VCD player and a video projector, so he needs the file saved in a format appropriate for this medium. Jim knows he needs an MPEG format for the VCD player, but realizes there are several formats ranging from DVD quality down to VHS-like quality. He isn't sure which MPEG format is best for the presentation.

- **a.** Start Premiere Elements if necessary, open the Dream Job Titles project you created from the drive and folder where you are saving files for this book, then save it as **Dream Job Final** in the *YourName* folder. (*Note*: If you did not create and edit this movie, consult your instructor.)
- **b.** Click File on the menu bar, point to Export, then click MPEG.
- **c.** In the Export MPEG dialog box, review each preset to find a format that is appropriate to play on a VCD player in the United States or Japan.
- **d.** Once you've found the right format, click OK, then save the file as **Dream Job for VCD**.

**Advanced Challenge Exercise**

ACE
- Create a still image file from any frame in the movie. Remember to deinterlace the frame before exporting it.
- Save the image as **Dream Job Final.bmp**.

- **e.** Save and close the project, then exit Premiere Elements.

## ▼ INDEPENDENT CHALLENGE 4

Your Internet Education video is ready for outputting. You've already burned a DVD of the movie for use at the conference. However, you want to excerpt a brief clip from the movie and export it as an animated GIF that can be posted to your cinema club's Web site. You need to choose a clip and then create the file.

- **a.** Start Premiere Elements if necessary, open the file Internet Titles and Credits from the drive and folder location where you are saving files for this book, then save it to the *YourName* folder as **Internet Education Final**.
- **b.** Choose a brief segment of the movie (not more than 150 frames) that you'd like to use to create an animated GIF. Choose a segment that is visually interesting; the clip will not contain sound.
- **c.** Adjust the work area bar to extend only over the segment you want to export.
- **d.** Click File on the menu bar, point to Export, click Movie, then in the Export Movie dialog box, click Settings.
- **e.** In the Export Movie Settings dialog box, change the File Type to Animated GIF, change the Range to Work Area Bar, then click OK.
- **f.** In the Export Movie dialog box, save the file as **Internet Education Web Excerpt.gif**.
- **g.** When you are finished, add the .gif clip to the end of the movie on the Timeline, then view it. (*Hint*: By default, Premiere Elements adds the clip to the Media panel, but if this option is not selected on your computer, add the file from your *YourName* folder.) Do not adjust the work area bar.
- **h.** Save your changes to the project, then close it and exit Premiere Elements.

## ▼ VISUAL WORKSHOP

Open the file PE G-4.prel from the drive and folder where your Data Files are located, then save it as **Butterfly DVD** in the *YourName* folder where you are saving files for this book. Using Figure G-25 as a guide, create a DVD menu based on a template and format it as necessary so that the Scenes Menu 1 menu matches the one shown in the Preview DVD window. (*Hint*: The template is available in the Templates dialog box. You will need to change the Thumbnail Offset of one menu button.) When you are finished, save your changes to the project, press [PrtScr], paste the image into your word-processing program, print a copy, then exit your word processor and Premiere Elements.

FIGURE G-25

# Source Files List

## Source Files folder

A Grey Day In Seaham.mp3
ActionA.wmv
ActionB.wmv
ActionC.wmv
ActionD.wmv
ActionE.wmv
ActionF.wmv
ActionG.wmv
ActionH.wmv
ActionI.wmv
ActionJ.wmv
ActionK.wmv
Bill.wmv
Brett and why he likes Fig.wmv
Cam1_a.avi
Cam1_b.avi
Cam1_c.avi
Cam1_d.avi
Cam1_e.avi
Cam1_f.avi
Cam2_a.avi
Cam2_b.avi
Cam2_c.avi
Cam2_d.avi
Cam2_e.avi
Chris.wmv
Client1.wmv
Client10.wmv
Client2.wmv
Client3.wmv
Client4.wmv
Client5.wmv
Client6.wmv
Client7.wmv
Client8.wmv
Client9.wmv
Common Buckeye.jpg
Django herding.bmp
Django.bmp
Dress for Success.wmv
Fantastic Plastic.wav
Fig sign.wmv
Fig street.wmv
Fritillary01.jpg
Fritillary02.jpg
Frodo.bmp
Interior travel shot.wmv
Jen and why she likes Fig.wmv
Jennifer.wmv
Kai.bmp
Kapoot1.jpg
Kapoot2.jpg
Kapoot3.jpg
Kapoot4.jpg
Kapoot5.jpg
Kapoot6.jpg
Kapoot7.jpg
Kapoot8.jpg
Lily.bmp
Lord McDonald Medley.wav
Megan.wmv
Michelle and why she likes Fig.wmv
Muffin Control.wmv
Painted Lady.jpg
Pipevine Swallowtail.jpg
Really Hot Coffee.wmv
Sad Song.wmv
Shannon teaching.bmp
Shannon with sheep.bmp
Shannon1.wmv
Sheep looking.bmp
Silent Breakfast.wmv
Singer Strange Theme.mp3
Staff pan.wmv
Still from Dress for Success.bmp
Still from The Mountaineer.bmp
Tax Help.wmv
The Pharaos Theme.wav
Theme Song.mp3
Tibbs.bmp
Twelve Empty Cups.mp3
Why Megan likes Fig.wmv
Zebra Longwing.jpg

## Extra Photos subfolder

Extra photo 1.jpg
Extra photo 2.jpg

## Genoa Photos subfolder

Frodo herding.bmp
Sheep looking.bmp
Shannon teaching.bmp
Shannon with sheep.bmp

# Data Files List

| Unit and Location | Data File Supplied | Student Saves File As | Student Creates File |
|---|---|---|---|
| **Unit A** | | | |
| Lesson 2 | none | n/a | Genoa Clients.prel |
| SR Step 2c | none | n/a | Clown PR.prel |
| IC1 | none | n/a | Film Fest.prel |
| IC 2 | none | n/a | My First Movie.prel |
| IC 3 | none | n/a | Dream Job.prel |
| IC 4 | none | n/a | n/a |
| VW | none | n/a | Butterfly Lecture.prel |
| **Unit B** | | | |
| Lesson 1 | PE B-1.prel | Genoa Clients Rough Cut 1.prel | |
| Lesson 5 | PE B-1.prel | Genoa Clients Rough Cut 2.prel | |
| Lesson 8 | Lord McDonald Medley.wav | (inserted in file) | |
| SR Step 1d | PE B-2.prel | Clown Rough Cut 1.prel | |
| SR Step 5a | PE B-2.prel | Clown Rough Cut 2.prel | |
| SR Step 8c | Fantastic Plastic.wav | (inserted in file) | |
| IC 1 | PE B-3.prel | Film Fest Rough Cut.prel<br>Film Fest Rough Cut ACE.prel | |
| IC 2 | none | n/a | My Documentary.prel |
| IC 3 | PE B-4.prel | Dream Job Rough Cut.prel<br>Dream Job Rough Cut ACE.prel | |
| IC 4 | none | n/a | Filmmaker Presentation.prel |
| VW | PE B-5.prel | Butterfly Slidehow.prel | |
| **Unit C** | | | |
| Lesson 1 | PE C-1.prel | Genoa Edit.prel | |
| SR Step 1b | PE C-2.prel | Clown Edit.prel | |
| IC1 | PE C-3.prel | Film Fest Edit.prel<br>Film Fest Edit ACE.prel | |
| IC2 | My Documentary.prel | My Documentary Edit.prel | |
| IC3 | PE C-4.prel | Dream Job Edit.prel<br>Dream Job Edit ACE.prel | |
| IC4 | none | n/a | Internet Education.prel |
| VW | PE C-5.prel | Butterfly Edit.prel | |

| Unit and Location | Data File Supplied | Student Saves File As | Student Creates File |
|---|---|---|---|
| **Unit D** | | | |
| Lesson 1 | PE D-1.prel | Genoa Effects and Transitions.prel | |
| SR Step 1b | PE D-2.prel | Clown Effects and Transitions.prel | |
| IC 1 | PE D-3.prel | Film Fest Effects and Transitions.prel<br>Film Fest Effects and Transitions ACE.prel | |
| IC 2 | My Documentary Edit.prel | My Documentary Effects and Transitions.prel | |
| IC 3 | Dream Job Edit.prel | Dream Job Effects and Transitions.prel<br>Dream Job Effects and Transitions ACE.prel | |
| IC 4 | Internet Education.prel | Internet Education Transitions.prel | |
| VW | PE D-4.prel | Butterfly Transitions.prel | |
| **Unit E** | | | |
| Lesson 1 | PE E-1.prel | Genoa Audio Adjustments.prel | |
| SR Step 1b | PE E-2.prel | Clown Audio Adjustments.prel | |
| IC 1 | PE E-3.prel | Film Fest With Soundtrack.prel<br>Film Fest With Soundtrack ACE.prel | |
| IC 2 | My Documentary Effects and Transitions.prel | My Documentary With Audio Adjustments.prel | |
| IC 3 | Dream Job Effects and Transitions.prel | Dream Job With Audio Adjustments.prel<br>Dream Job With Audio | |
| | | Adjustments ACE.prel | |
| IC 4 | Internet Education Transitions.prel | Internet Education With Soundtrack.prel | |
| VW | PE E-4.prel | Butterfly Soundtrack.prel | |
| **Unit F** | | | |
| Lesson 1 | PE F-1.prel | Genoa Titles and Credits.prel | |
| Lesson 4 | Django.jpg | (inserted in file) | |
| SR Step 1b | PE F-2.prel | Clown Titles and Credits.prel | |
| SR Step 4c | Kapoot4.jpg | (inserted in file) | |
| IC 1 | PE F-3.prel | Film Fest Titles.prel<br>Film Fest Titles ACE.prel | |
| IC 2 | My Documentary With Audio Adjustments.prel | My Documentary Titles and Credits.prel | |

| Unit and Location | Data File Supplied | Student Saves File As | Student Creates File |
|---|---|---|---|
| IC 3 | Dream Job With Audio Adjustments.prel | Dream Job Titles.prel<br>Dream Job Titles ACE.prel | |
| IC 4 | Internet Education | Internet Titles and Credits.prel | |
| VW | PE F-4.prel | Butterfly Title.prel | |
| **Unit G** | | | |
| Lesson 1 | PE G-1.prel | Genoa Stock & Training.prel | |
| Lesson 7 | | Genoa Stock for Web.wmv | |
| Lesson 8 | | Genoa Stock & Training.bmp | |
| SR Step 1b | PE G-2.prel | Kapoot Clown Theatre.prel | |
| SR Step 6f | | Kapoot Clown Theatre for Web.mov | |
| SR Step 7h | | Kapoot Clown Theatre.jpg | |
| IC1 | PE G-3.prel | Film Fest Trailer.prel<br>Film Fest Trailer for Windows Media Player.wmv<br>Film Fest Trailer for QuickTime Player.mov<br>Film Fest Trailer ACE.doc | |
| IC2 | My Documentary Titles | My Documentary Final.prel<br>My Documentary.mov (file extension may vary) | |
| IC3 | Dream Job Titles.prel | Dream Job Final.prel<br>Dream Job for VCD.mpg<br>Dream Job Final ACE.bmp | |
| IC4 | Internet Titles and Credits.prel | Internet Education Final.prel<br>Internet Education Web Excerpt.gif | |
| VW | PE G-4.prel | Butterfly DVD.prel | |

# Glossary

**.prel** Adobe Premiere Elements Project; file format for a Premiere Elements project

**Action-safe margin** In the Titler panel, indicates a frame within which content should be viewable on all television monitors.

**Amplitude** Describes the power of a sound vibration.

**Animate** Adjusts where an effect starts or stops in a clip so that the effect is applied to only part of the clip.

**Archive** To save a copy of a Premiere Elements project along with the project's source files so it contains everything needed to display and edit the movie.

**Artifact** Unintended data in a file that causes distortion.

**Assemble at timecode** When exporting to videotape, this option lets you move to a location on the tape within Premiere Elements rather than using the controls on the deck or camera.

**Audio waveform** A graphical representation of an audio signal.

**Auto-play DVD** Type of DVD in which the movie begins playing immediately when you insert it in a DVD player, and any additional movies on the DVD play in succession after the first one.

**Bars and Tone** A clip that consists of a standard television test pattern of color bars and a constant 1 kHz audio tone; used by video professionals to calibrate the video and audio levels on one source when outputting to another source.

**Bitrate** Amount of data space consumed by a second of video.

**Black Video** Command that adds a still black clip to the Media panel.

**Blur** Type of preset effect that blurs the beginning or end of a clip.

**Brightness** Setting that changes the relative exposure in a clip.

**Burning media** Writing video files to DVD.

**Bypass property** Setting that turns the effect off or on in the current clip.

**Camera operator** Person in charge of recording with a camera.

**Capturing** Process of transferring video from a camcorder to a computer's hard drive.

**Chapters** Links to scenes on a DVD.

**Clear** Type of deletion that removes a clip without closing the resulting gap in the Timeline.

**Clip instance** A duplicate of a clip on the Media panel, created when you drag the clip to the Timeline.

**Clip thumbnail** Small image that illustrates a clip, making it easier to identify.

**Clipping** Type of distortion that occurs when the audio signal exceeds the recommended range for output.

**Close-up** Shot in which the frame shows only the subject's head and shoulders.

**Codec** Type of COmpressor/DECompressor algorithm used in exporting a video file; Premiere Elements and other digital media programs use codecs to compress files for transferring and to decompress them for editing and playing.

**Color depth** The number of colors used to produce an image.

**Color Matte** Command that adds a still clip of the color you choose to the Media panel.

**Constant Gain** Audio transition that gradually increases the gain of the next clip while reducing the gain of the previous clip.

**Constant Power** Audio transition that creates a smooth, gradual crossfade from one sound clip to the next.

**Contrast** Setting that affects the distinctions between light and dark shades in a clip.

**Crawling** Title or credit text that moves left or right.

**Credits** Titles that identify, or give credit to, the cast and crew of a movie, and may provide additional information, such as the location where a movie was filmed, songs used, or a dedication.

**Cross dissolve** Transition that creates the effect of the previous image fading away while another appears on top of it and gradually replaces it.

**Crossfade** Audio transition in which the content from the previous clip and the next clip blend, with the previous clip fading out as the next one fades in.

**Current Task Progress bar** Shows the progress of the current task.

**Current-time indicator** Appears on the current frame on the time ruler and allows you to move to a different frame by dragging it.

**Decibels (dB)** A relative audio measuring system that describes signal drop-off over distance.

**Deinterlacing** Removes one field of data in a video frame and replaces it with a duplicate of the remaining field.

**Digital film** Common term for a video.

**Double-sided transition** Transition that overlaps frames from two clips at the edit point.

**Drop Shadow** Type of preset effect that adds a static or animated drop shadow to the frame of a clip.

**Dropped frame** A frame that doesn't get transferred from one medium to the other, usually due to a data transmission error.

**DVD markers** Adding these elements to a movie before creating a DVD allows the viewer to jump to specific points using his or her DVD player or remote.

**Edit** To assemble video, audio, and/or image clips in the order you want, add any special transitions and effects, or add a music soundtrack or make other audio enhancements.

**Edit point** Location on the Timeline where one clip ends and the next starts.

**Effects and Transitions panel** Window that contains special effects and transitions.

**Encoding Media** Compressing audio or video data.

**Export settings** When exporting to a video file, settings such as compression and frame size that affect the ultimate quality and size of a file.

**Fill** Inside color of an object.

**FireWire** IEEE 1394 cable, used to transfer data.

**Fixed effects** Basic properties, such as brightness, contrast, rotation, and audio volume that Premiere Elements applies to a clip when you add it to the Timeline.

**Frequency** The rate at which sound waves vibrate; measured in Hertz (Hz), or cycles per second.

**Gaffer** On a film or video shoot, the person in charge of the lighting and electrical team.

**Gain** Input audio level of a clip.

**Gate** Setting which specifies the level at which a sound must occur before it's affected by the current effect.

**Gradient** A blend of colors.

**Hold** Freezes a frame in a video clip as a still image.

**How To panel** Window that displays help topics for the current task.

**Hue** Setting that affects the relative color of pixels in a clip.

**In point** First frame of a clip or clip segment.

**Interlaced** A frame of video that consists of two fields of data combined to create the illusion of motion when all frames pass over the playback head.

**Interpolation** Process of calculating the values between two keyframes to create a smooth transition.

**J-cut** Type of edit in which the audio track starts before the video track, which resembles the letter J on the Timeline.

**Keyframes** Frames within a clip that control the path of an animation.

**L-cut** Type of edit in which the audio track ends after the video track, which resembles the letter L on the Timeline.

**Long shot** Shot in which the frame shows the subject's entire body.

**Loop** Setting that causes a clip to continue playing from the beginning when it reaches the end.

**Main menu** Menu that appears when you insert the DVD in a player.

**Marker** An icon you can place anywhere in the Monitor or Timeline time ruler to help in editing.

**Media** All video, audio, and image sources that can be used in a video.

**Media drop zone** Area on the Properties panel where you drag audio and video clips to add to a menu on a DVD.

**Media panel** Window that contains source clips you can add to a movie.

**Medium shot** Shot in which the frame shows the subject's waist up to the top of the head.

**Menu bar** Area near the top of the program window where Premiere Elements commands are organized into menus.

**Menus** Elements on a DVD that represent choices (such as scenes, bonus material, and so on).

**Mix** To combine or layer sounds together in an edit.

**Monitor panel** Window where you can view source footage and edited video, set in and out points, and add markers.

**Mono** One-channel audio

**Movie** A term for a finished video or film.

**MPEG-2** A high-quality file format that contains video, audio, and menu navigation data.

**Navigation pane** Window in Help that provides links to help contents.

**Noise** Extraneous or unintended sound such as hiss or distortion.

**Normalize** To automatically adjust audio levels in a clip to optimize the overall volume.

**NTSC** National Television Standards Committee; broadcast standard used primarily in the Americas, Japan, the Caribbean, and Taiwan. Specifies the pixel aspect ratio, frame rate, and other elements that control how an image is composed and displayed on a television screen.

**Object** Any text or graphic you can modify.

**Open** To load a file into Premiere Elements so you can work with it.

**Out point** Last frame of a clip or clip segment.

**Outputting** Converts a movie on the Timeline into a stand-alone video.

**Overlay** To replace frames on the target clip with the frames of a clip you are moving.

**PAL** Phase Alternating Line; broadcast standard used primarily in Europe and South America. Specifies the pixel aspect ratio, frame rate, and other elements that control how an image is composed and displayed on a television screen.

**Peak** The highest decibel reading of an audio clip.

**Picture-in-picture** Type of preset effect that superimposes a clip playing in a frame within another clip.

**Placeholder** Indicates suggested formatting and placement of text.

**Poster frame** Image that appears in a clip thumbnail.

**Preproduction** Planning and preparation that occurs before the start of a movie or video shoot.

**Preroll** When exporting to videotape, this option rewinds the tape by a specified number of frames, to allow it to get up to speed before recording starts.

**Preset effects** Preconfigured effects you can quickly apply to clips to create sophisticated results.

**Production crew** The people working together on a film or video shoot.

**Progressive scan** Another term for deinterlaced video, indicating that the data displays in sequential or progressive order rather than in alternating fields.

**Project Settings** Settings that control video and audio formats in a Premiere Elements project file.

**Properties panel** Window that displays information on the currently selected item.

**Properties** Attributes of a selected effect, transition, or clip.

**Rearrange** To relocate a clip by shifting existing clips to the right and closing the gap left by the moved clip.

**Reference** Shortcut to a media source that is added to a project when you add the source file, so that you can edit without using the computer resources necessary to copy and modify the actual file.

**Regain** To restore trimmed frames in a clip.

**Render** To process edits, compress information, recalculate each frame, and display the results in final form for previewing.

**Rip** To convert a file to a format compatible with the current editing program.

**Ripple deletion** Type of deletion that does not result in a gap on the Timeline.

**Ripple-trim** Trims a clip so that frames trailing the clip automatically adjust so no gap results in the Timeline.

**Rolling** Title or credit text that moves up or down on the screen.

**Rough cut** Assembly of all the clips you plan to use in a movie arranged in the general order you plan to use them, but in the state before you've edited the clips and applied transitions and other fine-tuning.

**Sample** To use a tool to obtain a color displayed on the screen by clicking it with the mouse.

**Saturation** Setting that increases or decreases the strength of the colors in a clip.

**Scene** One related sequence of action or set of shots.

**Scenes menu** On a DVD, a menu that appears when you click the Scene Selection menu on the main menu.

**Scratch file** A file Premiere Elements generates automatically to improve performance while editing.

**Semitone** A half-step in pitch.

**Set dresser** On a film or video shot, the person who decorates the set.

**Shooting** Recording action with a video or film camera.

**Shot** Unit of recorded action, defined by the starting and stopping of the camera's recording mechanism.

**Show Video** Command that displays the current video frame for reference purposes when creating titles.

**Snap** Feature that automatically aligns a clip or edit to the nearest positioning milestone.

**Sound wave** A pattern that consists of amplitude, wavelength, and frequency.

**Source footage** Recorded videotape intended for editing.

**Source material** Video, audio, and image files you edit into a movie in Premiere Elements.

**Split** To divide a clip into two or more separate clips on the Timeline.

**Stack** Group of layered objects.

**Standard effects** Special video and audio alterations you can apply to a clip to change the way it looks or sounds.

**Stereo** Two-channel audio.

**Storyboard** Set of pictures that illustrate the important action or progression of a movie.

**Streaming media** Video or audio that begins playing before the entire file has downloaded.

**Stroke** Outline of an object.

**Take** One of multiple instances of the camera recording the same action.

**Target** When moving a clip, destination location of the clip you plan to move.

**Task bar** Contains buttons to switch among the workspaces in Premiere Elements.

**Thumbnail offset** Image that illustrates a DVD marker in a DVD menu.

**Time display** Displays the exact frame location of the current-time indicator and allows you to enter a different location.

**Time ruler** Measures movie or clip length and indicates current frame location.

**Timecode** Numeric code that measures the location of each frame of video, allowing you to navigate to a precise frame quickly and easily.

**Timeline panel** Window where you assemble and enhance clips.

**Title** Usually appears at the beginning of a movie to introduce it.

**Title bar** Area at the top of the program window that displays the program name and project name.

**Title sequence** Consists of two or more titles and can be used to introduce important information at the beginning of a movie.

**Titler panel** Window in which you can edit and format text and graphic elements.

**Titler** Common term for the collection of panels exclusive to the Titles workspace.

**Title-safe margin** In the Titler panel, indicates a reliable viewing area for text.

**Tool bar** Contains buttons for commonly used commands

**Trail** Clips that follow the current clip on the Timeline.

**Transient peak** The widest part of a transient.

**Transients** Thick, roughly triangular-shaped regions of a waveform, which represent strong bursts of sound.

**Transition** A setting that affects the beginning or end of a clip.

**Trim** To remove frames at the beginning or end of a clip.

**Video editing software** Program that includes tools for putting together footage recorded with a DV (digital video) camcorder, along with existing video, audio, and image files, to create a finished video and distribute it on DVD, video tape, or over the Internet.

**Video file** Stand-alone file that can be played in a media player, opened in another editing program, stored on disk, or posted on the Internet.

**Wavelength** Distance a sound wave travels in one cycle of vibration.

**Work area bar** Indicates the portion of a movie that will be rendered with the Render command, or exported using an export range.

**Workspace** An arrangement of panels, smaller windows containing commands or tools for completing tasks or obtaining information.

**Wrap** Text that automatically moves to the next line when it reaches the edge of the text box.

**Zooming in** Displaying a smaller portion of the Timeline at a detailed level, so you can navigate more easily from frame to frame.

**Zooming out** Displaying a larger portion of the Timeline in less detail, so you can easily jump ahead or back in the movie.

# Index

*Note: Page references in **boldface** denote pages where terms are defined.

## ▶D



## ▶E



## ▶F

## T



## U



## V

## ▶W



## ▶Z